"This is required reading for anyone grappling with the church's mission, evangelical identity, and public witness. Hill skillfully retrieves the antebellum witness of David Ruggles, Maria W. Stewart, and William Still by exploring their contributions to the abolitionist movement and extends their logic into the present to spark the contemporary Christian imagination into faithful prophetic action. A must-read!"

—**Walter R. Strickland II**, Southeastern Baptist Theological Seminary; author of *Swing Low: A History of Black Christianity in America*

"Today's Christians have a lot to learn from Daniel Lee Hill. His thoughtful analysis of Ruggles, Stewart, Still, and what they teach us about God, ourselves, and our callings in the world shows—perhaps counterintuitively—that righteousness in public life depends to a large extent on evangelical witness (grounded in the Bible) to the Lord's will with respect to social ethics. Let us learn to live and die well in service of God and neighbor as we make good use of the models and theological wisdom in this book."

—**Douglas A. Sweeney**, Beeson Divinity School, Samford University

"In our time of social fragmentation and political polarization, we might rightly wonder how the church ought still to speak. Even more pointedly, Hill asks how the evangelical church ought to testify to the good news of God's reign, without being another voice shouting into the crowd. With wisdom, care, and faithful guidance, *Bearing Witness* calls the church to a posture of bearing witness, inviting us to feast on the riches of the catholicity of the church that tells and enacts God's good story of redemption and restoration so that we, too, might faithfully engage in the time and space in which God has placed us. Hill shows us the profound ways that the 'blood and sweat' of David Ruggles, Maria W. Stewart, and William Still 'still speak,' inviting us to clear-eyed, hope-filled, and catholic listening and action."

—**Jessica Joustra**, Redeemer University

"The term 'evangelical' is all too often defined by the gifts and liabilities of those of European heritage. Daniel Hill shows how this good news tradition is also defined and displayed by three nineteenth-century African Americans named Ruggles, Stewart, and Still. These forebears show us an evangelical faith where the good news is not merely a matter of simple facts and private piety but indeed a public faith that involves bearing one another's burdens. Let Hill be your guide toward a better vision of a 'good news' faith."

—**Vincent Bacote**, Center for Applied Christian Ethics, Wheaton College

"*Bearing Witness* is a treasure. It reminds me of several proverb-like sayings. First, 'other' voices can be fellow voices when it comes to Christian community. We need to be open to learning from such voices and seeing life through their lenses. Second, never forget, or you will never grow. The self-criticism that hearing about the experience of slavery should engender can teach us much if we are good listeners. Third, lament is a striving for the better with God. Sanctification assumes growing in honesty about how we see the fallen world and then acting on the need to change. Not only does this book deliver on those points; it is a lesson on a painful period in our nation's history from which we must learn to do better. Read this book, listen, lament, and learn . . . and then imagine what could be."

—**Darrell L. Bock**, Hendricks Center, Dallas Theological Seminary

BEARING WITNESS

BEARING WITNESS

What the Church Can Learn
from Early Abolitionists

Daniel Lee Hill

Baker Academic
a division of Baker Publishing Group
Grand Rapids, Michigan

© 2025 by Daniel Lee Hill

Published by Baker Academic
a division of Baker Publishing Group
Grand Rapids, Michigan
BakerAcademic.com

Printed in the United States of America

Library of Congress Cataloging-in-Publication Data
Names: Hill, Daniel Lee, 1988– author.
Title: Bearing witness : what the church can learn from early abolitionists / Daniel Lee Hill.
Description: Grand Rapids, Michigan : Baker Academic, a division of Baker Publishing Group,
    [2025] | Includes bibliographical references and indexes.
Identifiers: LCCN 2024032768 | ISBN 9781540965936 (paperback) | ISBN 9781540968630
    (casebound) | ISBN 9781493449347 (ebook) | ISBN 9781493449354 (pdf)
Subjects: LCSH: Witness bearing (Christianity) | Antislavery movements—History. |
    Abolitionists—History. | Evangelicalism—History.
Classification: LCC BV4520 .H545 2025 | DDC 248/.5—dc23/eng/20240906
LC record available at https://lccn.loc.gov/2024032768

Cover design by Paula Gibson

Baker Publishing Group publications use paper produced from sustainable forestry practices and postconsumer waste whenever possible.

25 26 27 28 29 30 31   7 6 5 4 3 2 1

*

To Jessica,
my heart, my love,
my companion
along life's way

*

Contents

Acknowledgments

Where indeed to begin and end. I am a Christian, a claim that is perhaps unsurprising given the fact that this is a book in Christian theology. But to claim oneself as a Christian is to point out that one's life is indebted to that community of the faithful whose prayers and love have carried one along life's way. And so I am overwhelmed with gratitude to the pastors who have nurtured me and my family with the Word. Bobby and Danielle Kelly, I would not have crossed the finish line of my doctoral program without your prayers, support, and ministry. Chris and Betty Woodard, thank you so much for your encouragement and support. The folks at River of Life are so blessed to have you both. Gerald Hiestand, you and yours are always in our prayers. Throughout the COVID-19 pandemic, my wife and I would tune in to Calvary Memorial week after week to hear you faithfully proclaim the promise that God reigns. What a gift. Cameron and Emily, Peak Street will always have a special place in our hearts (as will *The Jesus Storybook Bible*!) because of you two. Thank you for your ministry of the Word, for your care, and for your comfort with the promises of the gospel. We miss you dearly. Bill and Kaitlyn Moody, thank you so much for welcoming us into your living room with open arms. You two were one of the first couples to reach out to us in our newlywed stage, and your kindness was such a gift to my wife and me. Patrick and Gabby O'Neil, I nurtured many of the ideas that animate this book in your living room. The love you two have for each other is palpable, and the manner in which you extended hospitality to our ragamuffin community group was such a powerful declaration of the gifts of Christian community. Patrick, I will never forget your digging around on the internet to find that article of mine on the Eucharist. And your book recommendations remain unmatched. Sam and Erica Doyle, Jessica and I are so privileged to be a part of the family at Greater New Light Missionary Baptist Church. We come each week excited to hear the preaching hour from a pastor who does indeed believe that the gospel is the power of God unto salvation, even for us central Texas gentiles. Thank you for your faithful care of souls.

I am forever indebted to my advisors, Marc Cortez and Daniel J. Treier. Marc, your support and guidance over the past seven years have formed me as a theologian in more ways than I can count, cat jokes included. Dr. Treier, I pray I always remember your injunction to return again and again to the text of Holy Writ. Matthew Levering, thank you for your support and insights and reminders to find a surer branch. And Mr. Dr. Foster, how could I ever forget you? A Virgil if there ever was one, you believed in me when no one else had the right to do so. Your absence leaves a hole and an ache, a longing for resurrected life.

Teaching theology is an incredible privilege and gift, and I have had some truly wonderful students. This volume benefited significantly from the attentive work of some of my graduate assistants, mentees, and former students: Lindsey Edwards, Noah Edmonson, Kaitlyn Schiess, and Anabella Martinez. Anabella in particular put in countless hours reading through the entire draft and offering insights. I am so very thankful for you all and look forward with bated breath to the creative work your futures will produce.

And of course there are those souls I am fortunate enough to name as friends. Theon and Amy Hill, the two of you are better friends than I ever could have hoped for. The laughter we've shared has added years and years to my life. Jeremy and Erin Mann, the two of you have indelibly marked my life. You are both such wonderful witnesses of the love of God in Christ. I always treasure my time living with you and your family, not to mention those memories of a certain young man asking me every morning if I had learned any new facts about animals.

Ty Kieser, my frequent collaborator and friend, I am so very thankful for you, brother. In your willingness to listen to my random theological rants peppered amid random texts on country songs and Chicago-sports themed lamentations, you display so many of the virtues to which I aspire, especially on those days that I still believe in such a concept. The fact that you read this volume in its entirety, despite the fact that I urged you otherwise, still makes me shake my head in gratitude. Sammy and Karina, you two are the gift that keeps on giving. Now please move down to Waco so Sammy and I can finally record our album. My brothers-in-parenthood-arms, Fellipe do Vale and Matt Jenson, I am so very grateful for both of you, especially these past few years. John and Michelle, Cody and Ashlyn, and Sam and Lydia, my life is so much richer for your friendships. Ever since our lives converged at Wheaton College, a convergence consistently reinforced by an overindulgence in blueberry muffins, you and your families have been the boon of boons. Still looking forward to the day when we're all living on the same street in Santa Fe, New Mexico.

R. David Nelson and Anna Moseley Gissing, thank you for acquiring, shepherding, and nurturing this project. It does not come into being without the two of you. Anna, your thoughtful feedback throughout the writing process has made this book sounder in its argumentation, clearer in its thesis, and eminently more readable in its prose. Thank you both, a thousand times. Melisa Blok went through the process of editing this volume for clarity and cohesion. It is so much better because of your attention and time. Thank you so very much.

I recognize that theologians increasingly find themselves homeless in the twenty-first century, yet I have greatly benefited from employment at two institutions: George W. Truett Theological Seminary and Dallas Theological Seminary. I am thankful for my colleagues, the leadership, and the staff at both institutions for granting me time and space to write. I am also especially thankful for colleagues such as Dustin Benac and Jamal Dominique-Hopkins. Dustin, while I half-heartedly apologize for all the punk rock that has rippled from my office to yours through our shared wall, I want you to know that our conversations in the hallway have been a gift these past two years. And Jamal, your Howard University affiliations notwithstanding, I count it such a blessing to call you and Karen friends.

Many of these chapters have benefited from the constructive feedback and pushback I received in presenting them as lectures and at academic conferences. Elements of chapter 2 were offered as part of a larger paper given at the Evangelical Theological Society in the fall of 2021. Significant portions of chapter 3 are from a presentation at St. Alban's Episcopal Church's Theology on Tap (2023). Chapter 4 was adapted from a lecture delivered at Redeemer University for its annual The World and Our Calling lecture (2023). I am thankful to the Albert M. Wolters Centre for Christian Scholarship, Redeemer University, Cardus, the Acton Institute, the Centre for Public Justice, the Henry Institute, the Council for Christian Colleges and Universities, and the Richard John Mouw Institute at Fuller Theological Seminary for making that gathering possible. Sections of chapters 3 and 4 were presented at the annual Protestantse Theologische Universiteit International Conference in spring of 2022. Sections of chapter 6 were given as part of the Frank Pack Distinguished Christian Scholar Lecture at Pepperdine University in the spring of 2023. The kindness I have received in each of these venues and in interacting with various members there is far more than I deserve.

Whenever I speak in a public setting, I ask to be introduced as "the son of Elliott and Patricia." The two of you invested so much into me, and even this expression of gratitude risks undermining the greatness of the debt I owe. Thank you so very much for all the love and kindness you've shown to me. To my "little" sister, Charis, I am so very thankful for you and your friendship. You are the best of us. Thank you for sticking with me. Greg and Gina, thank you for welcoming me into your family, teaching me the joys of (losing at) board games, and holding our little boy all through the night.

Last, but of course not least, to my wife, Jessica, and our son, Dominic. What can I say? While not all unmarried lives are half-full, barren wastelands, I cannot imagine the empty desert mine would be without you two. Of course, it is worth noting that my blitz rating would be *vastly* improved and many rooks would remain un-blundered, but perhaps that proves a minor sacrifice (pun intended) in the grand scheme of things. Perhaps. Jessica, my heart, to whom this book is dedicated, what a treat these past three years have been with you. From saving my half-baked recipes to long walks in the rain, my life is so much richer, so much better with you in it. I still don't quite understand why you said yes. Even still, thank you for your support and willingness to join this hapless theologian. Dominic, my son, being your father is one of the highlights of my life, something I dreamed of for years, and I am still pleasantly surprised at how much of a joy it has been. And who knows, one day, when wolves lie down with lambs, lions might in fact go "ooh ooh ahh ahh." At any rate, I look forward to calling you in the middle of the night to wake you up at any point for the rest of our lives. You'd better answer the phone.

Introduction

God gives good gifts, and one of these good gifts is the church. However we might understand its practices, its often tragic history, and the complicated people who constitute its membership, the church is a gift from the triune Lord of life, who is goodness itself. And this God only gives good gifts.

But God does not give the gift of the church to the church. Such a statement is almost nonsensical. Surely and truly, God does extend gifts to the church, such as the gift of fellowship with Christ, the gift of communion in the Spirit, the gifts of bread and wine, and the gift of hope in the resurrection of the body and the life everlasting, among many others (Eph. 4:7–13). God gives the gift that is the church *to the world* out of his love for the world: "As you have sent me into the world, so I have sent them into the world," Jesus prays in John 17:18, using language that evokes earlier passages, such as John 3. Just as the Father sends the Son into the world out of his love for the world so that the world might know him, so too does the Son send his disciples, and by extension the church, out into the world so that the world might come to know of the Son's mission and the incredible mystery of the wisdom of God's love (17:21–23; Eph. 3:8–10).

Of course, God also sends the church into the world because he loves the church. The two claims are not incommensurate. Having set the church free from bondage to sin and death, he also sets it free for a life with himself, both in the world as it is now and in the world without end. In sending the church into the world, God offers it an opportunity to know and share in the love of God in Christ, a love that is shown in the sending of the Son into this same world for its redemption (Rom. 5:8; 1 John 3:1). And this too is a good gift that he offers to the church.

So if God sends the church into the world out of his love for the world, what is the church called to do? And how does this in turn point to what God has done in Christ? To ask such questions is to inquire into the church's *vocation*—that is, the nature of its task in the present and how this task orders its life, a life it shares in common with "the world." Responding to these queries is the burden of this book. The church's task, its vocation, I will argue, is to orient its life so as to clearly indicate the nature of the gift of new life in the gospel that it has been given and to try as best as it can to correspond to the character of the gift Giver. "For freedom Christ has set us free. Stand firm, therefore," as Paul says in his letter to the Galatians (5:1). We will return to this text in what follows. Suffice it to say that the church is, in a sense, a community sent forth into the world to bear witness to *this reality* to the world—that is, to testify to the God of the gospel and the gift of freedom he has given his people in Christ. The church's vocation is one of bearing witness.

Thinking Theologically about Public Witness

Somewhat recently, Jennifer McBride has proposed that the Protestant church's public witness within the United States must take the concrete form of confession and repentance.[1] In shaping her argument, McBride builds on Dietrich Bonhoeffer's Christology—namely, his belief that Christ not only took on sinful human flesh but was willing to be reckoned "guilty yet sinless."[2] In so doing, Christ expresses solidarity with the world and "wills to take responsibility for the sin that humanity has generated collectively through time."[3] For McBride, following Bonhoeffer yet again, the church today is the concrete form and presence of Christ in the world—that is, the church is the *visible* form and *redeeming* presence of Christ within the world.[4] Accordingly, the church must move beyond discussions of who is guilty or morally culpable for which societal ill, debates that McBride worries seek to absolve the church of its responsibility within the world. Indeed, she argues that the church must resist the temptations to claim that it possesses the truth in and of itself, that it is morally superior to the world, and that it has the answers to the world's problems, all of which reflect a kind of ecclesiological triumphalism.[5]

---

1. McBride, *Church for the World*, 6.
2. McBride, *Church for the World*, 82.
3. McBride, *Church for the World*, 86.
4. McBride, *Church for the World*, 119, 122.
5. McBride, *Church for the World*, 29–37.

For McBride, the church's public witness takes on the specific vector of confession of sin unto repentance. This takes place in two key ways. First, the ecclesial community's public witness involves the concrete action of confessing sin in the form of prayer, wherein the church names and exposes social sin as that which Christ has come to redeem.[6] Yet, second, confession of sin must lead to public action in the pursuit of justice—that is, it is confession unto repentance. Repentance, for McBride, involves taking responsibility for social/structural sin and the church's involvement within the broader world, "as the church community immerses itself in the complexities of public life while acknowledging its solidarity with fallen humanity."[7] In engaging in acts of repentance, the church is enabled to serve as a conduit of the redemptive work of Christ, leading to healing transformation of both the church in particular and the broader society as a whole.[8]

McBride's account of public witness is equal parts brilliant and inspiring as she attempts to shape an ecclesiology that is attentive to the present moment of religious pluralism and takes accountability for the church's involvement in social sin.[9] In fact, there is much to commend. Yet in what follows, I have opted for a somewhat different route. I think it both important and proper to maintain a stronger distinction between the agency of God and the agency of the church, a conviction that gives me a certain discomfiture with some of Bonhoeffer's ecclesiological proposals. It also significantly delimits the expectation that the church's public witness will bring about any sort of "healing transformation" of the broader society in which the church exists. So instead, I will argue that the church's public work of bearing witness takes the form of speaking the truth about the world as it is in light of the judgment and redemption of God and of bearing the world's burdens, not its sins. Rooted in a dialogue with three figures from the abolitionary era, this book proposes that this "burden bearing" is achieved through extending, preserving, and cultivating temporal goods as a sign of God's love for the world and the freedom he offers it. There is coherence, of course, between the church and its Lord, but there is also a strong distinction, as Christ alone has carried the world's sins, reconciling it to God. It is to this fact that the church bears witness in its speech and actions.

6. McBride, *Church for the World*, 131.
7. McBride, *Church for the World*, 113.
8. McBride, *Church for the World*, 207.
9. There are, of course, conceptual problems attendant to the notion of "social sin." See Hill and Kieser, "Social Sin and the Sinless Savior."

An Evangelical Account of Bearing Witness

David Ruggles, a nineteenth-century freedom fighter whom we will return to in chapter 2, in the midst of his critique of the institution of slavery, his call for its abolition, and his admonition to churches to utilize ecclesial practices toward that end, proposed that if the monster of slavery was to be defeated, evangelical weapons were required. He writes, "All attempts to abolish slavery, or to diminish the iniquities which are inseparable from it, must be utterly inefficient, unless you combat that monster with *evangelical weapons*. Arguments drawn from political evils, or prospective dangers however certain, are of no importance among worldly sensual men, when put in competition with present emolument and lascivious indulgences."[10] As we will see, Ruggles is engaging in a bit of rhetorical flourish. He *does* attempt to elucidate the political evils and inhumanity of slavery. But here he notes that arguments drawn *strictly* or *merely* from humanism have failed to make a significant dent in the institution of slavery. In fact, even his adoption of, say, humanistic forms of argument must carry a particular evangelical flavor. There is something unique about the gospel, the moral law of God, and, for Ruggles, the practices of the church that must be brought to bear on our shared, common life and those participating within it. And for Ruggles, the tools required for dismantling slavery and ushering the enslaved into a life of freedom must be of the evangelical sort.

But what does it mean to be evangelical, and how does it give rise to a very specific vision of bearing witness in our common life? Answering these questions lies at the heart of this project. But for now, it is important to merely observe in passing that figures such as Ruggles understood themselves as evangelicals and that this evangelical identity gave shape to a particular sort of witness in shared space. This is not a conclusion they argued *for* as much as it was a premise they argued *from*. In their minds, evangelical Christian identity had something very much to do with the way Christians organize their lives and how they attest to the reign of God in Christ in their life together. Somehow it amounted to risking their lives to help fugitive slaves find freedom, unwaveringly asserting their status as image bearers, and proclaiming that the gospel is indeed good news for those in bondage.

This, of course, raises an important preliminary question: What exactly is meant by the term "evangelical"? If there is such a thing as an evangelical approach to bearing witness in common life, what does it entail? Many a tome has been written in recent years about the essence of evangelical

---

10. Ruggles, *Abrogation of the Seventh Commandment*, 6.

identity and theology, a conversation that lies outside the purview of this introduction.[11] Yet to begin with, we might note that at minimum the word "evangelical" comes from a transliteration of the Greek word *euangelion*, meaning "good news." In the first century, the term "gospel" was tied to the imperial cult of Rome. Heralds were often sent out to proclaim the "good news" that a foe had been vanquished or that a new emperor had come to power, bringing glad tidings of a promised peace and prosperity for every citizen of the empire.[12] For Christians, the "good news" of God's reign is set up to both parallel and directly critique these claims of emperors. It is the Lord and not Caesar who brings peace, and it is peace that is grounded in what God has done in and through the death and resurrection of the Son of God. "The gospel is the announcement that God has made it possible for human creatures to enjoy fellowship with God forever because of the life, death and resurrection of Jesus Christ."[13]

The moniker "evangelical" intends to communicate an identity that is rooted in the gospel, the good news that the triune God—Father, Son, and Holy Spirit—has acted in Christ to reconcile all things to himself (Col. 1:20).[14] As John Webster writes, "An evangelical theology is one which is evoked, governed, and judged by the gospel."[15] To be evangelical is to be a part of a people defined by the radical and cosmic work of reconciliation that God has accomplished in Christ Jesus. God has set us free in Christ, free from sin and free for a life with him. Yes, as many have noted, evangelicals are a people of the book.[16] But to be an evangelical is to be, first and foremost, a person of, for, and animated by the gospel of freedom.

Yet, in one sense, that hardly distinguishes evangelicals from other Christians. Catholics and Eastern Orthodox alike believe that the work of God in Christ is fundamental to their self-understanding as the people of God. So in order to further delineate how the term "evangelical" might function, we can continue by distinguishing it on historic and theological

11. As Daniel Treier notes, "Debates about . . . 'evangelical' identity seem interminable" (Treier, *Introducing Evangelical Theology*, 18). Treier's sentiment may indeed be an understatement.

12. Boring, *Mark*, 30.

13. Vanhoozer and Treier, *Theology and the Mirror of Scripture*, 64.

14. A. Johnson, *Atonement*, 179. Stanley Grenz writes, "Evangelicals are a gospel people. They are a people committed to hearing, living out, and sharing the good news of God's saving action in Jesus Christ and the divine gift of the Holy Spirit, a saving action that brings forgiveness, transforms life, and creates a new community." Grenz, *Renewing the Center*, 337.

15. Webster, "Self-Organizing Power of the Gospel," 191.

16. Richard Briggs writes, "To be evangelical can involve holding many different convictions, but affirming some kind of central role for the Bible has always been one of them." Briggs, "Bible before Us," 15.

levels. Historically, the term "evangelical" denotes a movement branching out from some elements of orthodox Protestantism, particularly the doctrinal distinctives of justification by faith and sanctification, beginning in the eighteenth century.[17] As these doctrinal distinctives combined with elements of seventeenth-century Pietism, a new movement emerged that emphasized the personal nature of the Christian faith.[18] While there is debate about whether proto-evangelicals existed before the revivals of the 1700s, this need not concern us here. Timothy Larsen helpfully identifies five distinctives of evangelical Christianity, stating that an evangelical is an (1) orthodox Protestant, (2) in the tradition of eighteenth-century revival movements of Wesley and Whitefield, who (3) holds a preeminent place for Holy Scripture as the divinely inspired authority for matters of faith and practice, (4) emphasizes reconciliation with God through Christ's atoning work, and (5) stresses the work of the Holy Spirit for conversion, fellowship with God, service to others, and evangelism.[19] These emphases on genuine conversion, the work of the Spirit, and sanctification led to a genuine belief that faith in Christ ought to transform the way a person lives. For someone like Maria Stewart, a nineteenth-century abolitionist and educator in Boston, and others like her, there is something about the good news of God's reign, something shared by those inheritors of the revivalistic movements of the seventeenth and eighteenth centuries, that enabled collaboration across denominational lines.

Yet the term "evangelical" need not function only descriptively. There also seems to be a manner in which the term reflects a theological program and disposition, what Kevin Vanhoozer and Daniel Treier refer to as a "mere evangelicalism."[20] Evangelicals are not just those who sit as heirs to the revivals of the eighteenth century and lay claim to them as their inheritance; they are also those who employ a particular theological vision. For Vanhoozer and Treier, "evangelical theology designates an aspiration and ambition. . . .

---

17. Hutchinson and Wolffe, *Short History of Global Evangelicalism*, 25–47.

18. Anizor, Price, and Voss, *Evangelical Theology*, 2. See Grenz, *Renewing the Center*, 26–33. This differs slightly from the definition David Bebbington has proposed. Timothy Larsen, among others, has wondered if Bebbington's Quadrilateral is too inclusive. Larsen has observed that such boundaries are broad enough to include Coptics and Catholics alike (Larsen, "Defining and Locating Evangelicalism," 1–2). In the well-known description, Bebbington proposes that evangelicals have displayed "a common core that has remained remarkably constant down the centuries. Conversionism, activism, biblicism and crucicentrism form the defining attributes of Evangelical religion" (Bebbington, *Evangelicalism in Modern Britain*, 4–5).

19. Larsen, "Defining and Locating Evangelicalism," 1.

20. See Vanhoozer and Treier, *Theology and the Mirror of Scripture: A Mere Evangelical Account*. The phrase "mere evangelicalism" is borrowed from C. S. Lewis's famous text *Mere Christianity*.

The chief task of evangelical theology is to say, on the basis of Scriptures, what God is doing *in* Christ, and then to indicate how to live it *out*. Stated differently: the purpose of evangelical theology is to help make communities of disciples who come to understand and correspond to the reality of the gospel."[21] They propose that evangelical theology should be understood as an anchored set, rooted in the faithfulness and veracity of the God of the gospel who has "kept his word" in Jesus Christ—that is, grounded in the Trinity and in the person and work of Jesus Christ.[22] Vanhoozer and Treier identify two characteristics of a mere evangelical theology. First, on the level of substance, a mere evangelical theology is creedally orthodox, catholic in scope, and Protestant. Here, Vanhoozer and Treier affirm the supremacy of Holy Scripture as a mirror of divine truth while also recognizing that there are certain conciliar judgments that exercise a "ministerial authority" over the church insofar as these judgments are part and parcel of what it means to confess belief in the Spirit's work in the church.[23] Second, stylistically, a mere evangelical theology is rooted in the gospel and its evangelistic imperative, irenic in its appreciation for and recognition of human diversity, and joyfully fueled by the Holy Spirit.[24]

This theological vision, which guides how to read, interact with, embody, and perform the logics of Holy Scripture, has a natural extension into the spheres of the life we share with our neighbors. The Christian faith has always been "public" and publicly performed.[25] As Kristen Deede Johnson avers, "Christianity is at its heart a communal and public enterprise: the Church is comprised of a group of people sharing the common interest of worship of God and love of neighbor."[26] Baptism, proclamation, remembering the poor, caring for orphans and widows, partaking of the Eucharist, and even conversion are all things that are done "in public," activities that are grounded in the saving action of God in Christ.[27] And so whatever it means to *be* gospel people will invariably give some shape to what it means to *live* as those who bear witness to the resurrection of Jesus Christ and the hope of God's coming

---

21. Vanhoozer and Treier, *Theology and the Mirror of Scripture*, 45.
22. Vanhoozer and Treier, *Theology and the Mirror of Scripture*, 52, 80.
23. Vanhoozer and Treier, *Theology and the Mirror of Scripture*, 115.
24. Vanhoozer and Treier, *Theology and the Mirror of Scripture*, 52.
25. Throughout this book, I employ the terms "public" and "public witness" somewhat loosely, using them synonymously with "shared life" and "common life." This is not intended to index a particular allegiance to a so-called public theology that demands we relegate religion to the realm of the private and engage the public square on neutral terms.
26. K. Johnson, *Theology, Political Theory, and Pluralism*, 220.
27. Jason Sexton makes the observation that the public nature of baptism typifies the church's Spirit-ed call to engage in public action as it bears witness to the good news of the gospel and the hope of cosmic renewal. Sexton, "Public Theology," 431.

redemption.[28] Accordingly, this book seeks to provide something akin to a mere evangelical account of bearing witness to the gospel of freedom in our common, shared life as an aspiration and ambition. Just as we might argue prescriptively for a mere evangelical theology, we can argue for an aspirational, mere evangelical account of public witness.

Nurturing a Tradition

The purpose of this book is to highlight and retrieve the key insights of abolitionary figures for the sake of articulating how evangelicals might bear witness to the gospel of freedom in their shared, common life. This book seeks to remember and listen to some of these voices of the past so that they might help inform how we live in the present. As a theology of public witness, it presupposes that whatever is meant by the term "public" and whatever it might mean to bear witness to the resurrection of Jesus Christ "in public," these concepts must be theologically defined and situated within the broader schema of the Christian story of redemption.[29]

Listening to Our Ancestors

First, this project seeks to listen to the voices of nineteenth-century Christians in order to understand the goods they have to offer for the construction of an evangelical account of public witness. In one respect, the tasks of this project are rather simple: the goal is continued reformation; the method is retrieval. In telling the story of nineteenth-century freedom fighters, I hope to inspire their descendants to return *ad fontes* in order to discover their rich, vibrant, and creative modes of inhabiting an incredibly tumultuous context and then extend this legacy into the present. While these figures were consigned to the margins of society with limited voice and fewer resources, they strove to bear faithful witness *as Christians* to the manner in which the Christian faith, creeds, worship, and witness confront the social order with the good news that Christ reigns. The goal, to borrow from George Kalantzis, is to examine the hopes and concerns of these Christian figures of the abolitionary era and, in so doing, to see if

28. Sexton, "Public Theology," 431.
29. Charles Mathewes proposes that "a theology of public life defines 'the public' theologically, exploring its place in the created and fallen order and in the economy of salvation." He goes on to note that his primary audience is "Christian believers unsure of the religious fruitfulness of civic engagement" and argues "that they can become better Christians, and their churches better Christian communities, through understanding and participating in public life as an ascetical process of spiritual formation." Mathewes, *Theology of Public Life*, 1–2.

we might identify concerns we still ought to worry about and futures for which we still ought to hope.[30]

The figures engaged throughout this work make appeals of varying kinds at disparate points in their careers as they argue against the institution of slavery. Still they are fundamentally bringing Christian commitments to bear on the cultural, social, and economic realities of American life. Their work is kaleidoscopic and improvisational in both form and method. Sometimes they build on concepts of Christian humanism and other times they appeal to explicitly theological categories such as the *imago Dei* or the values and mores of natural law. Their pamphlets are at times polemical and prophetic and at other points autobiographical. Regardless of the shape their appeals take, these authors are explicitly theological in their critiques of the warped and vicious ways we organize our lives together. These abolitionary figures present us with a theology formed on the road by those following the drinking gourd, scraping and clawing to carve out some resonance of freedom. It is the theology of a people in search of place, in search of home.

As a work of theological retrieval, this project begins with a return to abolitionary history. It is imperative that we pay careful attention to the contexts in which these figures operated, the events that surrounded them, and the manner in which they responded. These historical events, then, do not exist as bare, naked facts but require interpretation in their own right. As Rowan Williams observes, "So far from history being an innocent attempt to list events in a sort of neutral space, history tries to identify more clearly what its own subject is. . . . We don't have a single 'grid' for history; we construct it when we want to resolve certain problems about who we are now. We use narratives to define a subject."[31] This is all the more true for interpreting the development of a particular tradition. As we look back and remember, we have no choice but to be selective and discriminate, normally an act undertaken in light of our present values and perceived needs. Accordingly, this selectivity is often indicative of incipient values we wish to accentuate and a particular narrative arc we hope to preserve. Williams goes on to note that "church history, like all good history, invites us into a process of questioning and being questioned by the past; the difference is that the Christian past is unavoidably part of the Christian present in such a way that we have to be extra careful not to dismiss, caricature or give up the attempt to listen."[32] The hope of this book is that in listening to the voices of those saints who have

---

30. Kalantzis, *Caesar and the Lamb*, 2.
31. Williams, *Why Study the Past?*, 4–5.
32. Williams, *Why Study the Past?*, 28.

gone before us, we might be challenged by their lives, instructed by their work, and encouraged to perform the way of Christ in the present in new, creative, and increasingly faithful ways.

Yet this is not a historical work, not mere history for history's sake. Rather, it is history in a theological valence. It seeks to *retrieve* the voices of the past, bringing them into the present so that we might give the dead a vote.[33] As G. K. Chesterton observes, in his characteristically pointed prose, "Tradition means giving votes to the most obscure of all classes, our ancestors. It is the democracy of the dead. Tradition refuses to submit to the small and arrogant oligarchy of those who merely happen to be walking about."[34] Eric Gregory echoes Chesterton's sentiments, writing, "The dead can reeducate us, if we let them. Of course, we might be amused, troubled, or simply confused by their concerns that we do not share. We also can be surprised by how many of our concerns, for good or for ill, stem from theirs."[35] According to the Apostles' Creed, Christians believe not only in the Holy Spirit but in the church catholic and the communion of saints, saints that subsist in a *koinōnia* that transcends space-time itself. Here, in a work of theological excavation, we seek to engage and acknowledge some of our theological debts, at least insofar as they pertain to the church's public-facing enterprise.[36] There is a story to be told here, one that says a great deal about how we understand evangelical Christianity in America today, the goods latent within that tradition, and the goals we can and should aspire to realize. My hope is to reengage these pamphlets of protest, these often glossed over and neglected works of political theology, in order to learn what it might mean for the church to bear faithful witness to the Spirit's work. In hearing how the Spirit *has* spoken in ages past, we might be better equipped to hear how he calls us to bear faithful witness even now.

Remembering the Past Faithfully

Yet I do not think merely remembering the work of our ancestors and forerunners is sufficient, at least insofar as we commonly understand the task of remembrance as an intellectual exercise. The evangelical tradition stands in need of consistent renewal, *ecclesia reformata, semper reformanda*. This is all the more the case in light of the fact that evangelical Christianity is often known for its lack of coherence around the idea of social action, especially in the past forty years or so. According to Charles Mathewes, evangelical

---

33. Jenson, *Theology in the Democracy of the Dead*, 2.
34. Chesterton, *Orthodoxy*, 85.
35. Gregory, *Politics and the Order of Love*, 7–8.
36. Williams, *Why Study the Past?*, 27.

Christians appear "haphazard in their civic engagement, and have not yet developed a 'social gospel' of their own; limited by their lack of a rich ecclesial and social imagination, they often end up with remarkably imbalanced and partial accounts of religious civic engagement, when they are engaged religiously at all."[37] Mathewes's observation is an apt if not pointed critique of the nature of evangelical participation in civic life, although undoubtedly this is in part due to the broadly transdenominational nature of evangelical theology.[38] Within the evangelical house, there are many rooms, ranging from independent Bible churches to confessional Lutherans and Presbyterians. Still, it is my estimation that there are resources within this tradition worth retrieving and worth engaging for the purpose of constructing an account of what it means to participate faithfully in public life.

This second concern, the desire to renew and continually reform the evangelical tradition, is tethered to the very nature of remembrance. When we study the contributions of our ancestors, it is a means of engaging in what Justo González identifies as "careful remembrance," a remembering that is intended toward action.[39] González contrasts this form of remembrance with "innocent readings" of history through which we engage the past for the mere sake of solidifying our own programs and commitments.[40] Instead, in carefully and faithfully remembering, we must recognize these saints as witnesses who call us to act and to carry on their legacy. If their blood and sweat still speak, they do so as a resounding call to awaken from our slumbers, dogmatic and otherwise, and follow in their footsteps. As we strive to hear them and acknowledge their contributions, we must also seek to carry forward their legacy, a legacy embodied in political action that seeks to extend social goods to our neighbors, especially those neighbors relegated to the margins (or worse) of our earthly politics. As a result, this is a work that seeks to retrieve these great voices of the past, recovering their insights for present action and for the work of tradition building.

In many ways, the evangelical tradition can be understood as an argument about the manner in which the gospel of salvation, as centered in the person and work of Christ Jesus, applied through the Holy Spirit, and attested to in Holy Scripture, transforms human life.[41] Far from being a *mere* collection

---

37. Mathewes, *Theology of Public Life*, 201–2.
38. See Treier and Shin, "Evangelical Theology."
39. González, *Mañana*, 79.
40. González, *Mañana*, 79.
41. Here, I am in part indebted to and building on Alasdair MacIntyre's work in *After Virtue*. There, MacIntyre argues that traditions are arguments carried out over time about the goods worth pursuing and the shape of our action. See MacIntyre, *After Virtue*, 205–55.

of static, ossified propositions that are transmitted from person to person, this tradition is carried along in the heroes we admire, the songs we sing, and the liturgical practices we adopt in our disparate churches. Evangelical Christianity is certainly not reducible to mere storytelling. Still, one reason we remember the past is to help account for our present, the goods we pursue, the ends we desire, and the standards to which we are held accountable.[42] Whether through examining the conviction of a John Wesley, the compassion of a C. René Padilla, or the patient courage of a Rosa Parks or a Harriett Tubman, we, in remembering these great titans of the faith, seek to pass on some virtue or ways of being human to subsequent generations, ways of navigating the world we believe they should aspire to emulate.

In choosing these three figures—David Ruggles, Maria W. Stewart, and William Still—I am, in no uncertain terms, making an argument about the very bones of the evangelical Christian tradition, particularly as it relates to the development and articulation of evangelical Christianity in America. Readers will soon see that all three figures share a common social location and vocation. All three were nineteenth-century abolitionists, living in the North in the United States, and of Afro-American ancestry. This is not an accident. As Neil Roberts has noted, while the literature of the abolitionary era has garnered renewed interest in English Literature and Black Studies departments, it has often been overlooked when it comes to the field of political theory.[43] We could extend this observation to the fields of political theology, Christian ethics, and Christian reflection upon the nature of public life. And even when these figures are engaged by political theorists, the strictly *theological* nature of their proposals is often diminished or overlooked.[44] On the one hand, this is understandable. There is a vast swath of literature to be engaged in the history of thought, and we have no choice but to be selective. Furthermore, many Afro-American writers, particularly those of the abolitionary era, wrote in a sporadic and occasionalistic manner, due in large part to their limited social capital, the urgency of the situations they addressed, and their lack of access to more traditional forms of publication.

On the other hand, in a very real sense the judgments emerging from this era are mestizo and mulatto in shape.[45] Many of our current arguments surrounding

42. MacIntyre, *After Virtue*, 213–17.

43. N. Roberts, *Freedom as Marronage*, 57.

44. Eric Gregory, in his illuminating study of Augustine, notes that this aversion is prominent within academic political theory on a general level, which tends to neglect theology and theological concerns altogether. Gregory, *Politics and the Order of Love*, 33.

45. Justo González provides a helpful articulation of what is meant by "mestizo." He writes, "To be a mestizo is to belong to two realities and at the same time not to belong to either of them. A Mexican-American reared in Texas among people of Euro-American culture is

freedom, humanity, representation, and human dignity are rooted in developments taking place within this era, developments that are conditioned on the very presence of Afro-American thinkers and writers who actively advocate for their place within American civic and political life. So while someone like anti-slavery activist and journalist Mary Ann Shadd Cary encouraged fugitive slaves to flee to Canada and make it their permanent home, other liberated blacks dissented, seeking to build a life in the nascent nation that once held them in bondage. These counterarguments illustrate that something is hidden in the sediment of history, of which we sit at the tail end. The fossils of an argument lie buried in the rocks, waiting to be unearthed and recovered. It is an argument about what it means to be a people, what it means to live faithfully as Christians, and what it means to be free. And it is an argument worth engaging so that we might learn what it means to live as their descendants.

Here, then, I am presenting an argument about who we have been and a case for who we must be if we are indeed to be faithful to those who have laid the stones of our foundation. Ralph Ellison, in his essay "What America Would Be Like without Blacks," notes that notions of black and white identity are inextricably intertwined and mutually reinforcing. Ellison argues that a great deal of American history, ranging from economic developments to creative tensions in literature and the arts to the construction of American English, is dependent on the dialectical and dialogical relationship that blacks and whites have had with one another. He writes, "Materially, psychologically and culturally, part of the nation's heritage is Negro American, and whatever it becomes will be shaped in part by the Negro's presence. Which is fortunate, for today it is the black American who puts pressure upon the nation to live up to its ideals."[46] Ellison's argument, in effect, is that black and white

---

repeatedly told that he is a Mexican—that is, that he does not really belong in Texas. But if that Mexican-American crosses the border hoping to find there his land and his people, he is soon disappointed by being rejected, or at least criticized, as somewhat Americanized . . . for being a *pocho*" (González, *Mestizo Augustine*, 15). Similarly, the term "mulatto" refers to someone of mixed racial ancestry—that is, someone with one parent who is black and another who is white. Importantly, as Brian Bantum points out, categories like mestizo and mulatto complicate the neat binaries of racial purity. "Mixed-race children were in between the categories of colonizer and colonized, human and nonhuman, slave and free" (Bantum, *Redeeming Mulatto*, 15). In describing the judgments of this era as mixed or mulatto, I am attempting to highlight the reality that they emerge from a panoply of factors that defy neat categorization. Of course, even describing something as "mixed" seems to presuppose the combination of two separate essences. This resorts once again to the fictitious notions of racial essentialism. Albert Murray makes a similar observation about the broader American project, noting that *all* the inhabitants of the United States are mulatto whether they acknowledge it or not. See Murray, *Omni-Americans*.

46. Ellison, "What America Would Be Like without Blacks," 581. Ellison's friend and contemporary Albert Murray echoes this sentiment: "Identity is best defined in terms of culture, and the culture of the nation over which the white Anglo-Saxon power elite exercises such

Americans are bound together as one people. They cannot be separated or divided around neat, racial lines. They together form one people, each person as thoroughly American as the other. "Despite his racial difference and social status, something indisputably American about Negroes . . . aroused the troubling suspicion that whatever else the true American is, he is also somehow black."[47]

This work seeks to extend the judgments of Ellison and apply them to the evangelical Christian tradition. David Ruggles, Maria W. Stewart, and William Still, figures we will engage in the pages ahead, all resisted the aspirations of the American Colonization Society in different ways and on different terms, believing that there was a way to make a place *here*. Segregation was not an option, and neither was, as we will see, deportation to Liberia or immigration to Canada. Hope demanded that their imaginations come up with an alternative.[48] Whatever evangelical Christianity is today and whatever it is to become in the future, it stands downstream of figures like Ruggles, Stewart, and Still, among countless others, figures whose lives have been poured out in the pursuit of freedom. We would do well to remember that.

A Map of the Way Forward

This project unfolds in two sections. The first section engages in the act of historical remembrance and reflection. In it, I will mine the thoughts of three abolitionary figures to see what they might teach us about the task of pursuing Christian public witness in common life and the virtues required to do so. The goal here is not so much to critique each figure, and there are certainly aspects of their thoughts that are worthy of critique, but to learn from them so that we might bear faithful witness in the present. Here, the task is primarily descriptive. In the second section, I seek to build on the insights gleaned in order to construct an evangelical account of public witness. This will require some theological engagement with the text of Scripture and the implementation of the concerns, questions, and guiding principles gathered along the way. Engaging with Holy Writ is all the

---

exclusive political, economic, and social control is not all-white by any measurement ever devised." Murray goes on to state that *"American culture, even in its most rigidly segregated precincts, is patently and irrevocably composite. It is, regardless of all hysterical protestations of those who would have it otherwise, incontestably mulatto. Indeed, for all their traditional antagonisms and obvious differences, the so-called black and so-called white people of the United States resemble nobody else in the world so much as they resemble each other." Murray, Omni-Americans, 23, emphasis original.

47. Ellison, "What America Would Be Like without Blacks," 587.
48. Hauerwas, *Christian Existence Today*, 211.

more appropriate due to the pride of place it holds in the work of the three abolitionary figures.

The first chapter serves as a historical introduction, setting the scene for what lies ahead. The past—even the recent past—is a foreign land, and we must work to remember its foreignness. As we will see, the nineteenth century was a time of crisis and upheaval. It was a time of runaway slaves and kidnapping gangs, of calls for revolution and succession. Yet as Rowan Williams is careful to remind us, this distant era is not utterly unintelligible, but it is *very* different from the present day.[49] The goal of this chapter, then, is to reframe some of that intelligibility and strangeness, explicating the historical context of these nineteenth-century figures and the issues that were boiling within the nation. It is a necessary step in contextualizing the figures so that we might better understand their goals, the options they chose, and the visions they pressed forward to realize.

Chapter 2 presents the work of the first abolitionary figure: David Ruggles. Ruggles was a freeborn abolitionist who spent most of his life working in New York City, devoting much of his time to advocating on behalf of fugitive slaves and combating the efforts of the kidnapping clubs of New York. From Ruggles's life and work, we learn how to "read" the world in light of its effects on Christian life and praxis. We also find a creative reimagining of social agency. First, Ruggles challenges us to attend to the ways that Christian life in the broader polis deforms Christian witness and then to reason backward to make conclusions about larger social structures on a more general level. Second, Ruggles recognizes that figures on the margins, be they fugitive slaves, freeborn blacks, or women, have the ability to effect meaningful social change in spite of their marginalization. Ruggles offers a challenge to our notions of social agency as he invites every member of society to participate in the pursuit of the abolition of slavery. As a founder of the New York Committee of Vigilance and a frequent contributor to various pamphlets of protest, Ruggles alerts us to the need for cultivating habits of ingenuity and creativity as we seek novel methods and approaches to extending social goods to our neighbors.

The third chapter engages the life of abolitionist Maria W. Stewart. Stewart recognizes the difficulty and complexity of Afro-American life in the antebellum era. On the one hand, she encourages her readers to become a community of character through the cultivation of civic virtue and the employment of social practices that cultivate a kind of independence. For Stewart, renewal starts from the bottom up, in the work of building new institutions and renewing old ones. On the other hand, Stewart is adamant that the work

49. Williams, *Why Study the Past?*, 10–11.

of cultivating a community of character is an act of enduring the current times, one that longs for and anticipates the transformation of our present politics. In other words, the cultivation of communal virtue is undertaken with the hope of appropriating the goods of emancipation and extending them to those who have been excluded from participation in civic life. Stewart shows us how communal virtue is an act of public witness and how we can appropriate the goods of the present to form and renew institutions to address present social concerns.

The fourth and final descriptive chapter engages the work and thought of William Still, the so-called father of the Underground Railroad. In Still, we see a call to hopeful renewal and loving preservation. As an abolitionist and contributor to the Philadelphia Vigilance Committee, Still served as a stop along the Underground Railroad and helped almost one thousand slaves follow the drinking gourd to freedom. But as inspiring as his story is, what is more pressing for our purposes is Still's work as a historian and his meticulous archives of those who passed through his station. Still's record of the Underground Railroad contains numerous details of fugitive slaves, ranging from their family tree to their physical description. For Still, this record was imperative if he were to enable the "reuniting and comforting [of] fugitives with their families" when slavery was ultimately abolished.[50] Still calls us to commit to the act of careful preservation, to envision a future beyond the present crises, and to prepare for that way of life by reweaving the social fabric and remembering well. If Stewart calls us to effectively use the goods of the present, Still encourages us to prepare for a life beyond it.

From there we turn our attention to the task of theological construction, which I have broken into two chapters. Through a theological reading of texts such as Romans 8 and Galatians 5–6, we will see that the Spirit of God brings the church into being as a creature of the Word to bear witness to the Word. Given the extent to which our abolitionary forerunners centralized the text of Holy Scripture in their work, we will follow their lead and engage in sustained meditations on these two texts. For Stewart and Ruggles in particular, thinking through the church's public witness must involve exegesis of and integration with Holy Writ. Here, we will see that the church is, by virtue of its very being, a sign of what God has done in Christ. But the church is also given a particular vocation, a task to undertake in the power of the Spirit. First, as outlined in chapter 5, it is to bear witness to the present age as one of suffering, futility, and decay. The church speaks the truth about the world as it is: one standing in desperate need of a promised transformation and renewal.

---

50. Kashatus, *William Still*, 83.

Yet the imperiled nature of the time in which we exist leads the church not into despair but into hopeful lament, for it rests in the promise of God as given in Christ Jesus. Second, the church is called to bear witness to the freedom God has realized in Christ, which, in our common life, entails the vocation of becoming a particular kind of community and bearing the burdens of the world. The goal of chapter 6 is to articulate the nature of bearing the world's burdens in common life as articulated in the tasks of extending, preserving, and cultivating temporal goods.

Conclusion

An earlier draft of this introduction began with a series of personal anecdotes. In it, I recounted stories from my past and from the generations that have preceded me, stories that sought to highlight the tension of living as a Christian in the world. Originally, I included those stories in order to trace a legacy from our three dialogue partners into the present, showing how their quest to form a life shared with others in a broken world is one echoed in my life, my father's life, and my grandfather's life. But on further reflection, I decided to go a different route. Those stories and any attendant damage or pain pertaining thereto are my own. I carry them with me and will pass them on to my children. But they are not for sale. What is more important is that my story and the many others like it are folded into a larger story, a story that asks looming questions: What has God done in Christ, and how does that reorient the very fabric of the way we share our lives with others? What is this freedom that Christ has led us into, and what does it mean to throw off the yoke of slavery and "stand firm" in freedom as it relates to our common life? After all, the gospel of God is in fact good news for those in bondage (Luke 4:18) and offers freedom to those enslaved (Gal. 5:1). The pressure of answering these questions is all the more acute in those hallow spaces that claim to be sealed and preserved by Christ, spaces in which he has promised to meet his people when two or three gather together.

In an era in which we attempt to think with increasing profundity about notions of the inclusion and presence of marginalized figures, about the place of the Afro-American people in particular within the greater argument that is unfolding in our body politics and our ecclesial traditions, figures such as David Ruggles, Maria W. Stewart, William Still, and others like them stand tall, straight-backed with narrowed eyes and set jaws, proclaiming, "We have been here all along." Often autopsies of evangelicalism and evangelical theology portray Afro-Americans as outsiders to this tradition of thought, as if they have no place in a home they helped build. Far from being relegated to the place of voiceless outsiders, these evangelical Christians find themselves as participants in an ongoing debate about what it means to be a people and a nation, about what it means to seek our neighbor's good as Christians who have both feet planted in the good news that God reigns. It is their sweat and tears—their salt, to echo Toni Cade Bambara's wonderful imagery—that are folded into the very fabric of our ecclesial and public life.[51] In the words of American Methodist Episcopal founder and bishop Richard Allen (1760–1831), "This land, which we have watered with our tears and our blood, is now our mother country and we are well satisfied to stay where wisdom abounds, and the gospel is free."[52] What is true of the land is true of the people who inhabit it and the traditions they participate within. What is required, then, is recognition, reflection, gratitude, and, ultimately, retrieval. The dead have something to say indeed. It is time we let them vote. It is our task to peer down into the strata of bygone days to the granite and clay where the bones of our ancestors lie entombed and recognize that our God is the God of the *living* and that our ancestors have indeed been with us all along.

51. Bambara, *Salt Eaters*.
52. Allen, "Letter from Bishop Allen," 134.

PART 1

GIVING *the* FAITHFUL DEAD *a* VOTE

1

Freedom in the Time of Slavery

"No Sir; for I would observe, that though the apostle acted with his prudent reserve, the unreasonableness of perpetual unconditional slavery may be easily inferred from the righteous and benevolent doctrines and duties, taught in the New Testament. It is very evident, that slavery is contrary to the spirit and nature of the Christian religion."[1] Abolitionist Daniel Coker wrote this in 1810 in one of the more curious abolitionary tracts of his time: a scholastic dialogue between an Afro-American minister and a Virginian slave owner. In a style similar to Anselm of Canterbury's *Cur Deus Homo*, Coker sets up the slave owner as a foil to the black minister, one whose wisdom, logic, and biblical knowledge cause the Virginian to continually stand back in awe. "Hold sir, you have said sufficient," the slave owner remarks in admiration. "I am so sorry I mentioned the text [of Scripture]: but I had no idea of your being able to give such an explanation of it. Pray sir, where did *you* study divinity!"[2]

Coker's dialogue is an esoteric (if not eclectic) approach to debating the legitimacy of the continued enslavement of black peoples in America. Coker inverts the slave/master relationship to show, in part, that Holy Scripture speaks to the people of God irrespective of skin color. It is the black minister, and not the dumbstruck slaveholder, who is the scholar of divinity and right

1. Coker, "Dialogue between a Virginian and an African Minister," 59.
2. Coker, "Dialogue between a Virginian and an African Minister," 59.

exegete of Holy Writ. It is the black minister, and not his friendly interlocutor, who sits as a master of the sacred page and can peer into the heart of the Christian message. If nothing else, Coker's text helps illustrate the narrow straits that Afro-Americans had to navigate in the antebellum era.

Many Afro-American abolitionists adamantly wanted to declare that they were fully human and capable of participating in common, civic life. In contrast to the common perception that they were incapable of civility and culture and were animalistic, they argued that they too could robustly contribute to the continued development of the American experiment. This would seem to require the passage of legislation and the transformation of public opinion. But at the same time, as slaves and second-class citizens, what they and many of their companions earnestly desired was freedom—that is, freedom from bondage, freedom from slavery, freedom for life. Waiting for the halls of Congress to decide one's fate is easier said than done when there are real bodies, real families on the line. So how does one pursue social change with limited social agency? How does one actively resist the tyranny of slavery and persuade slave owners at the same time?

In this chapter, I will present a cursory overview of the national landscape in which the three abolitionary figures operated. It is commonplace to acknowledge that brief historical surveys, like the one presented in this chapter, often obscure and flatten details more than they provide clarity. Still, the hope here is to prepare readers for what lies ahead so that they might gain an understanding of a few governing issues that Ruggles, Stewart, and Still had to face as free blacks pursuing freedom, a pursuit that they understood to be the form that Christian witness takes in public. As we will see, the Revolutionary War, the American passage of the Act Prohibiting Importation of Slaves in 1807, and the slave revolts taking place in the Caribbean all dramatically raised the temperature of American conversations concerning the legitimacy of slavery as an institution and the prospects of offering freedom to blacks.[3] While the importation of slaves from Africa was banned in the early 1800s, this merely transformed the slave trade within the United States from an international to a domestic enterprise. The end of the United States' participation in the transatlantic slave trade did little to resolve the tensions and questions surrounding the presence of Afro-Americans in the United States. As time passed, battle lines were increasingly being drawn between pro-slavery and anti-slavery apologists. And while Afro-American freedom was threatened by disenfranchisement on all sides, men and women mobilized within the church to begin building a better life together.

---

3. While the bill was passed in 1807, it did not go into effect until 1808.

The Landscape of American Slavery

Slavery in a Fledgling Nation

The eighteenth and nineteenth centuries introduced rapid changes to the makeup of American life. After the outbreak of the Revolutionary War (1776) and its subsequent resolution (1783), a new nation began to emerge from the smoldering rubble of a war that had lasted almost a decade. As the dust began to settle, many blacks took advantage of the subsequent chaos to flee with the retreating British.[4] As Gary Nash has noted, "With the gigantic movement of both civilian and military populations in and out of nearly every major seaport city from Savannah to Boston between 1775 and 1781, urban slaves had unprecedented opportunities for making their personal declarations of independence."[5] Thousands fled with the fleeing British into Canada. Samuel Birch's *Book of Negroes* (1783) details the exodus of over three thousand slaves who crossed British lines to evacuate with them to Nova Scotia in response to the Earl of Dunmore's promise of freedom to any enslaved African who chose to fight with the British (1775). Another five thousand slaves are estimated to have left with the retreating British when they fled Charleston in 1782, traveling to ports in Saint Lucia and Jamaica, among other locations.[6] Historian Casandra Pybus conservatively estimates that around twenty thousand slaves fled with the British in the turmoil surrounding the war's end.[7] And this does not begin to account for the untold number of slaves who escaped as stowaways in secret. In the words of Benjamin Quarles, "Whenever the defeated British made their final withdrawals, whether by land or sea, thousands of slaves went with them."[8] The same pattern held around

---

4. It is also worth noting that a great number of slaves opted to fight on behalf of the British during the American War of Independence. As Maya Jasanoff observes, "British officers offered freedom to slaves who agreed to fight. Approximately twenty thousand slaves seized this promise" and joined the British ranks. As Jasanoff goes on to note, this made "the revolution the occasion for the largest emancipation of North American slaves until the U.S. Civil War" (Jasanoff, *Liberty's Exiles*, 8). As Gary Nash observes, this is in part because the British made it a policy to offer freedom to any escaped slave, a policy undoubtedly intended to shift the tide of the conflict (Nash, *Race and Revolution*, 60).

5. Nash, *Race and Revolution*, 59.

6. Quarles, *Negro in the American Revolution*, 167.

7. Pybus, "Jefferson's Faulty Math," 261.

8. Quarles, *Negro in the American Revolution*, 158. As Quarles notes, the exodus of slaves with the British was so expansive that General Washington and General Weedon took active steps to deter this migration. Pybus is critical of Quarles for basing his estimate in the reports of slaveholders and for failing to scrutinize the context and motivations that may have engendered these claims (Pybus, "Jefferson's Faulty Math," 245). Furthermore, she estimates that since many slaves were not inoculated against smallpox, about twenty-five percent of those fugitives would have most likely died before reaching freedom.

thirty years later during the War of 1812. Thomas Malcomson estimates that another five thousand slaves escaped their bonds, stowing away with the British to the Caribbean or Nova Scotia.[9] While the American Revolution was originally viewed as a patriotic struggle for freedom from British tyranny, it quickly became an opportunity for many enslaved blacks to pursue a kind of self-emancipation, both within the newly formed United States and abroad.[10]

Still, this mass exodus made but a small dent in the slave population within the United States. Indeed, in spite of the several thousand slaves who made or attempted escape, these escapees made up only a small percentage of the broader slave population. Accordingly, slavery was still an integral part of American life.[11] Before the War of Independence, roughly one in five Americans was enslaved.[12] Around the time of the nation's founding in 1776, there were approximately 600,000 slaves in America. That number would grow to somewhere in the vicinity of 3.9 million by the eve of the Civil War in 1860. Black slaves were conscripted into a variety of services depending on their location. As David Davis observes, slaves in the South were typically used to help harvest tobacco and cotton, the latter of which became vital to the Southern economy after Eli Whitney's invention of the cotton gin (1793). Things were somewhat different in the North. "What mainly distinguished Northern 'societies with slaves' from Southern, West Indian, and Brazilian 'slave societies' was the lack of staple crops to export."[13] Crops such as cotton, tobacco, sugar, and rice could not grow in the climates of the Northern states and colonies, rendering an economy based around slave labor untenable. This of course did not eliminate the use of slaves altogether. As Davis goes on to note, "Northern farming, stock raising, and rural industry, including tanneries, salt works, and iron furnaces," provided Northerners with plenty

9. Malcomson, "Freedom by Reaching the Wooden World," 390.

10. Noll, *History of Christianity*, 139. Steven Hahn cautions us against reading the abolition of slavery in the North and the South as two distinct phases of emancipation; they must be understood as a longer, prolonged movement: "We ought to imagine emancipation not as two relatively discrete phases, but rather as a connected and remarkably protracted process." Hahn, *Political Worlds of Slavery and Freedom*, 6.

11. As David Davis notes, the extraordinary complexity of slavery being woven into American life almost defies categorization. He argues that "any overview of American slavery must move beyond official restrictive laws and leave room for slaves who rented out their labor, slaves who employed white workers as they transported cargoes on Mississippi River boats, and even slave doctors and midwives who treated upper-class white patients." He goes on to state that "one can find exceptions to virtually any generalization made about slave occupations, treatment, families, resistance, population growth, and many other matters." Davis, *Inhuman Bondage*, 124.

12. Burin, *Slavery and the Peculiar Solution*, 6.

13. Davis, *Inhuman Bondage*, 128.

of opportunities to appropriate the bodies and labor of enslaved black peoples.[14] Across the nation, many slaves lived on large plantations. Still, the possession of personal, household slaves was not uncommon, so much so that in the 1760s, black slaves made up around 75 percent of Philadelphia's servant class.[15] Nearly every member of the white elite class along with numerous members of the white middle class owned slaves who functioned as household servants.

Needless to say, whatever seeds had been planted in the War of Independence, seeds that would lead to the emancipation of slaves in states such as Vermont (1777) and Connecticut (1784), slavery was very much a part of America's social fabric. Yet even here the word "emancipation" must be uttered with a caveat and an even larger footnote, as many of these Northern states did not technically free slaves. Instead, they proposed freeing "the *children* of those who were enslaved (*post-nati* emancipation, as it was known), and only when they reached a certain point in their adulthood."[16] *Post-nati* emancipation enabled slave owners to continue reaping the benefits of slave labor during their slaves' most productive years to compensate them for their eventual loss of property and labor.[17] So while the shape and scope of slavery differed from region to region, slavery was still very much a part of the *entire* nation's social imagination and common life until at least the 1840s, when it began to die out in the Northeast.

Of course, this is not to say that the Revolutionary War failed to change the national conversation surrounding the enslavement of black people. In many ways, the American War of Independence was often understood to be a war over the Enlightenment ideals of freedom, self-determination, and human liberty. Some abolitionists viewed the Revolutionary War and the ideals articulated within the United States Constitution as providing the grounds on which subsequent appeals to the liberation of slaves could be made. For example, James Forten (1767–1842) begins his appeal for emancipation with a direct quotation from the Declaration of Independence and the American Constitution, proposing that the bondage of any human person is a "direct violation of the letter and spirit of [the American] constitution."[18] Forten goes on to note the disregard of the slave's "inalienable rights" and how the slave experiences the violation of their property, ideas that are intrinsic to the founding documents of the United States. Similarly, Coker, whom we have

---

14. Davis, *Inhuman Bondage*, 128.
15. L. M. Harris, *In the Shadow of Slavery*, 11–14; and Hodges, *Root and Branch*, 41.
16. Hahn, *Political Worlds of Slavery and Freedom*, 8, emphasis original.
17. Hahn, *Political Worlds of Slavery and Freedom*, 8.
18. Forten, "Series of Letters by a Man of Colour," 68.

already mentioned, argues that enslavement is an infringement of the slave's right to property (self-ownership) and stands in direct contradiction to the nation's identity as a "Christian government."[19] Frederick Douglass, many years later, typifies this trajectory of thought. In his famous speech "What to the Slave Is the Fourth of July?" (1852), he highlights the incongruence between the ideals of the American Revolution and the continuation of chattel slavery: "Fellow-citizens, pardon me, allow me to ask . . . what have I, or those I represent, to do with your national independence? Are the great principles of political freedom and of natural justice, embodied in that Declaration of Independence, extended to us? . . . Would to God, both for your sakes and ours, that an affirmative answer could be truthfully returned to these questions!"[20] For Douglass, the ideals of freedom and natural rights sat in contradiction with the institution of slavery. Still, the relationship between the colonial desire for freedom from British rule and the desire of slaves to obtain freedom from their masters was by no means obvious.[21] While the Revolutionary War and the US Constitution brought many of these questions to the fore, they did little to bring about material resolution of the debate for or against slavery.

With all the debate surrounding the legitimacy of slavery, American opinions were far from unanimous with regard to the nature, scope, and legitimacy of the enslavement of black peoples. One of the more monumental moments in this larger conversation involved a series of anti-slave-trade legislation between 1774 and 1807, effectively extricating the United States from the international slave trade. After legislation prohibited American participation in the slave trade in 1774, anti-slave-trade legislation was passed in 1807 banning the import of slaves across US borders.[22] Whereas New York and Charleston had previously served as primary places for the importation of African flesh, appropriated for forced, manual labor, with the passing of this legislation, the transatlantic slave trade ended for the United States of America. David Ericson observes that Congress did not initially dedicate

19. Coker, "Dialogue between a Virginian and an African Minister," 54, 59.

20. Douglass, "Speech at Rochester," 192.

21. Matthew Mason writes, "After the Revolutionary War, abolitionists continued to agitate for abolition, but their appeals to the ideals of the Revolution met with continued failure." Mason, "Necessary but Not Sufficient," 15.

22. David Davis argues that this general restriction on the expansion of the slave trade cannot be disconnected from the larger context of human trafficking within the Americas and the shifts taking place around the globe. "In 1775, at the start of the American Revolution, racial slavery, meaning the slavery of Africans and people of African descent, was a legal institution from Canada to Chile, and there were no restrictions on the expanding slave trade from Africa to most parts of the New World, but by 1825 Britain and the United States had outlawed their Atlantic slave trades." Davis, *Inhuman Bondage*, 142.

financial resources to the endeavor.[23] Yet in spite of this dearth of financial investment, the federal government was able to effectively end its involvement in international slave trading. "The federal government would now regulate imports as part of its broader responsibility for controlling the nation's borders. Federal officials were relatively successful in accomplishing this task," so much so that "slave smuggling into the United States virtually ceased in the early 1820s."[24] While enslaved Africans were still occasionally imported into the United States through various forms of subterfuge, these legislative changes were largely successful. The federal ban on slave imports brought an end to American participation in the international slave trade and drastically reduced the number of African slaves trafficked across US borders.

Bringing an end to American participation in the international slave trade introduced a much larger change into the nature of the slave economy within the United States.[25] The United States would no longer officially tolerate the *importation* of black men and women from Africa across its national borders. But human trafficking was still legal, as long as it took place domestically—that is, as long as it occurred *within* the United States' borders. Without any newly imported slaves to replenish the population, the United States turned the institution of chattel slavery and the corresponding activity of trafficking human persons between plantations into thoroughly indigenous enterprises. While not without its hiccups, this transition from international to domestic human trafficking was partly intuitive. Given the millions of blacks in bondage, the industry of slavery had become largely self-sustaining and self-perpetuating. Enslaved blacks would inevitably reproduce and have children. These children, even those fathered by slave owners or other free whites, would sustain the population of the enslaved insofar as enslavement proved hereditary and was understood to be a function of human nature. Accordingly, the population of enslaved Afro-Africans continued to grow, and the trafficking of human flesh still proved to be an economically viable mode of business. As Steven Deyle avers, "By the early nineteenth century, not only had the domestic slave trade made human property the most valuable form of investment in the South and made many slave traders rich, but it had also transformed southern society in another important way. Namely, it made the buying and selling of

23. Ericson, "Slave Smugglers, Slave Catchers, and Slave Rebels," 185.
24. Ericson, "Slave Smugglers, Slave Catchers, and Slave Rebels," 185.
25. Steven Deyle writes, "Before the Revolution, slave traders were wealthy and respected merchants who generally viewed their African and West Indian purchases as they did any other cargo. . . . By the nineteenth century, the slave trade had changed dramatically. It was no longer conducted in the North; most of the slaves traded had been born in America; and few slave traders were men of high social and political stature. For Americans, the slave trade had become an indigenous operation." Deyle, *Carry Me Back*, 16.

men, women, and children a regular part of everyday life."[26] In other words, the practice of selling and buying slaves was not abolished altogether. Rather, such endeavors were confined to the nation's borders. Even as the United States extricated itself from the transatlantic slave trade, the trafficking of human persons was still very much a part of American common life.

Changes in Slavery in the Surrounding World

While American life was undergoing a series of changes with respect to the international slave trade, conflict was erupting around the globe, simultaneously stoking fears of a black uprising within the United States and fueling the hope of those Afro-Americans who dedicated their lives to the abolitionary cause. One of the most unique and obvious instances is the Haitian Revolution (1791–1804).[27] In 1791, thousands of slaves and maroons gathered together and launched a revolt in retaliation for the cruelty they had experienced at the hands of their masters. Within a few days, thousands upon thousands of slaves joined the revolution. Thus began a multiyear campaign against their masters and, at varying times, the French, Spanish, and British armies. United around figures such as Toussaint Louverture, Henri Christophe, and Jean-Jacques Dessalines, the Haitian Revolution took place over the course of thirteen years—bloody, violent years marked by mass executions and constant carnage. Finally, in 1804, the Haitians wrested control of the island after the British departed (1798) and maintained their independence as Napoleon attempted a second invasion in 1802. Although the French infiltration led to the capture of Toussaint, the French admitted defeat after their supply lines from the British were cut off (1804).[28] That same year, the remaining Haitian generals declared the formation of the New Republic of Haiti, adopting a constitution a year later that made slavery illegal.

The Haitian revolt is remarkable in its own right, being one of the few successful slave revolts in modern history. Yet what is more pertinent for our

26. Deyle, *Carry Me Back*, 144.

27. Historian Franklin Knight describes the Haitian Revolution as "a unique case in the history of the Americas: a thorough revolution that resulted in a complete metamorphosis in the social, political, intellectual, and economic life of the colony" (Knight, "Haitian Revolution," 105). Haiti was also unique in its demographic. As Neil Roberts points out, the revolt may have in fact been conditioned on, at least in large part, the immensely large number of slaves in Haiti with respect to the general population. "Halfway into the 1700s, slaves outnumbered whites by 150,000 to 14,000. A few decades later, in the late colonial phase, two years before the revolution's start, there were approximately 31,000 whites, 28,000 free people of color, and 465,000 slaves. The slaves of Saint-Domingue [one of the population centers in Haiti] had grown to nearly 90% of the population" (N. Roberts, *Freedom as Marronage*, 91).

28. Blackburn, "Haiti, Slavery, and the Age of the Democratic Revolution," 647.

purposes is the effect of the Haitian Revolution on the American understanding of the abolitionary movement. On the one hand, the success of the Haitian Revolution fueled fears of slave uprisings and the division of the United States into two nations. As James Lynch notes, "For Americans, the slave revolt [in Haiti] represented the danger of their own revolutionary principles. While the early stages of the French Revolution validated American revolutionary ideology, the thought of a free black nation in North America shocked northerners and horrified southerners."[29] Slaves in Haiti vastly outnumbered the population of whites, giving them a kind of strength in numbers that mitigated against any scarcity of munitions.[30] As the slave population continued to grow in Southern and Northern states alike, some feared that a similar revolt could take place on the continent, significantly dampening abolitionary sympathies. Edward Rugemer writes, "From 1797 through 1835 white Americans had absorbed the lessons of Caribbean writers that abolitionist agitation caused slave rebellion. The news of West Indian rebellions, which most newspapers presented as black rebels killing whites at the instigation of radical abolitionists, shaped public opinion in the United States."[31]

On the other hand, the success of the Haitian Revolution along with the success of other anti-slavery efforts in the West Indies appears to have stimulated the Afro-American imagination. For some, the events taking place on the island of Haiti inspired the hope that they too could experience freedom and liberation.[32] Many abolitionists still preferred to resource "moral suasion," a tactic used to persuade outsiders of the moral wrongness of slavery.[33] Organizations such as the Anti-Slavery Society prioritized this tactic, believing that it was the best way to achieve the necessary legislative change that would bring about the end of chattel slavery. Yet others had become dissatisfied with rhetorical appeals to slave owners and wanted action. They were able to view Haiti as a template that could be followed in the pursuit of freedom. For example, Prince Hall in 1797 called on his listeners to see what was occurring in the West Indies as a source of hope. "My brethren, let us not be cast down under these and many other abuses we at present labour under: for the darkest is before the break of day. My brethren, let us

29. Lynch, "Limits of Revolutionary Radicalism," 192.
30. N. Roberts, *Freedom as Marronage*, 91.
31. Rugemer, *Slave Law and the Politics of Resistance*, 97.
32. Gilroy, *Black Atlantic*, 13.
33. Kirkland, "Enslavement, Moral Suasion, and Struggles for Recognition," 244. For a discussion of Frederick Douglass's thoughts on war and freedom, see Levine, "Frederick Douglass, War, Haiti." Douglass would continually call black slaves to resist their masters, but, as Robert Levine notes, he "was aware that the specter of black violence reinforced whites' stereotypes of black savagery." Levine, "Frederick Douglass, War, Haiti," 1865.

remember what a dark day it was for our African brethren six years ago, in the French West Indies. Nothing but the snap of whip was heard from morning to evening. . . . But blessed be God, the scene is changed."[34] For Hall and others inclined toward his way of thinking, the Haitian Revolution was proof positive that the days of slavery were indeed coming to a close. It also served as motivation to continue to pursue the cause of slavery's abolition. Similar calls, as we will see below, were made by figures such as David Walker, Frederick Douglass, and Henry Highland Garnet, albeit with differing points of emphasis and differing perspectives on the appropriateness of armed slave revolts.

The Haitian Revolution was not the only event that took place in the Western world with respect to slavery. In 1794, slavery was abolished in France, perhaps in part as a response to concerns emerging within its Caribbean colonies. In the midst of France's tumultuous and often violent revolution, the National Convention abolished slavery in 1794 in all of the French colonies. Given the lack of follow-up and follow-through, slavery would need to be abolished in France for a second time in 1848. A few years earlier, slavery had been on its way out in Great Britain due to the painstaking work of figures such as William Wilberforce and the Anti-Slavery Society. After abolition bills had repeatedly failed to pass Parliament, public opinion began to shift in favor of emancipation.[35] Eventually, in 1833, the British Parliament passed the Slavery Abolition Act, which emancipated slaves in the majority of British colonies, extending the efforts of the Slave Trade Act (1807). This 1807 act had made participation in the slave trade illegal for citizens of the British Empire. While the emancipation of slaves did not bring an end to the disenfranchisement that black persons experienced in Britain, France, or any of the colonies, it did signify that times were changing.

The abolitionary movement appeared to be gaining steam throughout the wider Western world, both in continental Europe and within its colonies, encouraging abolitionary efforts within the United States.[36] For example, abolitionist James McCune Smith, reflecting on the emancipation of slaves in Europe, remarked that "this transaction is one of the most cheering that has occurred in the history of abolitionism."[37] In a sense, abolition and emancipa-

---

34. Hall, "Charge," 47.
35. Drescher, "Whose Abolition?," 141.
36. For a discussion of the changing scope of slavery in some of the far eastern reaches of the various European empires, see Seijas, *Asian Slaves in Colonial Mexico*. As Seijas points out, the changing dynamics of chattel slavery were not limited to the Americas but were also taking place in the Philippines and in Spanish colonies.
37. J. M. Smith, "Abolition of Slavery."

tion were in the air, and it seemed as if the sun was setting on the institution of chattel slavery in the United States.[38] In part, this may have been due to the continued influence of post-Enlightenment philosophical distinctives that emphasized the inherit rights and worth of the individual. Yet these broader, global changes regarding the legitimacy of slavery would take some time to take root in the American imagination. In the meantime, it seemed that in the United States many political and social actors were determined to preserve the institution of slavery as an integral part of American life, undertaking legislative processes to extend its lifespan.

Black Freedom and Its Dissidents

In both 1793 and 1850, the United States Congress passed a fugitive slave act that entitled masters to pursue runaway slaves while penalizing and fining local officials who failed to arrest alleged fugitives. According to Richard Blackett, "The passage of the Fugitive Slave Law in 1850 changed the terms of the debate over slavery by providing for the first time in the nation's history a national system of enforcement, one which had the full backing of the federal government."[39] This reoriented the still legitimate practice of human trafficking so that it took place on a domestic level. As noted above, given the somewhat ambiguous nature of "black citizenship" within the United States on a political and legal level, an unintended consequence of ending American participation in the transatlantic slave trade was that it put the free status of any Afro-American in jeopardy. While many Afro-Americans were actively seeking to realize the promise of liberty, the rights of citizenship, and the opportunities participation in public life afforded them and their kindred, numerous hurdles continued to present themselves.

The passage of fugitive slave laws was intended to address a very obvious problem: the numerous slaves who fled plantation life in pursuit of freedom.[40] Throughout the late eighteenth and early nineteenth centuries, thousands of slaves fled their bonds and risked their lives to escape plantation life, some traveling across the border into Canada and others seeking refuge in Northern states where slavery was illegal.[41] Yet the realization of freedom through flight was difficult and contingent. Many slaves required the assistance of others. Once they left the confines of their plantations or towns, many slaves

---

38. Mason, *Slavery and Politics*, 158.
39. Blackett, "Underground Railroad," 275.
40. In reflecting on the story of Seymour Cunningham, Jonathan Wells observes that "African Americans' desire for liberty was a potent force in American politics." J. Wells, *Blind No More*, 16–17.
41. Blackett, "Underground Railroad," 284.

often found themselves in an unfamiliar environment without the requisite resources to navigate the treacherous road toward freedom. Additionally, running away was far more successful for those living in states like Virginia, Maryland, and Kentucky, states where freedom was only a few miles and rivers away. For slaves in the Deep South, the journey was often too long, dangerous, difficult, and uncertain to undertake.

Of course, the desire to pursue and obtain freedom was not limited to slaves. Freeborn blacks and those newly emancipated frequently found themselves in search of a more concrete and substantial form of human liberty. For Afro-Americans, both freeborn and runaway, freedom was always precarious and very much in process.[42] Even in Northern cities like Pittsburgh and New York, Afro-Americans lacked political representation and faced systemic disenfranchisement. Robert Purvis (1810–1898) notes the cruel irony that blacks were forced to pay taxes while being deprived of the right to vote for the very representatives they financially supported.[43] In Philadelphia, William Still, as we will see in chapter 4, fought for the right of Afro-Americans to have access to housing and the railcar system. In each instance, Still and Purvis noted that even those blacks who were "free" lacked access to public goods and faced social and political disenfranchisement. In other words, the realization of black freedom was still in the making.

Freed slaves and freeborn blacks in slaveholding states were sometimes threatened with enslavement if they did not relocate. As Cheryl LaRoche comments on the community of Lick Creek, Indiana, "As early as the 1740s, people of color had migrated to Indiana coming primarily from Kentucky and the eastern states of Maryland, Virginia, and North Carolina. Freedom seekers, driven to escape restrictive state laws mandating that newly freed men and women leave their slave states, usually within thirty days or face reenslavement, escaped and mixed among these early pioneers."[44] Abolitionist Theodore Wright argues that the passage of these kinds of state laws was linked in part to the events of Nat Turner's Rebellion and the growth of colonization rhetoric that had spread across the country. He writes, "Immediately after the insurrection in Virginia, under Nat Turner, we saw colonization spreading all over the land; and it was popular to say the people of color must be removed. . . . Maryland passed laws to force out the colored people. It seemed proper to make them go, whether they would or not."[45] Free black people in states such as North Carolina, Virginia, and others

42. Hahn, *Political Worlds of Slavery and Freedom*, 13.
43. Purvis, "Appeal of Forty Thousand Citizens," 96.
44. LaRoche, *Free Black Communities*, 57.
45. T. Wright, "Progress of the Antislavery Cause," 86.

were often at risk of being reenslaved if they stayed put, effectively forcing them to migrate elsewhere. All over the republic, free blacks were trapped in a precarious position in which they could, at any moment, be thrust back into the vortex of slavery. Lacking significant institutional agency and adequate governmental representation, these free blacks were citizens only in a nominal sense.[46]

Further complicating this pursuit of freedom was the profitable business of slave catching in what has been referred to as the Reverse Underground Railroad.[47] Jonathan Wells notes, "The closing of the Atlantic slave trade after 1809 reshaped the domestic slave economy and created a profitable opening for whites looking to abduct free blacks and sell them into bondage."[48] Slave catchers would travel to Northern cities and free black communities in pursuit of fugitive slaves. The intent, at least in theory, was to find runaways and return them to their masters for a profit, a profit that only increased as the price of slaves increased over time.[49] However, if fugitive slaves were in short supply, slave catchers would often resort to kidnapping free black men, women, and especially children in order to sell them into slavery. Some of these slave catchers, rather than working as merely independent operators, formed "kidnapping collectives," and given the ability of blacks to present themselves as "kin" to unsuspecting children, slave catchers worked with "several black or mixed race women to lure away credulous African-American children" from their homes.[50] Kidnapping gangs like those led by Joseph Johnson and Patty Cannon captured hundreds upon hundreds of blacks and sold them into slavery in the Deep South, far away from their homes and family members. According to Julie Winch, during the 1820s, forty to sixty black children were kidnapped every year in Philadelphia alone.[51] The development of steamboats

---

46. Luke Bretherton is helpful here in that he distinguishes varying dimensions of citizenship. First, citizenship refers to a legal status and the social, political, and civil rights and powers that are included with that status. Second, citizenship refers to participation in a system of government and the corresponding relationship between the governing and the governed. Third, citizenship involves the aligning of oneself with a particular community, entailing the subjective perception of the individual in relationship to the larger polis. Fourth, citizenship refers to "the performance of a vision of politics. . . . Citizenship involves doing certain things." And finally, citizenship refers to the processes of ascertaining and deliberating a particular vision of a shared, good life and the goods pertaining thereto. See Bretherton, *Christ and the Common Life*, 100–102.

47. Bell, "Counterfeit Kin," 202.

48. J. Wells, *Blind No More*, 19. Wells gives a date of 1809, though the Act Prohibiting Importation of Slaves was passed in 1807 and went into effect in 1808.

49. J. Wells, *Blind No More*, 19.

50. Bell, "'Thence to Patty Cannon's,'" 663.

51. Winch, "Philadelphia and the Other Underground Railroad," 4.

and railroads only made things worse, as these technologies enabled kidnappers to quickly and effectively traffic free black people.[52]

Responding to the Crisis of Slavery

Richard Carwardine observes that immediately following the American War of Independence, anti-slavery sentiments spread throughout many of the northern parts of the country.[53] Indeed, even in the South, slavery was beginning to be viewed as an institution that would eventually die out.[54] As Eric Burin notes, "Ideological, economic, and social forces slowly disintegrated slavery in the northern states. Chattel bondage collapsed first in New England, where it was weakest."[55] The hope of early proponents of abolition was that Southern, slaveholding states would eventually see the error of their ways and abolish slavery on a state-by-state basis.[56] At first, this strategy seemed to be working. By the 1820s, most Northern states had passed a gradual abolition act, a law that stated that anyone born after its passage would eventually be set free on a specific date. The gears of abolition, however, soon got stuck as the movement tried to move southward. As the slave population increased and cotton became an increasingly profitable industry as a result of the cotton gin, many Southerners, Christian and non-Christian, began to view slavery as "neither transient nor evil, but a positive good."[57]

As Mark Noll has pointed out, the issue of slavery led to a series of crises within evangelical America with respect to how to interpret the Bible, the appropriateness of slavery, and the nature of Christian social engagement.[58] Evangelical Christians fell on both sides of the slavery debate and had various responses to the continuing reality of slavery and the perilous state of the enslaved. For some evangelical Christians, slavery was a staple of American life, was permitted by Scripture, and was necessary for the stability of the union.

---

52. Jones, "Petition of the People of Colour," 330–31.
53. Carwardine, "Antebellum Reform," 73.
54. Carwardine, "Antebellum Reform," 73.
55. Burin, *Slavery and the Peculiar Solution*, 7.
56. Paul Polgar summarizes the movement aptly: "Early national abolitionism was designed to break apart American bondage through a progressive enlightenment for black and white Americans together. As gradual abolition laws gave time for former slaves to make the transition into republican citizens, displaying their aptitude for freedom and virtue, antislavery activists aimed to persuade a skeptical and prejudiced white American public to extend the egalitarian promises of Revolutionary ideology to the nation's African Americans." Polgar, "'To Raise Them to an Equal Participation,'" 230.
57. Carwardine, "Antebellum Reform," 73.
58. See Noll, *Civil War as a Theological Crisis*.

For others, slavery was morally repugnant, a sin, and an obvious violation of the natural rights of God's creatures.

Christian Responses to Slavery

Christian responses to slavery, evangelical and otherwise, were in many ways as diverse and wide-ranging as in the rest of the American political environment, with evangelical Christians falling on both the pro-slavery and the anti-slavery sides of the debate. For some evangelical Christians, slavery was a part of the created order, permitted by Holy Scripture, economically necessary, useful for the sake of advancing pragmatic state and local interests, and socially acceptable. Evangelical defenders of slavery often used biblical texts to support the institution, despite the fact that this mode of argumentation had become increasingly contested throughout the rest of the Western world.[59] As Noll observes, "The power of the proslavery scriptural position—especially in a Protestant world of widespread intuitive belief in the plenary inspiration of the whole Bible—lay in its simplicity."[60] For many, the Christian Scriptures seemed to plainly support the institution of slavery in both the Old and the New Testaments. Old Testament passages such as Leviticus 25:39–46 and Deuteronomy 20:10–11 were seen as indicating that slavery was supported by God, since he, after all, was the giver of this Law. In regard to the New Testament, proponents of slavery highlighted not only that slaves were given instructions on their conduct by both Peter (1 Pet. 2:18) and Paul (Eph. 6:5) but also that they were not told to seek their freedom and their masters were not told to set them free. This, in conjunction with the commonly held belief that Africans were descendants of Ham and therefore accursed (Gen. 9:25–27), seemed to rather plainly indicate that slavery was permissible.[61]

It is worth noting that pro-slavery advocates did not limit their arguments to appeals to Holy Scripture. A number of arguments in favor of retaining the institution were rooted in appeals to the common good and the lack of

59. Noll, *Civil War as a Theological Crisis*, 34.
60. Noll, *Civil War as a Theological Crisis*, 33.
61. There is also the larger issue, as Eva Sheppard Wolf points out, that slavery was viewed not only as permitted by Holy Scripture but also as economically advantageous and in the best interests of the nation. Wolf writes, "In the 1760s and 1770s, for instance, the Quaker abolitionism that dominated anti-slavery discourse tended to assume that the morality of abolition trumped the advantages of slavery. Abolitionists argued, not only in print but face to face in Quaker meetings, that the evil of slavery demanded its end *even though* so many individual Americans found slavery personally and financially beneficial." Wolf, "Early Free-Labor Thought," 36.

civility in black peoples.[62] Calls for immediate emancipation were dismissed with a scoff. The idea of releasing millions of uneducated, illiterate, property-less, "uncultured" black men and women into the cities and towns of this fledgling republic was unsettling, especially in light of the conflicts erupt-ing in the Caribbean. At best, these newly minted citizens would become a burden to society. Their continued enslavement provided their masters with the opportunity to instill in them a sense of "culture" and instruct them in Christian doctrine.[63]

Other Christians, adopting the cause of abolition, viewed slavery as either a social evil or a source of moral corruption.[64] While there were certainly exceptions to this rule, Christians who opposed slavery typically used theo-logical arguments or ethical principles instead of relying strictly on biblical exegesis.[65] For example, Afro-American abolitionist Theodore Wright grounds his appeal for the abolition of slavery in the fact that the enslaved are image bearers of God.[66] New York City preacher Robert Alexander Young points to the inherent rights God has given to every human being, slaves and freeborn alike.[67] William Lloyd Garrison calls for the instructions and teachings of Scripture to be measured by "its reasonableness and utility, by the probabilities of the case, by historical confirmation, by human experience and observation, by the facts of science, by the intuition of the spirit. Truth is older than any parchment."[68] Note here that for Wright, Young, and Garrison, among others, the appeal to abolish slavery is not rooted in providing contrasting exegesis of the slave codes in Leviticus or the teachings of the New Testament. Rather,

---

62. Burin, *Slavery and the Peculiar Solution*, 7.

63. Carwardine, "Antebellum Reform," 74.

64. Carwardine argues that the formation of the Liberty Party in the 1840s typifies this approach. He writes, "The new party was a quintessential product of socially concerned, re-vivalistic Protestantism. Its agenda sprang from seeing slavery as moral corruption, not just a social evil; from regarding government not as a neutral arbiter but as a vessel of righteousness. America's rulers, to avoid the judgment of the Almighty, had to stand up squarely to slavehold-ers." Carwardine, *Evangelicals and Politics*, 136–37.

65. Noll writes, "The primary reason that the biblical defense of slavery remained so strong was that many biblical attacks on slavery were so weak. To oversimplify a complicated picture, the most direct biblical attacks on slavery were ones that relied on common sense, the broadly accepted intuitions of American national ideology, and the weight of 'self-evident truth.' They were also the easiest to refute." Noll, *Civil War as a Theological Crisis*, 40.

66. T. Wright, "Prejudice against the Colored Man," 91.

67. "But learn, slaveholder, thine will rests not in thine hand: God decrees to thy slave his rights as man" (Young, "Ethiopian Manifesto," 88). It is worth noting in passing that it is a bit reductionistic to identify Young as "merely" appealing to principles. The entire framework of his pamphlet is rooted in the scriptural promise that "Ethiopia will soon stretch forth her hands unto God" (cf. Ps. 68:31).

68. Garrison, "Thomas Paine," 186.

the argument for emancipation is rooted in an appeal to "a universal human-ism and the struggle for the rights of all oppressed peoples."[69] While there is nothing inherently wrong with such a line of reasoning, it did leave something to be desired in the minds of many Christian readers and pro-slavery apolo-gists. As Matthew Mason summarizes aptly, "Antislavery in North America began with objections to slavery as antithetical to such precepts as the Golden Rule."[70] Appeals to ethical concepts or theological principles over the biblical text itself left abolitionists open to the charge that they had jettisoned the biblical tradition in favor of liberal principles or sentiments. Indeed, it was common for abolitionists to appeal to particular forms of biblical argument in conjunction with appeals to a particular interpretation of the United States Constitution.[71] This cocktail of argumentation did little to persuade their op-ponents, however, as many Christian proponents of slavery simply believed that the Bible was on their side.[72]

Resist, Resist, Resist: The Quest to Realize Emancipation

While politicians, constituents, and legislators debated the merits of slavery and emancipation, some abolitionists prepared to take matters into their own hands. For some, like Reverend Henry Highland Garnet, the perpetuation of the institution of slavery was simply not an option. When Garnet took the stage in 1843 at the National Convention of Colored Citizens in Buffalo, New York, he called on slaves to rise up in protest, following in the footsteps of the American Revolution.[73] He said, "Brethren, the time has come when you must act for yourselves. . . . You can plead your own cause, and do the work of emancipation better than any others."[74] Given the limited agency and political voice the enslaved possessed, Garnet appealed to the honor

69. Moses, *Creative Conflict in African American Thought*, 41.

70. Mason, "Necessary but Not Sufficient," 12.

71. See Watkins, *Slavery and Sacred Texts*, 110–17, 176–82.

72. While the historical accounts of slavery can frequently lapse into a North/South dualism, Burin observes that many of the arguments against abolition began in the North and were then appropriated by Southerners in their defense of slavery. "The first and most coherent defenses of slavery were developed by northerners during the late eighteenth and early nineteenth cen-turies. The institution's supports claimed that economic necessity, private property rights, and the Bible itself justified the continuation of chattel bondage. Southern apologists would later employ all of these arguments." Burin, *Slavery and the Peculiar Solution*, 7.

73. Garnet, "Address to the Slaves," 148.

74. Garnet, "Address to the Slaves," 146. Throughout Garnet's address, he alludes to Patrick Henry's speech at the Second Virginia Convention (1775), which is frequently credited with persuading the convention to send troops to participate in the Revolutionary War. The phrase "liberty or death" is directly stated three times in Garnet's speech and alluded to numerous other times.

of the enslaved, encouraging them to actively resist the desecration of their families, the exploitation of their labor, and the sexual assault of their loved ones.[75] Reminding his audience of the slave revolts of figures such as Denmark Vesey and Nathaniel Turner, Garnet argued that a violent uprising was necessary in order to bring an end to slavery. "Let your motto be resistance! Resistance! Resistance! No oppressed people have ever secured their liberty without resistance."[76] Garnet, tired of the middling efforts of those who preferred moral suasion and gradual abolition, called enslaved Afro-Americans to arms and action, a call that resonated with many of his listeners.[77] Freeborn blacks like Theodore Wright in New York City had grown weary with the slow effects of anti-slavery efforts. Following in the tradition of David Walker's *Appeal* (1829), Garnet's speech called for Afro-Americans of all stripes and castes to be ready and willing to shed their blood for the cause of freedom.

Garnet was a skilled orator, and his speech tapped into the anger and frustration that were simmering within the abolitionary movement. Of course, the effect of Garnet's speech was not solely positive. In fact, the speech left many abolitionists and slaveholders feeling uneasy, especially given its grounding in and affirmation of the insurrections of Nathaniel Turner and Denmark Vesey. The concern for slaveholders is fairly obvious. Slaves possessed intimate knowledge of plantation life and had access to the sleeping quarters and loved ones of their masters. Despite the fact that many slaves were illiterate and would not be able to read the publication of Garnet's speech, slaveholders were concerned that Garnet's speech would lead to violent uprisings, putting their families and livelihoods at risk. Many abolitionists also found Garnet's appeal troubling. They were concerned that if slaves did follow Garnet's advice, a violent and most likely failed uprising would quickly erode any sympathy the movement had taken such pains to cultivate. In fact, Frederick Douglass actively suppressed the publication of Garnet's speech, fearing it could lead to an insurrection that would ultimately undermine the abolitionary cause.[78]

75. Garnet, "Address to the Slaves," 146.

76. Garnet, "Address to the Slaves," 149.

77. Garnet's address led to larger concerns within both the pro-slavery and the anti-slavery movements that Garnet's ideas would spread and take root within enslaved minds, leading to a large-scale revolt.

78. Wilson Jeremiah Moses suspects that Douglass's opposition to Garnet's call to violent resistance may also have stemmed from both Douglass's opposition to wholesale revolt and his egotistical desire to leave a memorable impression at the convention (Moses, *Creative Conflict in African American Thought*, 28; see also Schor, "Rivalry between Frederick Douglass and Henry Highland Garnet"). Still, Moses notes that there are curious similarities between Garnet's speech at the National Convention of Colored Citizens in Buffalo, New York (1843), and Douglass's later speech, "What to the Slave Is the Fourth of July?" at the Corinthian Hall in Rochester, New York (1852).

Such fears were legitimate given the tendency among white, pro-slavery advo-cates to identify a causal link between abolitionary activity and slave revolts.[79] Still, Garnet's speech and the concerns it raised are indicative of a change in the national landscape. Southern slave owners were becoming increasingly resolute in their belief that slavery was a part of American life and here to stay. Northern abolitionists were becoming more and more convinced that the union would not be able to stand over the issue.[80]

The American Colonization Society

So what was to be done about the "slave question"? If violent revolt stood at one end of the spectrum, the American Colonization Society (ACS) stood at the other.[81] Formed in 1816, the ACS proposed that blacks and whites could not live in the same country and that the former needed a land of their own.[82] Its premises were not exactly novel. Long before the founding of the ACS, figures such as Thomas Jefferson and James Madison had already sown the seeds of its basic premises. Jefferson surmised that while blacks lacked the disposition and intellectual faculties required to thrive in civilization, the "total emancipation" of enslaved blacks was inevitable, albeit through the eventual consent of their masters.[83] What was needed, then, according to both Jefferson and Madison, was an African colony where manumitted slaves could be sent to realize their freedom. For Jefferson, this would happen only after slaves were of a certain age. When black women reached the age of eighteen and males the age of twenty-one and after they had been sufficiently trained in the arts and sciences, Jefferson surmised that these educated, "enculturated" individuals could be sent off to play their part in colonial life.[84] According to Jefferson, this sort of colonization was not just beneficial; it was necessary. Due at least in part to the "deep rooted prejudices entertained by the whites; ten thousand recollections, by the blacks, of the injuries they have sustained," which would inevitably "divide us into parties, and produce convulsion which

---

79. Rugemer, *Slave Law and the Politics of Resistance*, 96.

80. Jonathan Wells writes, "Just as the white South had become more absolute in its determi-nation to defend bondage in the 1820s and especially after Nat Turner in the 1830s, northerners had shifted in their stance on the legitimacy of the constitutional compromise over slavery." J. Wells, *Blind No More*, 50.

81. Mason, *Slavery and Politics*, 161.

82. There are conceptual similarities here with how the United States was responding to the presence of indigenous peoples. Indeed, the "enculturation" of Native Americans and their segregation from the rest of the population were viewed as something of a template for the ACS's aspirations in Africa.

83. T. Jefferson, *Notes on the State of Virginia*, 96, 174.

84. T. Jefferson, *Notes on the State of Virginia*, 147.

will probably never end but in the extermination of the one or the other race," the two groups could not coexist on the continent.[85]

The ACS recognized the growing number of blacks who populated the United States and the problems this could potentially pose for national unity.[86] If blacks and whites could not share a common life, then the only option was to send one group away.[87] Formed by Presbyterian minister Robert Finley, the ACS proposed that Afro-American slaves be sent back to Africa.[88] Finley writes, "We should be cleared of them; we should send to Africa a population partially civilized and Christianized for its benefit; our blacks themselves would be put in a better situation."[89] Eventually, the ACS saw the colony of Liberia as a viable option for black emigration and, with federal funds and the backing of Congress, began a series of ventures to relocate blacks to the new colony.[90] As Carwardine notes, "Setting freed men and women in West Africa would offer them the chance of self-government and self-improvement denied to them in the United States. Civilized Liberia would become a millennial beacon for the rest of the African continent."[91]

As a political movement, the ACS attempted to garner public support from pro- and anti-slavery advocates. Davis notes that the ACS attempted to unite those many whites who loathed the idea of living with free blacks and feared the contamination of the white race through amalgamation (interracial

---

85. T. Jefferson, *Notes on the State of Virginia*, 147.

86. Of course, the events in Haiti had not been completely erased from the national memory. While many of the early supporters of the ACS had abolitionary sympathies, other supporters were perhaps afraid that the growing number of freed blacks would lead to slave insurrections that would be reminiscent of the scenes unfolding in the Caribbean.

87. Davis notes that this abolitionary ethos would eventually lead to the movement's undoing. He writes, "Since many of the early Northern leaders of the ACS were sincere abolitionists, there were good reasons why representatives from the Deep South were the ones who finally, in the 1820s, killed any prospects for the federal funding that would have been essential for colonization. In the eyes of South Carolinians, especially, the ACS was a Trojan Horse designed to undermine and slowly destroy slavery." Davis, *Inhuman Bondage*, 68.

88. Matthew Spooner has raised questions in recent years as to whether Robert Finley can actually be credited with forming the society. For Spooner, it is important to note that the ACS was not novel in its proposals, as Afro-American slaves had been returned to Africa as early as 1646. Spooner, "'I Know This Scheme Is from God,'" 561.

89. Brown, *Biography of the Reverend Robert Finley*, 99–100.

90. David Ericson notes that "from 1819 to 1865, the ACS received a total of $763,198 in federal assistance. That sum represented 37 percent of the society's receipts of $2,057,133 over those forty-seven years" (Ericson, "American Colonization Society's Not-So-Private Colonization Project," 111). Presidents such as James Monroe and James Buchanan backed this federal-private partnership, offering to cover transportation costs and "settling costs" of any runaway slaves who were recaptured and stationed in Liberia (112).

91. Carwardine, "Antebellum Reform," 72.

copulation).[92] To those pro-slavery advocates who feared black uprisings or the economic and social burden of uneducated, traumatized black people, the ACS offered an avenue for cleansing the nation of black people by deporting them to Africa. Believing that the major obstacle to abolition was the prospect of millions of blacks being set loose in a country that belonged to whites, the ACS argued that blacks should be emancipated and then repatriated to Africa.[93] Yet at the same time, the movement also tried to appeal to abolitionists. The ACS recognized that prejudice and interracial tensions were not likely to disappear overnight, even if slaves were released from bondage. Emigration to Africa offered a tangible hope to the enslaved for their future generations and would effectively bring about the end of slavery in the United States.[94] The ACS hoped to combine these two groups into one coalition, formed around the ideas of emancipation and emigration, as it offered to send freed blacks back to Africa so that they could carve out a country of their own.[95] In other words, the ACS proposed that it could be an organization that served the interests of blacks, whites, abolitionists, and slave owners.

Afro-American Assessment of the ACS

Some Afro-American thinkers and writers were persuaded of the merits of the ACS's proposal.[96] But for many blacks, the ACS's offer ran afoul of the very nature of their appeals for freedom. Gary Nash observes that many Afro-Americans in the North, both slave and free, "did not regard their requests for freedom as appeals to a merciful master class but as a demand for the restoration of inherent rights unlawfully taken from them."[97] Moreover, many Afro-American abolitionists and civic leaders were able to peer through the veil of the ACS's pseudo-benevolence to see the organization's true roots in a fear of blacks. For example, civil rights activist and abolitionist William Hamilton remarks, "There is formed a strong combination against the people of colour, by some who are the master spirits of this day. . . . You can but

92. Davis, *Inhuman Bondage*, 66.

93. Raboteau, *Fire in the Bones*, 47.

94. Raboteau, *Fire in the Bones*, 67.

95. Before the formation of the ACS in 1816, figures such as Anthony Benezet and Thomas Paine proposed in the early 1770s that emancipated or freed blacks be sent to settle in the land across the Allegheny Mountains. Nash, *Forging Freedom*, 102.

96. Figures such as Prince Saunders saw emigration to Haiti as a viable option for forming a free, black nation that was unstained by the problems of prejudice, slavery, and racism. Mary Ann Shadd Cary, in contrast, invited blacks to move north into Canada, far removed from the issues of chattel slavery in the American South, viewing the situation in the United States as unviable for black people. See Shadd, "Plea for Emigration."

97. Nash, *Race and Revolution*, 55.

perceive that I allude to the Colonization Society. However pure the motives of some of the members of that society may be, yet the master spirits thereof are evil minded towards us. They have put on the garb of angels of dark."[98] Hamilton suggests that the ACS was attempting to appeal to Afro-Americans as a benevolent organization when it was in reality operating with mal-intent; he even goes so far as to compare the members of the ACS to demonic spirits (2 Cor. 11:14). Hamilton argues that evidence for this claim can be found in the fact that while the ACS promised opportunity to blacks in a new land, it worked behind the scenes to stir fears of race wars, convince legislators to deny blacks civil rights, and fought to ensure that "the higher branches of education" remained closed off for black peoples.[99]

Despite the ACS's best efforts, many blacks refused to view the attainment of freedom as a gift of benevolence from their masters. For many slaves and Afro-American abolitionists, freedom was theirs by divine right. Moreover, many blacks recognized their immense contributions to the American way of life and found the very notion that they should be sent elsewhere, as the ACS proposed, offensive. As Davis notes, "Most free blacks expressed pride in their American heritage and identity. Many had fought or had fathers who had fought in the War of Independence and then the War of 1812. Black leaders were well aware that their people's labor had been essential in creating the nation."[100] Nineteenth-century abolitionist Robert Roberts argues in the *Liberator* that the ACS operated on the fabled notion that Africa, and not the United States, was the Afro-American slaves' true home. "O ye schemers! Why do ye undertake to impose on the free people of color by telling them that Africa is their native soil, when our fathers fought for liberty, and received nothing for it, and laid their bones here? We claim this as our native soil, and not Africa."[101] This land and all its prosperity, both future and present, had been developed through the labor, exploitation, and deaths of black slaves. If the nation emerged from the salted earth in which their ancestors lay buried, how could it be just for blacks to have to leave and form a life elsewhere? If their forefathers had laid down their lives in the fight for freedom, how could it be good and right for them to be forbidden from enjoying its fruits? No, for Roberts and others like him, that simply would not do. If leaving the United States was not a viable option and slavery persisted throughout much of the country, the question for many abolitionists was how to pursue emancipation through creative resistance.

98. Hamilton, "Address to the National Convention of 1834," 112.
99. Hamilton, "Address to the National Convention of 1834," 112.
100. Davis, *Challenging the Boundaries of Slavery*, 62.
101. R. Roberts, "Texts for Meditation."

Conclusion

As the post–Revolutionary War years dragged on, the United States saw for the first time an increasingly large, free Afro-American population.[102] Advocates of emigration believed that the question of slavery could be resolved only through the return of slaves to their "native land."[103] But the ACS was increasingly addressing blacks who had been born in the United States and had lived here for generations. They were no more "African" than their slave masters were. Many Afro-Americans were less than enthralled with the idea of recrossing the Middle Passage, especially since so much of their ancestors' blood and sweat had soaked into the soil of the continent. Yet the continuation of the institution of slavery was not a viable option either. The question, then, for Afro-Americans, both enslaved and free, was in the words of William Hamilton how to "frustrate the purpose of so awful a foe."[104] As their numbers grew, so did their social agency and their capacity to engage in pluriform, improvisational resistance.

By referring to black resistance to the reality of slavery as "improvisational," I am borrowing a concept from Samuel Wells's *Improvisation*. For Wells, the motif of improvisation in the theater helps explain the manner in which the followers of Christ are called to engage and address new situations, using the narrative of Holy Scripture, as they await the consummation of redemption at Christ's second advent. He explains, "When improvisors are trained to work in the theater, they are schooled in a tradition so thoroughly that they learn to act from habit in ways appropriate to their circumstance. This is exactly the goal of theological ethics."[105] Wells maintains that this does not necessitate that the canon is open or that the text of Scripture is unfixed. Rather, Christian ethics is about forming "habits and disciplines" that will enable the church to respond to certain crises and dilemmas that occur over time.[106] The goal of improvisation is not to repristinate the past but to enable the church to embody the Christian story in its life together. So what does improvisation look like in the abolitionary era? And what does it look like to live in faithful memory of our ancestors while recognizing that the past is not something we ought to simply and uncritically repristinate? Describing and then appropriating abolitionary resistance and reform are the tasks of the chapters that lie ahead.

In what follows, we turn our attention to the pluriform and polyphonic nature of Afro-American improvisational resistance as blacks sought to carve out

---

102. Goodman, *Of One Blood*, 2.
103. Goodman, *Of One Blood*, 2.
104. Hamilton, "Address to the National Convention of 1834," 112.
105. S. Wells, *Improvisation*, 65.
106. S. Wells, *Improvisation*, 213.

a home in the early stages of a new nation. All throughout the United States, slaves, fugitives, and free blacks creatively used their limited social agency to pursue a common life. It was not merely that these men and women sought to free their immediate family members or relatives, although some certainly sought to do so, but that they fought to advance the goods American people held in common. In hearing about and learning from their lives and work, we hope to both honor and retrieve the wisdom of our ancestors so that we might better bear witness to all that God has done in Christ.

2 ✳ ✳ ✳

David Ruggles

Learning to Read and Reimagine the World

"He has literally worn himself out in humanity's struggle. . . . His loss is irreparable. We look in vain for another to fill his place," Frederick Douglass noted in memoriam at the death of the famed abolitionist and provocateur David Ruggles.[1] In hindsight, it is easy to see why Douglass held this particular friend in such high esteem. Not only had Ruggles played a vital role in Douglass's escape from slavery, providing Douglass with shelter, respite, and financial assistance when he arrived in New York, but Ruggles had also played a pivotal role in Douglass's reunion with and subsequent marriage to his wife, Anna.[2] Years earlier, in his second autobiography, Douglass had made a similar assessment of Ruggles's life and witness. Douglass writes,

> I was relieved from [my distressed situation] by the humane hand of Mr. David
> Ruggles, whose vigilance, kindness, and perseverance, I shall never forget. I am

1. As quoted in Hodges, *David Ruggles*, 200. Similar sentiments abounded in the months and years immediately following Ruggles's untimely death. A few months after Ruggles's death, William Lloyd Garrison and Isaac Knapp wrote, "We have not the materials for a biographical notice of this remarkable man, such as deserves to be written, and preserved in permanent form. Identified with the colored population by complexion and destiny, he contended successfully with difficulties, he conquered obstacles, he performed exploits, he encountered perils and sufferings, in the spirit of a hero, and with the courage [of] a martyr." Garrison and Knapp, "Death of David Ruggles," 202.

2. Douglass, *Narrative of the Life of Frederick Douglass*, 108–9.

glad of an opportunity to express, as far as words can, the love and gratitude I bear him. Mr. Ruggles is now afflicted with blindness, and is himself in need of the same kind offices which he was once so forward in the performance of toward others. I had been in New York but a few days, when Mr. Ruggles sought me out, and very kindly took me to his boarding-house.[3]

And so we come to the first of our three abolitionary figures: David Ruggles. David Ruggles was born to a family of free Afro-Americans in Norwich, Connecticut, in 1810. He was the son of a respected blacksmith and a highly regarded cook, and his parents most likely experienced a unique standing in the community due to their respective vocations.[4] Growing up in the community of Bean Hill, a town just north of Norwich, Ruggles appears to have attended the local, integrated Methodist church, even though slavery was still legal in Norwich well into his adult years.[5] Around the age of fifteen, he relocated to New York, where he began life as a mariner before opening a small grocery store from which he operated, making a living while publishing abolitionary sentiments through advertisements.[6] Eventually, in 1833, he left his grocery business behind to participate in abolitionary efforts, working with the likes of Samuel Cornish and Theodore Wright to combat the efforts of the American Colonization Society, address the widespread kidnappings of fugitive and free blacks taking place in New York, and pursue the cause of emancipation. He helped form the New York Committee of Vigilance in 1835, serving as its secretary until, after publicly accusing boardinghouse owner John Russell of participating in the kidnapping of black sailors and losing Russell's subsequent lawsuit, he was forced to resign.[7] Disgraced, losing his eyesight, and destitute, Ruggles moved to Northampton, Massachusetts.[8] There, he founded the nation's first hydropathic center, and he remained in Northampton until his death in 1849.[9]

---

3. Douglass, *Narrative of the Life of Frederick Douglass*, 109. In a subsequent edition of Douglass's autobiography, *My Bondage and My Freedom*, Douglass describes Ruggles as "a whole-souled man, fully imbued with a love of his afflicted and hunted people, and took pleasure in being to me, as was his wont, 'Eyes to the blind, and legs to the lame'" (274).

4. Hodges, *David Ruggles*, 12–14.

5. Slavery was effectively abolished in Connecticut with the passing of "An Act to Prevent Slavery" in 1848. For a discussion of Connecticut's progressive abolition of slavery, see Menschel, "Abolition without Deliverance."

6. Hodges, *David Ruggles*, 43.

7. L. M. Harris, *In the Shadow of Slavery*, 214. See also Ruggles, "Plea for 'A Man and a Brother.'"

8. Friends of Ruggles, such as William Lloyd Garrison and Isaac Knapp, tried to raise funds to help the ailing abolitionist. See Garrison and Knapp, "Meeting for David Ruggles."

9. L. M. Harris, *In the Shadow of Slavery*, 215. Ruggles's financial woes were due in part to his involvement in the Derg case. Accused of "aiding and abetting the slave [Thomas Hughes]

In this chapter, we turn our attention to the life and work of David Ruggles as a resource for the church's public witness. First, as we will see, he is critical of the institution of slavery, particularly in light of the way that Christian participation in it led to a drastic compromise of the Christian community's witness. It is this proliferation of vice within the *Christian* community that serves as evidence, from Ruggles's vantage point, of a larger need to address the vicious nature of chattel slavery. Second, Ruggles extends a call to action to the margins, asking women, fugitive slaves, and freeborn blacks to participate in the struggle against slavery in meaningful ways. Whether it is women in church appropriating the power of "the ban" or free blacks pooling resources for fugitive slaves, Ruggles believes that the marginalized can combine their agency creatively and powerfully. His life and work call us to reimagine the possibilities for human action, both individually and collectively, in pursuit of social transformation.

Interpreting the World with Holy Writ and Christian Ethics

Slavery and Christian Ethics

To provide an overarching critique of slavery as an institution, Ruggles, using the long-standing prophetic principle of moral suasion, first seeks to establish that slave owners are behaving viciously (e.g., in *The Abrogation of the Seventh Commandment*). Moral suasion, as Frank Kirkland observes, "is *prima facie* the use of rhetoric to persuade others about the wrongness of slavery and the moral rightness of abolition."[10] Ruggles observes how slave owners consistently violate moral law, here typified in a failure to observe the Ten Commandments. He points to the manner in which their beliefs and practices deform them and the tacit acceptance of this moral compromise within the larger community. For example, Ruggles notes that slavery leads to violation of the seventh commandment: do not commit adultery (Exod. 20:14). He observes that the large number of "mixed race" offspring on plantations indicates that masters have been copulating with their female slaves, an act of obvious infidelity to their wives.[11] He writes, "In addition to all the most odious and criminal attributes of American slaveholding, a licentiousness of intercourse between the sexes, constant, incestuous, and

---

in robbing his master, and concealing the fugitive," Ruggles was arrested and forced to pay thousands of dollars in legal fees. "Examination of the Black Man, Ruggles."

10. Kirkland, "Enslavement, Moral Suasion, and Struggles for Recognition," 244.

11. As Loren Schweninger notes, "Although it is not possible to know how often slaveholding husbands engaged in sexual relations with one or more of their slaves, we know from various sources that it was not unusual." Schweninger, *Families in Crisis in the Old South*, 19.

universal, exists. . . . This direful calamity is an essential portion . . . of that debasing bondage in which colored women are held, and by which they are defiled and destroyed."[12] Notice that Ruggles identifies the defiling of black women as an "essential portion" of institutional slavery. This suggests that he sees some kind of logical and perhaps even causal connection between the degradation of the humanity of black women and their sexual exploitation. It is slavery itself that is generative of this kind of vice. Ruggles argues that this constant assault of black women and their subsequent subjugation, "in the most flagrant forms of turpitude, without the possibility of complaint or redress," are illustrative of a moral failing on the part of their masters.[13]

Elsewhere, Ruggles argues that the institution of slavery is founded on the violation of two other commandments: do not steal and do not covet (Exod. 20:15, 17). According to Ruggles, the commandment not to steal is applicable to the practice of "man stealing"—that is, the taking possession of a person's self as property.[14] For Ruggles, "Any thing that is thy neighbour's, anything which he holds in his possession, whether lawfully or not, is no concern of thine. . . . The command is to us to do our duty in relation to our neighbour."[15] Slavery violates this commandment in that the slaveholder appropriates another person's labor, rights, children, and spouse, claiming them as their own.[16] Ruggles also applies the logic of the commandment not to covet to the act of owning another human being as property. According to Ruggles, a slave owner covets their neighbor's body in their desire to possess the other person as property. In so doing, they lust after something that belongs to another by divine right: their very self.[17] In holding their neighbor as property, the slave owner has effectively stolen what rightly belongs to another. Of course, undoubtedly, few masters would have viewed the slave/master relationship through the lens of neighborliness and negated the very proposition that slaves possessed self-ownership. Yet Ruggles is adamant that slaveholding is "man theft" in any and every case and that it violates the very logics that undergird a Christian community.[18]

---

12. Ruggles, *Abrogation of the Seventh Commandment*, 4.
13. Ruggles, *Abrogation of the Seventh Commandment*, 4.
14. Ruggles, *Antidote for a Poisonous Combination*, 5.
15. Ruggles, *"Extinguisher" Extinguished!*, 26.
16. Ruggles, *Abrogation of the Seventh Commandment*, 21.
17. There is a larger question here of whether we do in fact belong to ourselves. As Luke Bretherton observes, "The intrinsic value of every human is determined through how each human is always already situated in and open to relation with God. By implication, one's humanity is not owned like a piece of property, and so it cannot be revoked or alienated." Bretherton, *Christ and the Common Life*, 309.
18. Ruggles, *Antidote for a Poisonous Combination*, 8.

The application of Christian moral law to the slave/master relationship is particularly intriguing. Ruggles consistently points out the failures of *Christian* slaveholders to exercise *Christian* charity in regard to their enslaved neighbors.[19] In many ways, then, he identifies the manner in which Christian agents fail to embody the spirit and standards of their own creeds and confessions.[20] Yet what is subtle here is the manner in which Ruggles subverts and delegitimizes the social hierarchy, a hierarchy that renders such behavior acceptable. Ruggles takes for granted the fact that slaves are persons and neighbors. It is not a proposition he feels inclined to argue *for* as much as a self-evident claim he argues *from* throughout the course of his writings. In other words, Ruggles presupposes that the ethic that is used to govern the interaction between fellow citizens must accord within the slave/master relationship, which implicitly proposes that slaves have certain rights of citizenship. Furthermore, Ruggles accuses slaveholders—those who would have argued that slavery was advantageous to the enslaved, granting them access to the Christian faith, restraining their "barbaric" behavior, and offering them the opportunity to be trained in civility—of an even greater barbarism.[21] In so doing, he cryptically inverts these very categories of brutality and civility, painting slave owners and their supporters as those who exhibit a bestiality unbefitting their status as human creatures. The goal, of course, is social reformation and the abolition of slavery. But to reach this end, Ruggles strives to demonstrate how the Christian community is failing to live up to its own standards.

A Polluted Church in a Disordered World

For Ruggles, the violation of specific commandments is indicative of slavery's larger perversion of the human social life, as evidenced in the communal disregard and contempt for God's moral law, the acceptance of these

---

19. Ruggles, *Antidote for a Poisonous Combination*, 11.

20. Ruggles, *Abrogation of the Seventh Commandment*, 14.

21. Immanuel Kant can here serve as a representative figure. According to Kant, "The Negro race, one could say, is exactly the opposite of the American; they are full of affect and passion, very lively, talkative and vain. They acquire culture, but only a culture of slaves; that is, they allow themselves to be trained. They have many incentives, are also sensitive, afraid of beatings, and also do many things out of honor" (Kant, *"Menschenkunde,"* 320). Kant's schema, one affirmed by the likes of Johann Blumenbach and other anthropologists, argues that phenotypic differences are indicative of *essential* differences, such that blacks (Negros) are consigned to a place of inferiority in a racial hierarchy. As Justin Smith points out, one way of accounting for the phenotypic and cultural distinctions of different people groups was through a narrative of degeneration—first through differences of diet and climate and then, eventually, through degenerate morals and practices, including but not limited to copulation with the members of other species. See J. E. H. Smith, *Nature, Human Nature, and Human Difference*, 114–39.

violations, and the resulting deformation that occurs. Ruggles makes an appeal here to something akin to the idea of natural law, arguing that there are certain institutions (e.g., the family and marriage) that God has ordained for the flourishing of civil society. Yet enslavement actively opposes both institutions and, by extension, leads to the perversion of society. Regarding marriage, Ruggles notes that Christians have traditionally valued the institution of marriage as necessary for human flourishing and that human trafficking directly undermines this commitment. While slaves could technically enter into marital relationships, their marriages were neither formally recognized nor legally protected.[22] Because slaves were subject to the proclivities of their masters, it is unsurprising that a large number of marriages ended in sale and were thereby effectively dissolved.[23] For Ruggles, this is problematic, given that it either consigns couples to perpetual infidelity or effectively violates slaves' marital bonds so that "the matrimonial connection among slaves is altogether nullified."[24] Ruggles exclaims, "You will remember also, that all those hideous and crying sins [mentioned in Amos 2:6–7] are the unavoidable result of the dissolution of the marriage compact: which overthrow the will and government of God, as it was announced at the creation of mankind, is sanctioned by the professed disciples of Christ; and by all those ecclesiastical associations who recognize slaveholders and slaves as good and acceptable members."[25] Ruggles uses the prophetic pronouncements of Amos to point out that since marriage is an institution that God has ordained and established, slaveholders, in violating and voiding slave marriages, are actively showing contempt for God's governance and nullifying his commands.[26] Involvement in one institution, slavery, has perverted Christians to the point that they hold antipathy toward the institutions God has ordained.

Ruggles makes a similar argument for the dissolution of the family, another institution that he believes is divinely ordained. Ruggles notes that from the beginning the procurement of slaves severs familial ties, as slaves are snatched from one nexus of relationships, transported across the Atlantic, and thrown into another.[27] He writes, "One of the greatest evils, and most undeniable effects of slavery or slaveholding, is the frequent separation of families and

---

22. Ruggles, *Abrogation of the Seventh Commandment*, 10.

23. Schweninger, *Families in Crisis in the Old South*, 22. David Brown and Clive Webb estimate that as many as a third of all slave marriages ended in sale, with many of the surviving marriages serving as a means to dissuade or manipulate those seeking manumission. Brown and Webb, *Race in the American South*, 138–39.

24. Ruggles, *Abrogation of the Seventh Commandment*, 5.

25. Ruggles, *Abrogation of the Seventh Commandment*, 14.

26. Ruggles, *Abrogation of the Seventh Commandment*, 10.

27. Ruggles, *"Extinguisher" Extinguished!*, 14.

dear friends and relations. No one will have the hardihood to deny that slavery is the parent of these evils."[28] Worse still, Ruggles points out the common practice of selling family members and spouses to neighboring plantations to deter a slave's pursuit of freedom. For Ruggles, intentionally manipulating familial bonds to "remove from many [slaves] the desire of running away"[29] again highlights the depth of social perversion. Ruggles believes this sets slaveholding in diametric opposition to the governance of God and those who participate in slavery in opposition to the very spirit of the gospel.[30]

Not only has society's moral fabric been compromised, but Ruggles also draws attention to the fact that there has been a tacit acceptance of this distortion within the larger community. Regarding the preponderance of adultery and sexual assault taking place on plantations, Ruggles notes that Southern women are unperturbed by their husbands' infidelity and abuse. He writes, "[Southern women] know all the odious and accursed miseries to which colored women are subject; and they connive at those violations of female honor and affection, by raising no voice of outcry, and making no effort for their deliverance."[31] For Ruggles, the problem is less one of unconscious participation and more one of blatant moral compromise. The fact that one woman is able to look on the sexual assault of another and remain unmoved is problematic and is indicative of a larger moral shift that has taken place, a shift that has untethered Christian social ethics from its biblical moorings. The result for Ruggles is fairly obvious, and we can critically look back from the effects (rampant adultery and rape) to the cause (the objectification resulting from slavery). For Ruggles, then, the acceptance of adultery and rape as part of the social fabric, one unhampered by the Christian moral landscape, serves as evidence that the larger social structure is in need of severe renovation.[32] Accordingly, the individual participants, the social institutions, and the ecclesial communities that exist within it must be purified.[33]

---

28. Ruggles, *Antidote for a Poisonous Combination*, 11.
29. Ruggles, *Antidote for a Poisonous Combination*, 9.
30. Ruggles, *"Extinguisher" Extinguished!*, 24.
31. Ruggles, *Abrogation of the Seventh Commandment*, 9.
32. As Schweninger observes, "The fact that some of the men, both slaveholders and non-slaveholders, boasted of their sexual prowess and appeared to care little about what others thought of their bragging about their 'conquests' not only reveals their own confidence that nothing could be done or would be done to punish such conduct but also suggests that their neighbors accepted such behavior as a normal by-product of the slave system." Schweninger, *Families in Crisis in the Old South*, 22.
33. Here we can see the influence of Ruggles's Methodist and revivalist upbringing. Continuing the legacy of John Wesley's abolitionary efforts in England, American Methodists originally disbarred slaveholders from membership, a stance more strongly held in the North than in the South. As Douglas Strong notes, "The Wesleyan Methodists' conception of entire

Systems of Vice

Of course, delineating the immoral acts committed by disparate immoral agents does not *necessarily* prove the viciousness of slavery on an institutional level. After all, Ruggles's critique could just as easily suggest that a change of behavior on the part of the slaveholder is sufficient. Yet Ruggles rejects this conclusion explicitly, arguing that it is the system of slavery that must be abolished because the system itself is evil.[34] Slavery necessarily produces these kinds of actions. Ruggles maintains that individual slaveholders and those free citizens who ignore the horrors of slavery are morally culpable for the institution's continued existence. But he also argues that culpability can be predicated *in virtue of* a certain kind of deep participation in the institution. As a result, the institution of slavery must be abolished because of the manner in which it encourages and incentivizes vicious behavior.

Ruggles takes pains to demonstrate that the vicious actions he has identified on the part of slaveholders is indicative of a vicious social system. For Ruggles, the problem is not the specific cases of adultery and theft, nor is deformation of individual agents the center of his critique. Rather, Ruggles is principally concerned with the manner in which the system of slavery incentivizes and encourages these sinful ways of being in the world. For Ruggles, this takes place in at least two distinct ways.

First, the objectification of black bodies delegitimizes the role social guilt and the justice system play in restraining immoral actions and shaping society morally. Both social guilt and the legal system, at minimum, are tools that seek to disincentivize certain forms of depraved behavior with the threat of punishment. Yet Ruggles notes that in the case of slavery, these two resources of communal formation have been removed and cannot serve their intended function of restraining vice. He argues that slave owners are actively encouraged to "habitually violate their nuptial vows and the laws of chastity, if they please, without forfeiting their moral or Christian character; because the enactments of slavery preclude the proof, and consequently the disgrace which conviction of the fact might produce."[35] According to Ruggles, the assault of black women has been legitimized and any social disgrace that ought to accompany it has been removed, since they are viewed as "no better than brutes."[36] Furthermore, the legal system was ill-equipped to prevent such action due to its relegating of blacks to the status of chattel and its

---

sanctification stressed purity of life, including the purity of social institutions." Strong, *Perfectionist Politics*, 101.

34. Ruggles, *Antidote for a Poisonous Combination*, 13.

35. Ruggles, *Abrogation of the Seventh Commandment*, 13.

36. Ruggles, *Abrogation of the Seventh Commandment*, 5.

refusal to grant them the rights of citizenship, having excluded blacks from participation in juridical and governmental spaces, having denied them the right to own property, and having refused to admit their testimony as evidence in court.[37] Accordingly, a slave had no legal recourse in the face of her attackers.[38] Prohibited from the justice system, these women were not afforded the protections it would offer legally recognized citizens. They could neither identify nor confront their attackers, let alone hold their masters accountable for their actions. Consequently, there was neither a social nor a legal consequence to the sexual assault of black women. While it is certainly a problem that individual agents are acting in malicious and sinful ways, the larger problem for Ruggles is that the institution of slavery encourages these immoral and deleterious ways of being in the world.

Second, the commodification of black bodies incentivizes sexual assault and other forms of vice (e.g., kidnapping, lying, human trafficking). As Kathryn Tanner observes, capitalism, like all social systems, has certain concomitants that direct and encourage particular actions in order to achieve a meaningful and valuable life.[39] These forms govern, encourage, and incentivize behavior in the hope of attaining more economic capital.[40] Because slaves were relegated to the status of chattel, marked as things instead of persons, they could be exchanged on the market for other commodities.[41] As noted in the previous chapter, the closing of the transatlantic slave trade in 1808 reshaped the domestic slave economy, providing an incentive for slave catchers to target and capture free blacks in order to sell them as runaways, with children being some of the most frequent victims.[42] Ruggles argues not only that the practice of "man-theft" is immoral, as we have already noted, but that the institution of slavery is perverse precisely because it incentivizes and rewards these kinds of actions. In a similar manner, the confluence of capitalism and slavery encourages a slaveholder to effectively instrumentalize the bodies of black women to create more capital. Racial categories were

---

37. Ruggles, *Antidote for a Poisonous Combination*, 8. See also Goring, "History of Slave Marriage in the United States," 303–4.

38. Less than ten years after Ruggles's death, the famous *Dred Scott v. Sandford* case would articulate these logics precisely. See Smedley and Smedley, *Race in North America*, 239–44.

39. Tanner writes, "Capitalism has cultural concomitants—beliefs, values, and norms—that direct conduct, that get people to do willingly what capitalism requires of them by encouraging them to see what they are doing—what they *must* do to get ahead—as meaningful, valuable, or simply inevitable. . . . Such cultural concomitants of capitalism amount to practical directives, helping to elicit and orient the very behaviors that capitalism mandates." Tanner, *Christianity and the New Spirit of Capitalism*, 99.

40. Tanner, *Christianity and the New Spirit of Capitalism*, 10.

41. N. Roberts, *Freedom as Marronage*, 59–60.

42. J. Wells, *Blind No More*, 19–20.

understood to travel along bloodlines, and the child of a slave would remain chattel. In light of this, Ruggles concludes that there is financial incentive to "multiply slaves" through any and every means since those children could be sold for profit or put to work on the plantation. In other words, it was profitable and advantageous for slaveholders to create children *through* their slaves in order to increase their slave populations.[43] According to Ruggles, this illustrates once again that the system of slavery encourages vice.

For Ruggles, culpability can then be predicated of those agents who support and profit from the system, as they are the ones who are engaging in sinful acts and succumbing to malicious temptations.[44] Yet Ruggles, as we will see below, by no means disavows the agency of the enslaved or marginalized. We might say, to borrow from more recent categories, that Ruggles delineates between deep participation and deep moral responsibility. Following the work of Susan Wolfe, Jesse Couenhoven argues that there is a distinction between being responsible, causally connected, and deeply, morally responsible, the latter of which is true of an agent who engages in an action of moral significance for which they justly deserve blame.[45] It is only those who are deeply responsible for the propagation of the system of slavery who are morally responsible for it on an institutional level. For Ruggles, the particular corrupt acts that slavery encourages and incentivizes cannot be abstracted from the institution of slavery itself and illustrate the malicious nature of the social system.[46] It is a system of vice that habitually encourages and incentivizes sinful human acts, typified in the blatant violation of the Ten Commandments.

A Call to Action

Ruggles reasons via retrospective analysis from the effects of slavery and slaveholding on the Christian community to explore the vicious nature of the institution. Yet Ruggles is unsatisfied with a mere critique of the viciousness of slavery or a description of its unjustness as a social system. And while many of the followers of William Lloyd Garrison were content to try to persuade citizens morally to commit to the cause of abolition and were skeptical of institutions, Ruggles opted not to follow them in this regard, calling for slaves, women, fugitives, and free blacks to engage in concrete acts of resistance.[47] For Ruggles, Christian charity takes the form of active resistance in

43. Ruggles, *Abrogation of the Seventh Commandment*, 5–6.
44. Ruggles, *Antidote for a Poisonous Combination*, 3.
45. Couenhoven, *Stricken by Sin, Cured by Christ*, 571.
46. Ruggles, *Abrogation of the Seventh Commandment*, 11.
47. Strong, *Perfectionist Politics*, 43.

the progressive pursuit of freedom. As Neil Roberts avers, "Resistance is the means through which an agent achieves [the] condition of emancipation."[48] According to Ruggles, the institution of slavery is an unjust social system that requires reformation and creative, resilient resistance. Both the church and those living on the margins of society possess their own tools of resistance, "evangelical weapons" that must be used to resist and reform the societies in which they exist.

Recall that, for Ruggles, the turning of the Christian community against God's rule and governance is evidence of slavery's viciousness. In light of this, Ruggles focuses on the two ecclesial practices of the Eucharist and the ban (excommunication), which he reads and applies politically. Appropriating 1 Corinthians 5:9–11 and its call for excommunication on the grounds of adultery, Ruggles calls Northern women to break communion with those who own slaves, permit the abuse of black bodies, and refuse to adhere to the commandments of Holy Scripture. In his view, the church must cleanse itself for the sake of its witness to the world.

On the one hand, Ruggles's emphasis is ecclesial as he calls for Christians to openly engage in the "arduous but indispensable duty of purifying the churches of this noisome pestilence."[49] For Ruggles, slavery pollutes the church on moral grounds, compromising the ecclesial community's purity, warping its shape, and perverting its goods. So, then, Ruggles seeks ecclesial reform.[50] On the other hand, ecclesial practices take on a political valence in Ruggles's thought, and correct praxis holds ramifications for society at large. For Ruggles, the proper administration of the sacrament and the exercise of the ban are intended to illuminate the moral compromise to which the Christian community has succumbed and then place a kind of theological pressure on Christians that will lead them to oppose the evils of slavery outside the church's walls. In other words, ecclesial praxis holds political significance for the community outside the church insofar as church members share a common life with those outsiders. Ruggles argues that proper ecclesial praxis is essential to the task of seeking "the immediate and universal emancipation" of slaves across the United States.[51]

Additionally, Ruggles recognizes the potential for social transformation to emerge from the margins of society. He calls women to exercise their voices within the church so that "all slaveholders of every grade and name shall be peremptorily excluded from the pulpit and the Lord's tables, in the churches

48. N. Roberts, *Freedom as Marronage*, 161.
49. Ruggles, *"Extinguisher" Extinguished!*, 19.
50. Ruggles, *Abrogation of the Seventh Commandment*, 20.
51. Ruggles, *"Extinguisher" Extinguished!*, 11.

to which they belong."[52] Women were politically marginalized, since they possessed little formal political or institutional power and were denied the rights of full citizenship and representation within governmental spheres. Yet Ruggles calls them to participate in forms of resistance, exercising social agency that he believes can effect meaningful social change. Ruggles asks, "It is nugatory to ask what can a small number of women do? *What cannot they do?*"[53] As Graham Hodges observes, Ruggles's proposal was revolutionary, even for his time. "At a time when American Protestant churches were splitting over the issues of slavery and abolitionism, Ruggles was not seeking a truce but demanding that northern congregations shun their southern communicants. He aimed his words right at women, who formed the majority of loyal members in most American churches."[54] According to Ruggles, the Christian, and by extension the citizen, must creatively engage society and take advantage of whatever "pockets of action" are available to them in order to pursue the good of the enslaved. He writes, "It is not a sufficient excuse for the Southern ladies to plead that they cannot destroy the system of slavery. *They can do it*; and if they were not callous . . . *they would do it.*"[55] The failure to recognize and actualize one's agency in pursuit of extending social goods to the enslaved, then, is principally a failure of the Christian political imagination.

Ruggles makes a similar move within his call for freed and runaway slaves to participate in the act of pursuing freedom and the rights of citizenship for the enslaved. In seeking to raise funds for the *Liberator*, a periodical dedicated to the cause of abolition, Ruggles writes, "Though ours is the 'Land of Liberty' *we are slaves* whose condition is but a short remove from that of two millions of our race who are pining in their bloody chains, and that our contest is for *freedom* and that the press is the weapon which we wield in behalf of our rights."[56] The importance of the press may again be an example of Ruggles's use of moral suasion as a tactic. Yet Ruggles also recognizes that the press can serve as a tool to combat the efforts of kidnappers or smugglers who seek to trick or abduct Northern free blacks and sell

52. Ruggles, *Abrogation of the Seventh Commandment*, 20.
53. Ruggles, *Abrogation of the Seventh Commandment*, 16–17, emphasis original.
54. Hodges, *David Ruggles*, 80. This demand for the immediate abolition of slavery is indicative of the *Liberator*'s perspective of slavery, a newspaper begun by William Lloyd Garrison. As David Brown and Clive Webb observe, "The abolitionist attack on the South became progressively fiercer, forcing a southern response that increasingly promoted a racial defence of slavery. . . . That uncompromising message bluntly stated that slaveholding was a sin and called for immediate emancipation." Brown and Webb, *Race in the American South*, 103–4.
55. Ruggles, *Abrogation of the Seventh Commandment*, 9, emphasis original.
56. Ruggles, "Appeal to the Colored Citizens," 637, emphasis original.

them into slavery for profit.[57] Leslie Harris notes that Ruggles uses the press to publicize the tactics of the New York Kidnapping Club and the names of its members while also raising awareness of the plight of fugitive slaves and free blacks.[58] As a founder of the New York Committee of Vigilance, Ruggles, along with other committee members, also informed runaway slaves of their right to claim freedom, offered financial support to fugitives, and provided legal aid in times of need.[59] Ruggles's appeal to Afro-Americans is instructive. Ruggles asks other blacks, including those who are freeborn, those who have escaped enslavement, and those who are currently in the pursuit of freedom, to support the *Liberator* financially and to contribute to its goal of abolishing slavery. Elsewhere Ruggles writes, "Admitting that we are moral agents and accountable beings, we have a duty to perform in relation to ourselves and to two million of oppressed brethren who are now 'in bounds.'"[60] Again, in light of the little social, institutional, and financial capital that Afro-Americans possessed in the antebellum era, this call is particularly illustrative of Ruggles's conception of social agency and the pursuit of emancipation. Moreover, Ruggles repeatedly sources this appeal in an account of communal solidarity that subverts the recognized *legal* distinction between freeborn and fugitive.[61] Ruggles refuses to acknowledge this distinction, placing runaway slaves and freeborn blacks on the same tier as friends, coadjutors, and brothers.[62] Again, this is an act of social subversion, as Ruggles rejects the very judgments regarding freedom and agency that the social structure in which he lives incentivizes and encourages. For Ruggles, the vestiges of citizenship that "free" blacks are offered is insufficient, and new understandings of public life are needed. As he writes in a letter to Frederick Douglass and Martin Delany:

> Let it be seen and felt, that while our brethren and sisters of the South are slaves to *individuals*, we, of the North, are slaves to the *mass*. Let the whole truth in regard to our real condition be so clearly shown, that our colored brethren, who believe themselves free, may understand that in the United States, there are no "*free* colored men"; and that there never can be, so long as there is no concert of action; and our *neutrality* continues to clog the wheels of the car— emancipation. On this subject, may the light of the North Star be like that of

57. Ruggles, "New York Committee of Vigilance," 147.
58. L. M. Harris, *In the Shadow of Slavery*, 212. See, for example, Ruggles, "For the Colored American."
59. J. Wells, *Blind No More*, 44.
60. Ruggles, "Appeal to the Colored Citizens," 645.
61. J. Wells, *Blind No More*, 38–39.
62. Ruggles, "New York Committee of Vigilance," 149–50.

the inflexible Sirius, that never waxes nor wanes, until our brethren, who are sleeping in calm security, shall awake to the dangers which surround them, and take such observations from the beacon-light as shall point them to the haven where they should be, in the full enjoyment of freedom, not slavery; rights, not privileges.[63]

Ruggles was even willing to mobilize the resistance on a larger scale and engage in extra-legal forms of it to try to secure a place for Afro-Americans within the broader society.[64] Ruggles and the New York Committee of Vigilance (NYCV), which sought to advance the cause of emancipation by utilizing the resources of Afro-Americans in conjunction with the resources of white abolitionists,[65] kept track of persons arriving from the South, the arrivals and departures of suspected slave vessels, the actions of potential kidnappers and slave agents, the arrivals of fugitive slaves, the abductions by kidnappers, and the release of colored persons and their property from kidnappers.[66] The NYCV challenged arrests and abductions in court, lobbied for changes in legislation, and organized mass protests in order to provide protection and legal aid to the Afro-American inhabitants of New York.[67] Raising money from within the black community to pay bail or legal fees, the NYCV eventually served as a paradigm for Afro-American resistance during the antebellum era, with its primary membership consisting of members of black churches.[68] Ruggles, however, was not averse to eschewing the nonviolent commitments of abolitionists in his task of defending the Afro-American community from outside attacks. At a public meeting with other members of the NYCV, Ruggles proposed, "We cannot recommend non-resistance to persons who are denied the protection of equitable law, when their liberty is invaded

---

63. Ruggles, David Ruggles to Frederick Douglass and Martin R. Delany, January 1, 1848, emphasis original.

64. The belief that slaves or marginalized blacks possess "indirect agency" was not limited to Ruggles alone. Of course, the manner in which this agency should be leveraged was a source of contention among abolitionists. Stanley Harrold notes that some of the objections to leveraging this agency in the form of revolt were pragmatic or moral (Harrold, *Abolitionists and the South*, 61). Moreover, Harrold proposes that some of the pessimism is indicative of racialist notions undergirding both white and black abolitionists, logics that presumed that "African Americans [were] incapable of the initiative required for gaining and exercising freedom" (48).

65. L. M. Harris, *In the Shadow of Slavery*, 210. Graham Hodges writes, "The Committee of Vigilance . . . served as a model for other cities, including Boston, Worcester, Rochester, Cleveland, and Detroit, among others, that established their own committees." Hodges, *David Ruggles*, 156.

66. Ruggles, "New York Committee of Vigilance," 149–50.

67. Ruggles, *Antidote for a Poisonous Combination*, 21–23. See also Singer, *New York's Grand Emancipation Jubilee*, 32.

68. Hahn, *Political Worlds of Slavery and Freedom*, 36–37.

and their lives endangered by vicious kidnappers."[69] This more radical element marks a movement in Ruggles's thought, one that eventually put him at odds with other members of the abolitionary movement.[70] Harris notes that this may have been Ruggles's attempt to find a middle ground between working-class Afro-Americans, who supported more aggressive measures, and middle-class blacks and white abolitionists who were reticent to engage in any form of violence.[71] In either case, Ruggles was willing to seek extra-legal methods of civic action, mobilizing the NYCV as a communal form of self-defense in order to resist the predatory attacks of kidnappers and illegitimate authority figures.[72]

As we have seen, for Ruggles the problem of slavery is not reducible *merely* to individuals; it is an unjust and vicious social system. Focusing on the manner in which it has polluted the Christian community and caused it to compromise the spirit of the gospel, Ruggles proposes that this vicious system must be resisted and reformed. Christian charity involves communal resistance in the pursuit of freedom and protection for Afro-Americans. For Ruggles, true liberty involves the pursuit of self-actualization and not the mere attainment of citizenship.[73] Women as well as liberated, fugitive, and enslaved Afro-Americans are called to join in the cause of emancipation. While the state may not recognize them as actors, Ruggles proposes that they can indeed contribute to the cause of abolition in meaningful ways, working from the bottom up to reorder and cleanse a vicious social structure. For Ruggles, resistance must be pluriform, emanating from the margins and from ecclesial spaces in the hope of expanding imaginative horizons in the progressive pursuit of freedom.[74] In this way, emancipation is as much existential as it is legal. It is a freedom won through resistance, emboldened in protest, and concertized in action.

69. Ruggles, "For the Colored American."

70. Ruggles, "For the Colored American." Perhaps the most memorable example of this divide is the dispute between Frederick Douglass and Henry Highland Garnet at the National Negro Convention of 1843. While Garnet and Theodore Wright sought to encourage slaves to revolt, Douglass demurred, believing it impractical. See Schor, "Rivalry between Frederick Douglass and Henry Highland Garnet."

71. L. M. Harris, *In the Shadow of Slavery*, 173.

72. Steven Hahn writes, "Organized self-defense was crucial. By the mid-1830s vigilance committees had been established by African Americans in the major cities of the East Coast, taking as their responsibility the harboring of fugitive slaves as well as the thwarting of 'slave agents and kidnappers.' To those ends, they monitored waterfronts for the arrival of runaways or of vessels suspected as 'slavers.'" Hahn, *Political Worlds of Slavery and Freedom*, 36–37.

73. L. M. Harris, *In the Shadow of Slavery*, 201.

74. As Ruggles argues in defense of the Anti-Slavery Society, "All the weapons which the Anti-Slavery Society use are the Bible, the Declaration of Independence, and the Bills of Rights of the different States, illustrated according to the most pacific principles of the purest moral philosophy." Ruggles, *Brief Review*, 12.

Retrieving David Ruggles's Vision of Public Witness

Ruggles's life and witness provide us with a number of theological goods as we move forward to build a theology of public witness. I will briefly highlight two in particular. First, David Ruggles invites us to engage in retrospective, critical analysis of the Christian community and its witness as a way of evaluating the broader polis in which it exists. While at times Ruggles focuses on the virtues or commands of Scripture, he consistently shifts his lens of analysis to ascertain the character of our social life and the manner in which lived theology fails to accord with the principal logics of Christianity. Second, Ruggles encourages us to reimagine our own *agency* and the possibilities for meaningful political action. We will deal with each in turn.

Retrospective Analysis and Christian Witness

As noted above, Ruggles advances his primary critique of the institution of human slavery in light of how it has led to the malformation of the Christian community. Put simply, Christians who own slaves are living lives marked by vice. Whether it is the denigration of the family or the violation of the prohibition against adultery, Ruggles highlights the fact that Christians are willing to compromise, which serves as evidence of the vicious nature of this social structure. This is similar to what Daniel Daly has proposed in recent years. Daly argues that theological ethics requires two new concepts in order to engage social structures: structures of virtue and structures of vice. Every social structure provides "restrictions, enablements, and incentives" in order to encourage some behaviors and discourage others.[75] According to Daly, a social structure is virtuous to the degree that it "in some way consistently [functions] to promote the human good and human happiness."[76] Moreover, a virtuous social structure encourages the internalization of particular moral habits in order to "consistently prescribe the human good, the common good, good moral character, and human happiness."[77] A social structure is vicious to the degree that it does the very opposite—namely, insofar as it functions to "prevent the human good, the common good, and human happiness, and . . . produce human unhappiness."[78] Of course, in a postlapsum world, things are never this tidy. Every social structure and institution is rife with vice insofar as it emerges

75. Finn, "What Is a Sinful Social Structure?," 153.
76. Daly, "Structures of Virtue and Vice," 355.
77. Daly, "Structures of Virtue and Vice," 355.
78. Daly, "Structures of Virtue and Vice," 355.

from the morally compromised actions of human agents who, on their best days, suffer the deleterious effects of sin.

One key difference between Daly's and Ruggles's proposals is worth highlighting. While for Daly the question is how a social structure shapes agents on a general level, Ruggles sets his microscope on the church. For Ruggles, the vicious nature of an institution (e.g., slavery) is illustrated in the way it encourages the Christian community to violate the law of God and destroy the institutions God has affirmed as good (e.g., marriage and the family). This is not to say that Ruggles is uninterested in bringing about the end of slavery on an institutional or legislative level. His life and activism testify to the very opposite.[79] Rather, it is to say that the sin of the world, on both a general and an institutional level, is exposed in the life of the church. As I have written elsewhere, "God's self-attestation in the church [highlights] the depth of the church's sinfulness as he holds its life up to the light of the Word, but this self-attestation also involves a denunciation of the church's sin."[80] God promises to come to his church in its gathering (Matt. 18:20), but in so doing he comes as both its Lord and its Judge (Rev. 2:5, 16), as the one who promises to forgive *and* to judge sin. The sovereign Lord's announcement of judgment on his church is an announcement of the church's acquiescence to "that which is earthly" in it—that is, the way its modes of life reveal an orientation to the world, its values, its ways of perceiving and judging and acting instead of being oriented by and to God.[81] As I go on to press, "God's announcement of judgment on the sin of the church is a judgment on the impurity and corruption that the church *shares with the world*."[82]

Appropriating Ruggles's insight, we might begin to critically analyze the church's life and witness, identifying the ways in which the Christian community has compromised its witness through its participation in various forms of life. Here examples abound, ranging from the cultus surrounding college test prep to youth sports culture to social media. Such critical examination can be used to clarify and reorient the church's witness. We must be a community whose life bears witness to the resurrection of Jesus Christ and the life he makes possible on account of the sending of the Holy Spirit. Yet at the same time, the church is able to look beyond its walls to

79. Shortly after Ruggles's death, the Anti-Slavery Society of Massachusetts described him as "an early, active, sagacious and persevering friend of the Anti-slavery cause—of one whose professional ability makes his decease a public loss, and whose position and success were doing much to weaken the cruel prejudice against color." Z. W. H., "David Ruggles" (in Works Cited under H., Z. W.).

80. Hill, "Bound Together in the Holy Fire," 196.

81. Hector, *Christianity as a Way of Life*, 46.

82. Hill, "Bound Together in the Holy Fire," 196.

the surrounding institutional and political forms of life it shares with others. It is in looking retrospectively—that is, in beginning with the *church's* compromised witness—that we might be positioned to make larger claims about society as a whole. In turning the magnifying glass on the Christian community *first*, we are then positioned to see the world around us for what it is, held up to the light of redemption. But even this judgment must begin with the household of God.

Reimagining Possibilities for (Communal) Action

Second, Ruggles provides us with resources for reimagining the nature and shape of the church's communal action. Recall that the primary audience of Ruggles's pamphlets and addresses are those on the margins, particularly women and freed slaves. While traditionally excluded from any form of robust participation in the body politic, the marginalized could, according to Ruggles, still meaningfully effect change from the bottom up. The church's public witness, then, is not reducible to forms of statecraft but involves an attention to creating and sustaining forms of common life that are realized in and through the maintenance of relationships.[83]

At times, as we will see later with Maria Stewart, this rejuvenated imagination will lead to the formation and creation of new institutions and communities capable of helping us better endure the world and "carry on."[84] In Ruggles's life, this took the form of participation in the Underground Railroad and forming the NYCV, both of which sought to aid fugitive slaves in their escape. But it is worth noting that, for the most part, Ruggles's invitation to act is extended to those excluded from formal legislative and political processes. He appeals to the women within the church to uphold the integrity of the Christian community. He exhorts free and fugitive blacks to support the abolitionary press. To appropriate his language from earlier, "It is nugatory to ask what can a small number of [Christians] do? *What cannot they do?*"[85]

Ruggles is calling on his audience to turn an eye toward the "friendless" and act with them and on their behalf, believing that such collaboration is capable of bolstering and renewing a community on a larger scale.[86] This is a key insight. What this vision and collaboration requires, if we are to think with and beyond Ruggles, is the formation of a kind of relational power with

83. Bretherton, *Christ and the Common Life*, 34.
84. The phrase "endure the world" is borrowed from Mathewes, *Theology of Public Life*, 12.
85. Ruggles, *Abrogation of the Seventh Commandment*, 16–17, emphasis original.
86. Luke Bretherton writes, "In political terms, the friendless are those with either a severely constrained capacity to act for themselves or who lack the ability to appear on their own terms." Bretherton, *Christ and the Common Life*, 44.

our neighbors that refuses to give in to the temptations of coercion and, in my opinion, violence.[87] The women he writes to and the free slaves he addresses are not currently in a meaningful relationship with the enslaved, the marginalized, and the assaulted. His audience cannot, or does not, see the scars they wear and cannot, or does not, imagine how collaboration with them can bring about meaningful renewal. So Ruggles is asking them, and us by extension, to reimagine the possibilities of relational networks and the possibilities these networks can realize on an institutional level. Attendant to this exhortation is an invitation to establish *new* and meaningful relationships with the other. Here, the formation and subsequent maintenance of these networks of relations that Ruggles envisions, say, between free, white women and the sexually assaulted slave or between free blacks and their enslaved brethren, are a necessary precondition for the abolition of slavery. But the goal is not simply to amass more legislative power in order to direct institutions or engage in acts of statecraft, imposing a form of life on the enslaved from without. The purpose of such relational networks is not, then, to try to exercise a kind of domineering power over our neighbors, even if they possess rival or incommensurate visions of the good life. Rather, Ruggles calls us to befriend the "friendless," those who "lack status, are economically, politically, and socially vulnerable; and are situated in relations of dependency."[88] And so this vision of the political is almost inherently collaborative, as "it is characterized by its good will and active openness toward the other" and attempts to preserve the conditions and means of communication between differing groups even in the midst of disagreement.[89]

Of course, there are necessary and important caveats here. The Christian community's task is not to save or redeem the world, a task that stands outside its purview and is extrinsic to its vocation. Ruggles, as I have noted, is also comfortable with resorting to forms of collective violence for the sake of one's neighbor, a position I find understandable given his context. Yet it is troubling nonetheless. We will return to this thread in this book's final two chapters, but here it is worth reiterating that only God can bring about the future he has promised, and he will do it (Zeph. 3:14–17). But the church has been sent into the world to *do* something: to bear witness to the resurrection of Jesus Christ. And so we might learn from Ruggles the ways in which collaboration and relational networks with the friendless enable creative and emboldened forms of bearing witness. Based on Ruggles, we might consider the ways we

87. Bretherton, *Christ and the Common Life*, 35–36.
88. Bretherton, *Christ and the Common Life*, 44.
89. Lee, *God and Community Organizing*, 180.

have grown accustomed or habituated to particular forms of life and how, through the formation and maintenance of relationships with the other, we might need to reimagine the ways we can meaningfully engage them.

Conclusion

In this chapter, I sought to remember and retrieve the work of abolitionist David Ruggles. A fierce advocate for the enslaved and organizer of the first vigilance society of record, Ruggles believed that the Christian community's participation in the institution of slavery led to drastic moral and ethical compromise, evidenced in the destruction of familial units and the disregard for the sanctity of marriage. This in and of itself illustrated the need for institutional change. Ruggles called men and women within the church to reorient their lives and witness around the law of God, an exhortation that he believed had immediate implications for the common life they shared. Insofar as this is the case, Ruggles provides us with theological goods worth retrieving and retaining. He offers us resources not only for evaluating the quality of the social structures we find ourselves in but also for reorienting and reordering them through meaningful, organized action.

3

Maria W. Stewart

Nurturing the Seeds of Change

In 1833, abolitionist, educator, and women's rights activist Maria W. Stewart stood up in front of a hushed audience to deliver her farewell speech to the colored community of Boston, Massachusetts. Just a few months earlier, Stewart had delivered a fiery speech at the African Masonic Hall, a speech whose reception may have been somewhat fraught.[1] These two speeches would be her last public addresses before she moved south, finally settling in Washington, DC. "My respected friends, you have heard me observe that the shortness of time, the certainty of death, and the instability of all things

1. There are hints of this in Stewart's farewell address, although we should be reticent to draw any strong conclusions. Stewart states, "For I find it is no use for me as an individual to try to make myself useful among my color in this city. It was contempt for my moral and religious opinions in private that drove me thus before a public. Had experience more plainly shown me that it is the nature of man to crush his fellow, I should not have thought it so hard" (Stewart, "Mrs. Stewart's Farewell Address," 70). Elsewhere, Stewart refers to being "wrongfully persecuted" by her enemies, which may also be a reference to what happened in Boston, although such a conclusion may be mere conjecture (Stewart, "Meditation XIII," 47). Still, there is some warrant to the belief that Stewart experienced some form of fallout due to her public speaking career in Boston and the content of her speeches. As Jameliah Inga Shorter-Bourhanou, commenting on Stewart's farewell address, writes, "Stewart was speaking publicly to 'promiscuous' audiences—that is, audiences of mixed race and gender—regarding race, gender equality, and social and political rights for black people. Stewart's farewell speech suggests that when she left Boston, she did so angrily and reluctantly." Shorter-Bourhanou, "Maria W. Stewart," 67.

here, induce me to turn my thoughts from earth to heaven. . . . I believe that a rich reward awaits me, if not in this world, in the world to come. O, blessed reflection."[2] And thus ended the public career of one of the first women, black or white, to lecture in front of an audience of both men and women in a public space on political topics.[3]

Yet in retrospect, what she said was rather curious given that her life and career of activism would last another forty years. While a rich reward may in fact have awaited her in the heavenly city, it turns out she had more work to do here on earth: teaching Sunday school, starting schools, and serving as the matron of a local hospital in DC.[4] Her speech in Boston was not in fact the end of the road, but her life and witness did take a decisive turn once she left Massachusetts behind and transitioned from a public spokeswoman in a bustling metropolis to a community activist. This was perhaps due in part to the backlash she had received from her speeches in Boston, after a public speaking career that had lasted roughly four years.[5] Her passion for activism would persist, albeit on a much more local scale.

Little is known about Maria Stewart's early years, a common side effect of life as an Afro-American woman in the nineteenth century. Born Maria Miller in 1803 in Hartford, Connecticut, Stewart endured a great deal of hardship and crisis.[6] Connecticut had formally committed to the process of gradual emancipation in 1784, meaning that any child born to a slave would be free, while their parents remained enslaved. So there were likely to have been large numbers of unenslaved Afro-Americans in the community in which Stewart was born and raised. In fact, neither of Stewart's parents was a slave, granting Stewart her own status as "freeborn." Unfortunately for her, both of them died tragically when she was only five years old, leaving her an orphan.[7]

---

2. Stewart, "Mrs. Stewart's Farewell Address," 65, 74.

3. Richardson, "What If I Am a Woman?," 192.

4. Bailey, "Letter from Henry Bailey," 96–97.

5. Many commentators note that Stewart may have received pushback from her audiences in Boston due to the content of her speeches and her depiction of the United States as a nation teetering on the precipice of divine judgment. Historian William C. Nell, writing to William Lloyd Garrison in 1952, comments that "Mrs. Maria W. Stewart . . . encountered an opposition even from her Boston circle of friends, that would have damped the ardor of most women" (Nell, "Letter from William C. Nell," 39). So Britany Sulzener concludes, "[Stewart] ended her brief public speaking career in 1833 due to the overwhelmingly harsh criticism she received for her revolutionary arguments, her public presence, and her apocalyptic vision" (Sulzener, "Night of Death, Morning of Rebirth," 624). Yet Sulzener seems to overestimate the degree to which Stewart receded from public life in the years that followed. Upon moving to Washington, DC, Stewart appears to have continued to write for the African Methodist Episcopal Church's periodical and engage in works of civil service.

6. Stewart, "Appendix D," 118.

7. Stewart, "Religion and the Pure Principles of Morality," 28.

Stewart was subsequently sold into indentured servitude to a local minister, living with him and his family until she turned fifteen.[8] She then moved to Boston, where she met and married James Stewart, a local shipping agent and war veteran, in 1826.[9] The marriage lasted only three years, as James died of illness in 1829.[10] Unfortunately for Stewart, things in Boston quickly went from bad to worse, as the executors of her husband's will swindled her out of the pension he had earned due to his service in the War of 1812, money that was rightfully hers.[11] It would take almost fifty years for the situation to be resolved.[12] One year after James's death, Stewart trusted in Christ.[13] After befriending David Walker and William Lloyd Garrison, Stewart enjoyed a brief career as a public speaker, teacher, and abolitionist in Massachusetts. In 1833, she left Boston behind, moving south, first to New York, then to Baltimore, and finally to Washington, DC, where she spent her final years as a schoolteacher and nurse in the Freedman's Hospital and Asylum until her death in 1879.[14]

While Stewart has received attention in the past few years for her contributions to political theory, significantly less attention has been paid to the theological and evangelical strata that underlie her public witness. As Marilyn Richardson astutely observes, "It is not possible, nor would it be appropriate, to separate [Stewart's] secular documents from the pervasive religious consciousness which informs her analyses. Stewart's intense piety shaped her decidedly evangelical style."[15] The dearth of attention to Stewart's evangelical convictions is all the more curious given the hymns, prayers, and allusions to and citations of Scripture that are spread throughout her speeches.[16] Even

---

8. Stewart, "Religion and the Pure Principles of Morality," 29.

9. James Stewart had served in the United States Navy on three naval vessels during the War of 1812. G. Palmer, "Appendix E," 119. See also Gardner, "Introduction," 156.

10. Stewart, "Appendix D," 118. Watching her husband die had a profound effect on Stewart, especially in conjunction with the fact that her dying husband was unconverted. She describes retrospectively, "O my soul thou has watched the sick-bed of one who was near to thee, even the half of thyself; thou has heard his dying groans, and seen his restless head turn from side to side in quest of ease; and his dim eye hath he turned upon thee and implored thee for relief. Alas, what could I do? . . . And he had no God to look to." Stewart, "Meditation X," 41.

11. Kristin Waters describes in harrowing detail the length that various individuals went to in order to appropriate James Stewart's earnings and property. See Waters, *Maria W. Stewart*, 196–98.

12. Gardner, "Introduction," 156.

13. Stewart, "Religion and the Pure Principles of Morality," 29.

14. Richardson, *Maria W. Stewart*, 84–85.

15. Richardson, *Maria W. Stewart*, xvii.

16. Stewart herself notes the strong role that Christianity plays in her speeches and writings: "I suppose many of my friends will say, 'Religion is all your theme,' I hope my conduct will ever prove me to be what I profess, a true follower of Christ; and it is the religion of Jesus alone that

Richardson's description of some of Stewart's essays and speeches as "secular" risks inserting a divide into Stewart's writings that would have been foreign to her understanding, as I will demonstrate below. For the purposes of this chapter, we are interested less in Stewart as a political theorist and more in the theo-political vision that undergirds her political activity. Accordingly, in what follows, I will argue that Maria W. Stewart presents humanity with a charge, one that requires us to create subterranean communities and to attend to the formation of those communities in virtue so that we can endure the present suffering of the world. If David Ruggles challenged us to think creatively about space and our agency within it, Stewart reminds us that change often happens at a deliberate pace and that we, in the meantime, need to engage in the work of cultivation and renewal.

A Common Humanity in Search of a Common Life

A number of key themes emerge from a quick perusal of Stewart's corpus: her belief in the full humanity of Afro-Americans, both men and women; her convictions regarding the nature of social agency; her encouragement to cultivate self-reliance; and her confidence in divine aid with respect to the state of the oppressed.[17]

Throughout Stewart's speeches and writings, there is a constant challenge to the prevailing ideologies of her day regarding the alleged inferiority of Afro-Americans. The attack is two pronged. First, Stewart challenges these notions on the grounds of their intellectual incoherence, critiquing the division of the human community along alleged essential lines in an attempt to undermine the conceptual grounds that reinforce slavery in its multivariate forms.[18] Second,

---

will constitute your happiness here, and support you in a dying hour" (Stewart, "Religion and the Pure Principles of Morality," 32). Additionally, two contemporaries of hers, pastors Henry Bailey and William B. Jefferson, both note her profound commitment to teaching Christian doctrine. In a letter that serves as one of the prefaces to her *Meditations*, Jefferson observes, "The aim of her life is to promote the glory of God and the welfare of men" (W. Jefferson, "Letter from William B. Jefferson," 95). Similarly, Bailey notes Stewart's commitment to teaching children "the wisdom of repentance, and also a knowledge of [God]" (Bailey, "Letter from Henry Bailey," 96). Jefferson and Bailey say such things in light of Stewart's life of activism *in conjunction with* her commitment to teaching Sabbath school multiple times a week at different churches. In other words, it seems that Stewart herself and those who knew her were thoroughly convinced of the sincerity of her Christian convictions and evangelical piety.

17. J. Ryan, "Spirituality and/as Ideology," 277.

18. Stewart is adamantly concerned with the continued enslavement of Afro-Americans, as we will see below, and casts herself as an abolitionist who seeks their freedom and release. But Stewart is also concerned that the "free status" of liberated blacks is little better. She writes, "Tell us no more of southern slavery; for with few exceptions, although I may be very erroneous

Stewart critiques the attendant conceptual framework that presumes that Afro-Americans are savages, incapable of developing moral character. For Stewart, this fails to take seriously humanity's formation in God's image. If it is indeed the case that Afro-Americans, both men and women, possess the powers of rationality and are capable of attaining virtue, then, she reasons, they must be included under the broader genus of humanity. Furthermore, if this is the case, then these nascent powers and capacities must be developed and nurtured so that these individuals have the opportunity to realize their God-given potential. This is a burden placed not on the individual as such but on the communities in which these individuals exist. Growth in virtue is a burden of the communal and relational nexuses in which we live.

One can hardly read the writings and speeches of Maria Stewart without noticing her continual affirmation of the full humanity of Afro-Americans and their subsequent right to participate fully in American common life. Two points of emphasis seem to emerge. First, Stewart attempts to demonstrate the full humanity of Afro-American men and women by demonstrating their possession of the powers and potentials that are inherent in the human race. Stewart takes for granted that human creatures are essentially rational and reasoning animals.[19] This is similar to many Enlightenment portrayals of the human person. Figures such as John Locke, Immanuel Kant, and René Descartes, among many others, had long since identified rationality as the essential power of the human creature qua creature, its presence setting humanity above the rest of the created order. Rationalizations of the enslavement of Afro-Americans frequently relied on the alleged intellectual inferiority of the members of this community, but Stewart argues that these same powers of reason exist within the members of the Afro-American community, both men and women. As noted in chapter 1, Afro-Americans were often viewed as lacking intellectual and cultural powers found in their Caucasian peers, the absence of which was used as a kind of ex post facto justification of their relegation to a particular stratum of the social hierarchy.[20] Stewart pushes

---

in my opinion, yet I consider our condition but little better than that." Stewart, "Lecture Delivered at the Franklin Hall," 45.

19. It is worth noting in passing that these Enlightenment understandings of the human creature as fundamentally a rational animal are not completely divorced from antiquity or the Christian tradition. Similar conceptions of the *imago Dei* appear in the work of Thomas Aquinas, Boethius, Augustine of Hippo, and Basil of Caesarea. Of course, the prominence of this particular understanding of the *imago* is not sufficient for adjudicating whether the substantial view of the *imago* is correct. To the point, such substantial accounts of the *imago* have come under a great deal of criticism in recent years, either for supposedly imposing metaphysical concerns on the biblical text or for the degree to which they exclude certain members of the human community.

20. Tran, *Asian Americans*, 78.

back on this ideology: "Many think, because your skins are tinged with a
sable hue, that you are an inferior race of beings; but God does not consider
you as such. He hath formed and fashioned you in his own glorious image."[21]
Appropriating and appealing to Psalm 8:5 and Genesis 1:26, Stewart leverages
the traditional language from the Christian doctrine of creation to argue that
the "sons and daughters of Africa" are made in the image of God and therefore
have intellectual powers: For God "hath bestowed upon [them] reason and
strong powers of intellect. He hath made [them] to have dominion over the
beasts of the field, the fowls of the air and the fish of the sea. He hath crowned
[them] with glory and honor; hath made [them] a little lower than the angels."[22]
Valerie Cooper observes, "Stewart brackets her claim that people of African
descent have 'strong powers of intellect' with two references to the creation
as detailed in Genesis 1, thereby underscoring her contention that people of
African descent shared that moment of creation with those of other races
of the earth. This shared creation imparts a shared dominion over the earth.
Although as slaves they are ruled by others, this was not God's intention."[23]
Stewart positions black dignity in relationship to God and, concurrently,
positions her interlocutors *against* God and God's work in creation.[24] The
slave owner and the pro-slavery apologist are unable to recognize the "glory
and honor" that the slave has been imbued with by God. Insofar as this is the
case, they are setting themselves against God and stand in the path of divine
judgment. Appropriating the rhetorical device of jeremiad,[25] Stewart warns

21. Stewart, "Religion and the Pure Principles of Morality," 29.
22. Stewart, "Religion and the Pure Principles of Morality," 29.
23. Cooper, *Word, Like Fire*, 45n17.
24. Elsewhere Stewart returns to this connection between the *imago Dei* and the relationship
Afro-Americans experience with God, writing, "For we also are His people and the sheep of His
pasture. He formed and fashioned us, and we are the workmanship of His hands. He knows
our griefs and our sorrows, our fearful apprehensions of the future, and like a father pitieth
his children, so the Lord pitieth them that fear Him" (Stewart, "Proper Training of Children,"
160). It is important to see here that Stewart again identifies her audience primarily in light of
their relationship to God.
25. "Jeremiad" refers to a rhetorical device used to warn of the impending judgment of
God on those who continue in sin. The term alludes to the prophetic figure Jeremiah in the
Old Testament, who repeatedly warned the people of God of their impending conquest due to
the proliferation of their idolatry and sin. So Jeremiah reads, "Thus says the LORD, the God
of Israel: I am going to turn back the weapons of war that are in your hands and with which
you are fighting against the king of Babylon and against the Chaldeans who are besieging you
outside the walls; and I will bring them together into the center of this city" (Jer. 21:4). God
explicitly describes this as a judgment on the people of God in light of their idolatry and failures
to keep the terms of the covenant (Jer. 10). Jeremiah accordingly warns that God will come
against his people in judgment. "For I have set my face against this city for evil and not for
good, says the LORD: it shall be given into the hands of the king of Babylon, and he shall burn
it with fire" (21:10). Afro-Americans frequently appropriated this device for their criticisms of

that a divinely ordained "day of reckoning" is coming.[26] And it is a judgment that will be applied particularly to those people and societies who turn a blind eye to the suffering of the enslaved and disenfranchised.[27] As Britany Sulzener observes, "In her conception, the black 'bondmen' and 'freemen,' rather than being punished along with the sinful rich men, sit with God while he punishes the 'Americans.'"[28]

Second, Stewart argues that Afro-Americans are capable of developing their nascent powers and potentialities in dynamic and creative ways, allowing them to contribute to American life. In short, they are capable of attaining virtue and contributing to the common life of the broader polis. This can be seen as attendant to and concomitant with her belief in the full rationality of her enslaved brothers and sisters. For Stewart, the reason the capacities and intellectual powers of Afro-Americans may not be readily apparent is not because of some genetic or ontological inferiority. Rather, the larger society in which Afro-Americans live has failed to provide them with the necessary and sufficient conditions for self-actualization. She writes, "Most of our color have been taught to stand in fear of the white man from their earliest infancy, to work as soon as they could walk, and to call 'master' before they could scarce lisp the name of mother. Continual fear and laborious servitude have in some degree lessened in us that natural force and energy."[29] The supposed inferiority of Afro-Americans is an indictment of the society they inhabit, one that is responsible for nurturing, developing, cultivating, and creating space for the actualization of their capacities and powers. While the skeptical onlooker may identify habits of speech, illiteracy, and so on as evidence of the sub- or inhumanity of the enslaved, Stewart proposes that such things

the institution of slavery. William Jeremiah Moses states, "The term 'jeremiad' [describes] the constant warnings issued by blacks to whites, concerning the judgment that was to come for the sin of slavery. Blacks ingeniously adapted their rhetoric to the jeremiadic tradition, which was one of the dominant forms of cultural expression in revivalistic ante-bellum America." Moses, *Black Messiahs and Uncle Toms*, 30–31.

26. Waters, "Crying Out for Liberty," 44–45.

27. Stewart writes, "My brethren, sheath your swords, and calm your angry passions. Stand still and know that the Lord he is God. Vengeance is his, and he will repay. It is a long lane that has no turn. America has risen to her meridian. When you begin to thrive, she will begin to fall. . . . Fret not yourselves because of the men who bring wicked devices to pass; for they shall be cut down as the grass and wither as the green herb" (Stewart, "Religion and the Pure Principles of Morality," 40). Commenting on this passage, Kevin Pelletier states, "Stewart provides consolation to black Americans by ensuring them that God will seek retaliation against their oppressors and soon free them from bondage. Not only will the Christian God exact vengeance, but he has also placed in America his surrogates . . . who symbolize this threat to southerners and who work on God's behalf." Pelletier, *Apocalyptic Sentimentalism*, 74.

28. Sulzener, "Night of Death, Morning of Rebirth," 625.

29. Stewart, "Address Delivered at the African Masonic Hall," 59.

are due to the conditions of the American social environment that black men and women are forced to endure. She writes:

> Most of our color have dragged out a miserable existence of servitude from the cradle to the grave. And what literary acquirement can be made, or useful knowledge derived, from either maps, books, or charts, by those who continually drudge from Monday morning until Sunday noon? O, ye fairer sisters, whose hands are never soiled, whose nerves and muscles are never strained, go learn by experience! Had we had the opportunity that you have had, to improve our moral and mental faculties, what would have hindered our intellects from being as bright, and our manners from being as dignified as yours? Had it been our lot to have been nursed in the lap of affluence and ease, and to have basked beneath the smiles and sunshine of fortune, should we not have naturally supposed that we were never made to toil?[30]

In short, the brutal conditions of chattel slavery and the perpetual disenfranchisement of freeborn Afro-American men and women are to blame for any failure of black people to self-actualize.[31] Stewart writes, "Give the man of color an equal opportunity with the white from the cradle to manhood, and from manhood to the grave, and you would discover the dignified statesman, the man of science, and the philosopher. But there is no such opportunity for the sons of Africa."[32] Stewart takes for granted that her Afro-American compatriots are capable of effectively contributing to American life. What is lacking for them is opportunity. The challenge to her audience, then, is to push for the civic and political rights of those of African descent so that their nascent powers can be cultivated.

"Talk, without Effort, Is Nothing": Subterranean Communities of Character

If it is the case that the enslavement and disenfranchisement of Afro-Americans precludes the actualization of intellectual and cultural powers, one might be tempted to think that Stewart places both blame and social agency squarely in the hands of her white audience members or the legislative branches of government. Yet nothing could be further from the truth. "I am sensible that there are many highly intelligent men of color in these United States. . . . But if they are blessed with wit and talent, friends and fortune, why have they

---

30. Stewart, "Lecture Delivered at the Franklin Hall," 48.
31. Stewart, "Address Delivered at the African Masonic Hall," 61.
32. Stewart, "Address Delivered at the African Masonic Hall," 59.

not made themselves men of eminence, by striving to take all the reproach that is cast upon the people of color, and in endeavoring to alleviate the woes of their brethren in bondage?" Stewart asks her audience. "Talk, without effort, is nothing; you are abundantly capable, gentlemen. . . . And this gross neglect, on your part, causes my blood to boil within me."[33] Instead, she calls on Afro-Americans to create something akin to subterranean communities that will enable them to take advantage of their economic, relational, and communal powers to extend temporal goods to their community members.[34] In so doing, she portrays the cultivation of piety and virtue as a burden of the community that is inherently public and as the necessary prerequisite to social change. In effect, Stewart calls her audience to become a community of piety and character, one capable of both enduring and taking advantage of the present even as they long for and await greater social change.

A Call to Communal Formation

First, Stewart calls her listeners and readers to the work of communal formation. The focus is less on the development of particular individuals and more on the creation of new institutions and communities that will then enable the expansion and expression of their various talents. For example, she laments the lack of opportunity that society affords young Afro-American women and the manner in which this lack of opportunity relegates them to a lifetime of servile labor. "Let our girls possess whatever amiable qualities of soul they may; let their characters be fair and spotless as innocence itself; let their natural taste and ingenuity be what they may. It is impossible for scarce an individual of them to rise above the condition of servants."[35] If there is no place for the free and the enslaved to develop according to their God-given potential, they cannot afford to wait for the intervention of outsiders. Instead, they need to create alternative institutions that will supply what is lacking.

Here, Stewart appears to draw inspiration from some of the benevolent societies that dominate American life. Stewart notes how "the American people . . . [thrive] in arts and sciences, and in polite literature. Their highest aim is to excel in political, moral and religious improvement."[36] For Stewart, these three—political, moral, and religious improvement—are intertwined and interdependent.[37] Stewart observes that American society demonstrates a

---

33. Stewart, "Address Delivered at the African Masonic Hall," 58.
34. Stewart, "Religion and the Pure Principles of Morality," 37.
35. Stewart, "Lecture Delivered at the Franklin Hall," 46.
36. Stewart, "Religion and the Pure Principles of Morality," 34.
37. Judylyn Ryan perceptively notes, "Stewart's written and oral addresses take the form of religious exhortations petitioning Black people to a Christocentric standard of moral behavior

concern for the well-being of the child, the orphan, the widow, and the impov-
erished, a concern that she argues is well and good. "And their poorest ones,
who have the least wish to excel, they promote! And those that have but one
talent they encourage."[38] For Stewart, this genuine concern within American
society for the well-being of its poor and vulnerable members is admirable.
But she laments a gaping hole in its application—namely, the failure of her
fellow citizens and Christians to extend this same concern across racial lines
to members of the Afro-American community. "But how very few are there
among them that bestow one thought upon the benighted sons and daughters
of Africa, who have enriched the soils of America with their tears and blood:
few to promote their cause, none to encourage their talents."[39] If political,
moral, and religious improvement are goods worth pursuing and extending
to others, then they should be extended to Afro-American men and women
as well. Yet while political and legislative change might be desired conditions
for the extension of these goods, Stewart calls Afro-Americans to take matters into their own hands, forming new ways of life that will address their
issues and concerns.

So Stewart does not stop with mere prophetic critique of the ways the social
world is organized. Instead, she goes a step further, calling for the formation
of "subterranean communities," communities that exist beside, underneath,
and within a specific social order to address the needs and concerns of the marginalized and the disenfranchised. She writes, "Let every female heart become
united and let us raise a fund ourselves; and at the end of one year and a half,
we might be able to lay the corner-stone for the building of a High School,
that the higher branches of knowledge might be enjoyed by us."[40] Elsewhere,
Stewart draws attention to the complicity of women irrespective of race and
across the strata of American life in the failure to provide opportunities for
black women and children as well as their contributions to the victimization
of black women and children.[41] As Sulzener notes, "Stewart repeatedly directs
her words to the 'daughters of Africa,' urging them to create new communities
funded and founded by black women."[42] Stewart envisages new possibilities
for Afro-Americans' common life but notes that doing so will require the
cultivation of particular habits and virtues within the disenfranchised as well

---

and to a degree of political, social, and economic analysis and self-reliance inextricably bound
to the former." J. Ryan, "Spirituality and/as Ideology," 277.

38. Stewart, "Religion and the Pure Principles of Morality," 34.
39. Stewart, "Religion and the Pure Principles of Morality," 34–35.
40. Stewart, "Religion and the Pure Principles of Morality," 37.
41. N. Wright, "Maria W. Stewart's 'The First Stage of Life,'" 152.
42. Sulzener, "Night of Death, Morning of Rebirth," 626.

as opportunities for political participation.[43] Accordingly, Stewart advises her listeners to combine their economic and social agency to provide educational opportunities for the next generation, opportunities that society as a whole has denied them. "Let our money, instead of being thrown away as heretofore, be appropriated for schools and seminaries of learning for our children and youth."[44] Yet it is important to note that the goal of these subterranean communities is to provide the opportunity for black men, women, and children to develop and express their latent talents.

A Call to Communal Cultivation

Second, Stewart calls her audience to engage in the work of communal cultivation. This is, after all, what the formation of subterranean communities is for: the cultivation of the various marginalized members of society who exist within a given community. Attempting to discourage her listeners from resorting to violence, Stewart encourages them to invest their energies elsewhere. "Far be it from me to recommend you either to kill, burn, or destroy," she pleads. "But I strongly recommend to you to improve your talents; let no one lie buried in the earth. Show forth your powers of mind."[45] According to Stewart, the formation of new social organizations is intended to result in the cultivation of the community.

Stewart believes that the creation of subterranean communities will ensure that Afro-Americans are able to nurture their faculties and grow in piety and morality. For Stewart, the project of freedom does not consist of merely the acquisition of social and political rights; it also involves the freedom to become a kind of people marked by morality and piety. Stewart is disgusted by the dearth of virtue and the lack of other-directed concern she sees in her own community. "It appears to me that there are no people under the heavens so unkind and so unfeeling towards their own, as are the descendants of fallen Africa. . . . Unless the rising generation manifest a different temper and disposition towards each other from what we have manifested, the generation following will never be an enlightened people."[46] Irrespective of whether the slave question is answered in the immediate future, Stewart calls free and fugitive blacks to attend to the ways they can renew the communities they inhabit. These communities must be marked by a concern for the vulnerable and a commitment to taking responsibility for the formation of the next generation.

43. N. Wright, "Maria W. Stewart's 'The First Stage of Life,'" 152.
44. Stewart, "Address Delivered at the African Masonic Hall," 60.
45. Stewart, "Religion and the Pure Principles of Morality," 29.
46. Stewart, "Address Delivered before the Afric-American Female Intelligence Society," 53.

So she asks "sons of Africa" to save and better invest their earnings so as to care for "the future welfare of their children."[47] Stewart says, "O ye sons of Africa, turn your mind from . . . perishable objects, and contend for the cause of God and the rights of man."[48] She adjures Afro-American women to improve their own intellectual powers while also attending to the needs of the children and households of which they are a part.[49] Marilyn Richardson observes, "[Stewart] called on black women to develop their highest intellectual capacities, to enter, without apology, into all spheres of the life of the mind, and to participate in all constructive activities within their communities, from religion and education to politics and business."[50] Stewart especially appeals to parents to tend to the needs of their children. She writes, "We are not always to bloom in youth and beauty, and God has wisely arranged that the old and the middle-aged, by their wisdom and discretion, should counsel and guide the young."[51] For Stewart, the goal of subterranean communities is to form a people in virtue who encourage and support "each other" so that the entire community might become "a thriving and flourishing people."[52] This cultivation of an other-directed community is nothing less than an exercise in hoping in God in the midst of crisis. It is nothing less than an exercise in clinging to the truth of their status as beloved image bearers of God as a brazen resistance to the ideological lies that surround them.[53]

Important to the logic undergirding Stewart's vision of communal cultivation is a conviction that Afro-American communities possess some semblance of social agency and communal responsibility. So these communities must be able to cultivate not only the habits of courage, perseverance, temperance, and the like but also the possibilities for meaningful social action. Stewart writes, "Under these circumstances, do not let our hearts be any longer discouraged; it is no use to murmur nor to repine; but let us promote ourselves and improve our own talents."[54] The community must be a place where its members are shown and taught how to act within the confines of an unjust social system. This involves cultivating one's powers of intellect and piety, developing one's

---

47. Stewart, "Address Delivered at the African Masonic Hall," 60.
48. Stewart, "Address Delivered at the African Masonic Hall," 60.
49. Stewart, "Religion and the Pure Principles of Morality," 31, 35–36.
50. Richardson, "What If I Am a Woman?," 194.
51. Stewart, "Proper Training of Children," 160.
52. Stewart, "Address Delivered at the African Masonic Hall," 62.
53. As Lisa Bowens astutely points out, "Aware of the many elements present in society and in public discourse aimed at dehumanizing African Americans, Stewart encourages her audience to resist the lies about their nature and their origin and to take charge of their destiny by proving to the world the fabrications regarding inferior black intellect and black subservience." Bowens, *African American Readings of Paul*, 126.
54. Stewart, "Religion and the Pure Principles of Morality," 35.

talents, and "turning [one's] attention to knowledge and self-improvement."[55] "Motivation to prove their intellectual prowess; the development of piety, morality, and virtue; and the pursuit of knowledge are all significant for Stewart's program of black uplift."[56] For Stewart, self-improvement functions as something akin to the terminus of virtue, for it enables the individual and the community to act meaningfully in social situations that are less than ideal.

Stewart's injunction, then, is to take seriously the need to become a particular type of people, and the impetus rests on every member of the community to engage in the work of cultivation. Stewart writes, "I am rejoiced to reflect that there are many able and talented ones among us, whose names might be recorded on the bright annals of fame. But 'I can't,' is a great barrier in the way. I hope it will soon be removed, and 'I will,' resume its place."[57] Lisa Bowens is perceptive here. Commenting on this passage, she writes, "When Stewart writes that she desires to see the phrase 'I can't' removed from the lips of her fellow African Americans and replaced by 'I will,' she advocates that blacks reject the prevalent notion that they are inferior and cannot change anything," a rejection that Stewart bases on the imperatives of the biblical text.[58] For Bowens, Stewart is calling Afro-Americans to reimagine themselves in light of the manner in which the biblical text addresses them. They are the audience of Paul's letters; they are the ones called to respond to the exhortations of the gospel.[59] And insofar as this is the case, they are also *able* to respond to the gospel's urgings.

Stewart's calls for the formation and the cultivation of alternative communities and institutions involve asking her listeners to reimagine the social landscape they inhabit, to view it as a land ripe with opportunity for economic, cultural, and moral development. Here, cultivation and piety take a sharp, political valence that witnesses to God's work in creation. Insofar as God has formed and fashioned the sons and daughters of Africa in his own glorious image, any demonstration of their "natural genius and talent" is a testimony to the work of God in them.[60] For Stewart, self-improvement and cultivation are necessary for the formation of alternative communities and institutions that will operate beside, underneath, and within the existing forms of civic life. If the general public and social order of the antebellum era will

---

55. Stewart, "Religion and the Pure Principles of Morality," 28.

56. Bowens, *African American Readings of Paul*, 126.

57. Stewart, "Religion and the Pure Principles of Morality," 35.

58. Bowens, *African American Readings of Paul*, 130.

59. Richardson notes that "Stewart called upon blacks to plan wisely for the future in this country by establishing strong, self-sufficient educational and economic institutions within their own communities." Richardson, "What If I Am a Woman?," 194.

60. Stewart, "Address Delivered at the African Masonic Hall," 62.

not extend opportunities to blacks, then the formation of new institutions and new forms of common life is needed. In the political climate of America in the nineteenth century, which excludes black men and women and abuses black children, Stewart's call for formation and cultivation is an act of political resistance. Communal formation and cultivation are ways of enduring and resisting the injustice of the present even as we look to God for our future, ultimate deliverance.

Retrieving Maria Stewart's Vision of Public Witness

Some might argue that there are strong notes of philosophical liberalism, Republican values, and the "cult of true womanhood" littered throughout Stewart's project, concepts that are strongly wedded to the anthropological assumptions of the Enlightenment and its commitment to human optimism.[61] Indeed, to a degree, we must admit that this in fact appears to be the case, especially in some of Stewart's earlier writings. Valerie Cooper provides helpful commentary on the complexity of Stewart's wrestling with the "cult of true womanhood," writing, "What Maria Stewart makes of questions of gender is complicated—even conflicted. On the one hand she advocates very traditional roles for women, as mothers and wives, for example. . . . However, Stewart is careful to draw distinctions between the lives of African American women and their white counterparts. . . . Finally, and perhaps most interestingly, Stewart clings to protestations of ladylike modesty even as she argues, with increasing boldness, that she, as a woman, has every right to a place in public discourse."[62] Here, one might point out that Stewart calls black women and mothers to take responsibility of their respective homes, embracing their role as *mothers*.[63] So Kristin Waters proposes that Stewart is struggling to disentangle some of the patriarchal conceptions of womanhood that she has uncritically adopted from the surrounding cultural environment.[64]

---

61. The "cult of true womanhood" refers to a set of ideals that were viewed as the *conditio sine qua non* of civility as it pertains to women. As Kristin Waters summarizes, "At this time, the notion of the ideal lady, what is sometimes known as the cult of domesticity or true womanhood that governed white women operated in full force. . . . The virtues demanded of white women were 1) purity, 2) piety, 3) obedience, and 4) domesticity" (Waters, *Maria W. Stewart*, 121–22).

62. Cooper, *Word, Like Fire*, 131. Waters argues that Stewart is "immersed" in this ideology (Waters, *Maria W. Stewart*, 122). For further discussion of this motif and trope in the eighteenth and nineteenth centuries, see Welter, "Cult of True Womanhood"; and Legates, "Cult of Womanhood in Eighteenth-Century Thought."

63. Stewart, "Religion and the Pure Principles of Morality," 35.

64. Waters, *Maria W. Stewart*, 121.

Bowens helpfully points out that this too could be a matter of pragmatic resistance: "In a society that often denies black familial status and refuses to see black families as equal to those of whites, Stewart urges black women to take care of their household and to make them a priority, something they could not do fully under slavery."[65] In an era when Afro-American families were easily separated and disintegrated due to the trading of slaves, the nature of running away, and predatory activity of kidnappers, Afro-American families were in a very fragile state. Bowens goes on to note, "Stewart encourages the free black women in her audience to exercise their freedom and focus on their home life. For Stewart, religion enables black people to be all they were created to be and to exist as full human beings in a world that constantly rejected their humanity."[66]

As Waters observes, both Maria Stewart and David Walker appear to adopt and revise "revolutionary language and ideas . . . , applying the Enlightenment concepts of liberal political theory to African Americans, diasporan Africans worldwide, and, in Stewart's case, to black women."[67] Waters notes that this is a direct attempt by Stewart to engage and combat "proslavery ideology."[68] Yet Stewart's use of these forms of thought, however creatively, does not negate the resources she makes available to us. We need not appropriate the totality of Stewart's intellectual heritage to recognize the goods she has to offer us in establishing a framework for thinking about what it means for Christians to inhabit public space in a way that bears witness to the redemptive work of God in Christ. We can identify at least two insights worth preserving. First, Stewart views the church's public witness as inherently bound up with the formation and cultivation of subterranean communities that enable the marginalized in our contexts to "carry on." Second, Stewart demonstrates that the development of communities of character and virtue is intrinsically an act of public witness to how we view ourselves in relationship to God and what God is doing in the world.

Institutional Formation, Renewal, and Communal Cultivation

First, we can seek to retrieve Stewart's call to engage in the work of forming institutions for the sake of cultivating communities of character. We saw in the previous section that Stewart is unwilling to accept the terms presented to her and her community members, terms that would relegate and confine them to

---

65. Bowens, *African American Readings of Paul*, 128.
66. Bowens, *African American Readings of Paul*, 128.
67. Waters, "Crying Out for Liberty," 36.
68. Waters, "Crying Out for Liberty," 36–37.

the margins of social life, awaiting deliverance from someone else. "Improve
your talents!" she repeatedly tells Afro-Americans, an injunction that she tethers
to the formation of new schools, new seminaries, and new benevolent societies
that will serve the interests and meet the needs of the disenfranchised and the
marginalized. If the social world her listeners inhabit refuses to provide them
with opportunities to grow, develop, and nurture their potential, then it will do
little good merely to bemoan the state of things or to lapse into a kind of nihil-
ism, one she sees pressing in on the black community of the antebellum era.[69]
Instead, the black community must organize its life to ensure the flourishing
of its members and those in its proximate contexts. And this is something they
can do here and now. Fathers and mothers must tend to the formation of their
children. Women must pool their resources and form their own institutions of
learning. As we saw above, the formation of new institutions is for the sake
of investing in the community and for the sake of cultivating forms of social
agency in order to pursue access to particular public goods.

With Stewart, the Christian community today might do well to view its
public witness as something that *requires* the forming of institutions and the
consistent renewal of those communities for the sake of extending temporal
goods beyond its walls.[70] Not reducible to the actions or vocations of isolated
individuals, the church is a community that is bound together, a community
that operates with certain shared values across local and supra-local levels.[71] We might think of institutional formation as a kind of commitment
to forms of shared life for the sake of extending particular temporal goods.
Communities exist, in large part, to address the needs of their members and
their contexts. But like everything else in a world warped by sin, they too
are prone to falling into disrepair. Stewart reminds us that formal networks
and organizations can serve as a means of bearing witness to the world as it
is, still in bondage to futility and decay, still in a present age that sits under
divine judgment. Yet, further still, Christian attempts to renew and revive
institutions can bear witness to God's commitment to the world and testify
to his judgments about the people living therein. In forming institutions that
seek to extend temporal goods and provide environments conducive to human
flourishing, however defined, Christians testify to God's refusal to abandon
the world and the depths of his love for its inhabitants.

---

69. Stewart, "Religion and the Pure Principles of Morality," 33.

70. Stewart, "Religion and the Pure Principles of Morality," 44.

71. Admittedly, here some of my Protestant and baptistic sympathies might be at work,
sympathies that tend to privilege the autonomy of the local church over against any institutional
framework that may supervene upon it. A defense of these ecclesiological commitments is well
beyond the purview of this present project.

Yet here we might think not just with but beyond Stewart. While many of Stewart's appeals are to the renewal of familial units, a call that is right and good, we might extend the logic to other communities we inhabit. Here, the church can function as a communal hub, as Dustin Benac has recently articulated. According to Benac, a hub refers to "a densely networked organizational form that anchors religious life within a particular community and facilitates webs of connection across a broader ecclesial ecology through partnership, education, and leadership development."[72] These hubs, according to Benac, are not reducible to parachurch ministries or megachurches.[73] Rather, Benac notes that they are intentionally collaborative constellations of relationships that, through partnership and friendship, can facilitate the transformative work the church strives to engage in.[74] Stewart gestures to such an idea at various points in her oeuvre, as we saw above, but her emphasis seems to rest squarely on viewing individual family units as sources of communal renewal and transformation. My point here is not to minimize the importance of the family. Rather, it is to suggest that the church can view the relational nexus of the immediate family as a kind of good it can share with the wider community.

Admittedly, formation and cultivation will take different shapes in different eras and contexts. The forms of participation in civic life afforded to those inhabiting a democratic republic differ drastically from the opportunities afforded to those living in a totalitarian regime or even those denied the rights of citizenship within a republic, a fact Stewart knew all too well. Because formation and cultivation often depend on the macropolitical climates we inhabit, this ought to chasten and restrain programmatic statements about what the formation and cultivation of institutions *must* look like. But still, we can recognize that networks of relationships are needed to better endure the world and to meet the needs of inhabitants. The question, then, is not whether the Christian community will engage in acts of institution building and renewal for the sake of testifying to the divine commitment to the goodness of creation but what form, structure, and shape these institutions will take at various points across space-time and how these institutions will adapt to changes in their social and political environments.

Virtue as Public Witness

Second, we can retrieve Stewart's vision of piety, of the character of the Christian community, as a form of public witness. The work of piety, for

72. Benac, *Adaptive Church*, 4.
73. Benac, *Adaptive Church*, 104.
74. Benac, *Adaptive Church*, 106.

Stewart, is a public practice. Yet before moving forward toward retrieving this insight, it is worth highlighting the fact that Stewart's program is a fundamentally *theo*-political vision. By that I mean that Stewart's belief in the pressing need of forming communities of character and of cultivating these communities flows from her Christian convictions and her engagement with the biblical text. While she never identifies herself as a preacher and her speeches are not sermons per se, her oeuvre is rife with allusions and references to and interpretations of the text of Holy Scripture.[75] As Cooper points out, "Maria Stewart understood her public speaking and writing very much as a religious vocation."[76] In other words, Stewart views herself as compelled by a kind of holy vocation, given to her by God, to preach a message of pure religion, a message calling her listeners to lives of virtue and piety.[77] Accordingly, Stewart's sense of holy calling and the attendant exhortation to her audience to a life of virtue and piety involve a constellation of social, political, and theological concerns. She writes, "I am more and more convinced that the cause of Christ will never be built up, Satan's kingdom will never be destroyed, the chains of slavery and ignorance never burst, and morality and virtue will never flourish, till pure and holy examples are set home, and the professing followers of Christ arise and shine forth, and prove to the world that there is a reality in religion, and a beauty in the fear of the Lord."[78]

For Stewart, there is a kind of Christian imperative at play, both in her life personally and in the lives of the people she hopes to reach.[79] It is this imperative and the corresponding desire to live in a manner that pleases the Lord that motivate Stewart to speak and preach in public.[80] For Stewart, the cultivation of piety is fundamentally undergirded by a theo-logic, based in

75. Cooper, *Word, Like Fire*, 4.
76. Cooper, *Word, Like Fire*, 106.
77. Stewart, "Religion and the Pure Principles of Morality," 32–33.
78. Stewart, introduction to *Spiritual Narratives*, by Stewart, Lee, Foote, and Broughton, 24.
79. Stewart, "Address Delivered before the Afric-American Female Intelligence Society," 50.
80. Stewart says frequently and increasingly boldly that she has been called by God to ministry. She states, "Methinks I heard a spiritual interrogation—'Who shall go forward and take off the reproach that is cast upon the people of color? Shall it be a woman?' And my heart made this reply—'If it is thy will, be it even so Lord Jesus!'" (Stewart, "Lecture Delivered at the Franklin Hall," 45). Elsewhere, after recounting her conversion experience and the feeling of the Spirit of God coming upon her, Stewart says, "Thus far I have every reason to believe that it is the divine influence of the Holy Spirit operating upon my heart that could possibly induce me to make the feeble and unworthy efforts that I have [in public speaking]" (Stewart, "Mrs. Stewart's Farewell Address," 67). Cooper provides a helpful comment on this theme in Stewart's work, noting that by the end of Stewart's career "she is ready to argue that women have a God-given place in public life and that she has a God-given place in public life" (Cooper, *Word, Like Fire*, 141). Cooper goes on to note that Stewart seems to view herself in line with the prophets of Scripture and the apostle Paul himself (149).

her convictions regarding divine rule and the Holy Spirit's authorization of her preaching. As evidenced in her *Meditations*, Stewart sees a strong need to cultivate holy affections. "I have just returned from church," she writes. "O, may what I have heard prove a rich and lasting blessing to my soul. Disrobe me, O God, of every impure and unholy affection, and make my soul a fit temple for thee to dwell in."[81] This emphasis on piety as personal devotion to God is prominent throughout Stewart's work. Unfortunately, in religious discourse, piety is often reduced solely to an internal feeling, an internal encounter with God, or the affections inspired from communing with God.[82] This is not the case with Stewart.

For Stewart, piety is not merely centered on the development of internal emotional feelings or spiritual affections, as important as these both may be.[83] Rather, piety is tethered to prudently and wisely navigating the world as creatures bound to God in Christ and destined to stand before him.[84] Piety is something that enables the individual and the community to navigate the numerous complexities that arise over the course of their lives in the world. As Richardson observes, Stewart's "religious vision and her sociopolitical agenda were intrinsically bound together, defined one by the other."[85] Accordingly, if the call on the Christian life and the Christian community is to cultivate piety—that is, to "make every effort to support your faith with

81. Stewart, "Meditation II," 27.

82. Many evangelicals have historically emphasized the internal, interior, and individualistic nature of piety, leaving the connection between piety and social action somewhat opaque. So Phoebe Palmer writes, "Holiness is a state of soul in which all the powers of the body and mind are consciously given up to God; and the witness of holiness is that testimony which the Holy Spirit bears with our spirit that the offering is accepted through Christ" (P. Palmer, "Entire Devotion to God," 196). While Palmer is adamant that such an internal devotion to God orients the Christian to act in particular ways, the point of emphasis is on internal and interior feelings. Piety, or holiness in Palmer's words, still has to do primarily with the "feeling of communion" with God and inwardness—that is, internal states of the soul. Stewart certainly has room for this kind of interiority. In fact, in her *Meditations*, she constantly returns to the need to cultivate holy and pure affection toward God. But as I will demonstrate below, her approach to piety is interwoven with involvement in a particular sociopolitical agenda.

83. The adverb "merely" is important here, for Stewart most certainly believes that the cultivation of particularly religious affections is a necessary part of the Christian way of life. Her devotional, *Meditations*, which we have referenced occasionally, places this emphasis front and center. For example, she writes, "My friends, I have been sorely troubled in my mind; and why? It is because I have seen that many, who professed the name of Christ, are not careful to discharge their duty faithfully to their dying fellow immortals around them. . . . Religion has become too unfashionable and too unpopular, even among the professing followers of Christ." Stewart, "Meditation I," 25.

84. The concept of "standing before the bar of God" is prominent in Stewart's work. See, for example, Stewart, "Address Delivered before the Afric-American Female Intelligence Society," 52.

85. Richardson, "What If I Am a Woman?," 196.

goodness [ἀρετήν] . . . and self-control with endurance, and endurance with godliness [εὐσέβειαν]" (2 Pet. 1:5–6)—for Stewart, this cultivation is bound up with an attendant vision of social and political action. We must become the kind of people capable of enduring the present, a people capable of resisting the malformations in our present social world and "carrying on" within it.[86]

What we see in Stewart's work, then, is what we might refer to as an account of "public piety"—that is, an understanding of religious piety that includes within it a call to engage in righteous conduct in dealing with one's neighbor and pursuing their social and political good. Of course, this seems fairly obvious. As Jason Sexton has observed, much of the Christian life, from baptism to burial, is lived "in public" and in spaces shared with others outside the Christian community.[87]

For Stewart, the cultivation of piety is intended to benefit the larger community in which we exist. Piety is ordered to our participation in a common life. "Never; no, never will the chains of slavery and ignorance burst till we become united as one and cultivate among ourselves the pure principles of piety, morality, and virtue."[88] The individual's and the community's piety, for Stewart, terminate in *political* and in *public* actions that bear witness to the tethering of one's life to the reality undergirding true religion. Again, she is worth quoting: "Permit me to ask you, my Christian friends, in the name of the Lord Jesus Christ, what progress are you making in the divine life? Are you bringing forth the fruits of righteousness, and proving to the world by your own conduct that there is a reality in religion, and a beauty in the fear of the Lord?"[89] These "fruits of righteousness" include caring for one's family members, developing one's talents, pursuing the political good of the disenfranchised, and attending to the social, material, and physical needs of one's neighbors. These fruits are a natural extension of the transformation brought about as a result of the miraculous renewal

---

86. Stewart explicitly uses the language of flourishing. I am somewhat less bound to such language. At times, it seems to me, the best we can do in a postlapsum world is to strive to carry on and encourage one another to do the same. It is difficult for me to conceive of what it might mean for the enslaved of yesteryear or of today to flourish. But there is a consistent commitment to carrying on even as one hopes that God will split the heavens asunder and come down, that the mountains might quake at his presence (Isa. 64:1). The evidence of such a commitment is found in nothing less than the existence of their descendants, children born in hope that their tomorrows would be materially different from those of their parents. I am indebted to Jonathan Tran for this language.

87. Sexton, "Public Theology," 431.

88. Stewart, "Religion and the Pure Principles of Morality," 30.

89. Stewart, "Meditation VI," 31.

that occurs in conversion, a conversion she describes in language common to the evangelical tradition.[90]

Stewart draws a strong connection between religious convictions and the activity of anti-slavery societies: "These Anti-slavery societies . . . will soon cause many grateful tears to flow, and many desponding hearts to bound and leap for joy. And is it the applause of men that has prompted these benevolent ones to take their lives in their hands, as it were, to plead our cause before the great and powerful? Ah, no! It is that holy religion . . . whose precepts will raise and elevate us above our present condition."[91] Based on this, we can say that according to Stewart, the cultivation of piety and a commitment to "holy religion" carry with them a clear commitment to particular kinds of action in political and social environments. Of course, the nature and scope of this action will depend in large part on the kinds of options one's political and social environments afford. For example, in speaking to a group of men and women, she notes the limited political agency that women, especially Afro-American women, have in her time period.[92] This should serve as motivation for their "beloved brethren," on whom they depend, to advocate on their behalf. Still, Stewart believes that black women possess a semblance of political agency in the form of "influence."[93] Stewart refuses to accept the proposition that dependence and marginalization can serve as a sufficient excuse for inaction. She calls for women to exercise a kind of creative wisdom even within their limitations. All of this is connected to the themes of religion, piety, and the cultivation of virtue. In essence, she calls Afro-Americans to become people capable of inhabiting their social location, flourishing within it, and somehow, hopefully and expectantly, navigating around the boundaries that society has impressed upon them.

The pursuit of virtue focuses on growth in godliness, both individually and collectively, and also the cultivation of a community's powers and persons. It requires men to advocate on behalf of their "sisters" and to create opportunities for them to flourish. It requires women to use their relational influence and to take advantage of whatever power they are afforded to act.

90. See Stewart, "Religion and the Pure Principles of Morality," 29; and Stewart, "Mrs. Stewart's Farewell Address," 67. As Cooper notes, Stewart approaches Scripture with a schema common to the evangelical tradition, viewing the whole of it as inspired by God and addressing her in her time and place. Cooper, *Word, Like Fire*, 4, 103.

91. Stewart, "Cause for Encouragement," 43.

92. Stewart, "Lecture Delivered at the Franklin Hall," 48.

93. Stewart writes, "My beloved brethren . . . it is upon you that woman depends; she can do but little besides using her influence; and it is for her sake and yours that I have come forward and made myself as hissing and a reproach among my people." Stewart, "Lecture Delivered at the Franklin Hall," 48.

And it requires the liberated and the freeborn to pursue the interests of the enslaved. Yet Stewart's belief is not that Christian virtue is reducible to the pursuit of the neighbor's good, as important as she believes that pursuit to be. Rather, growth in piety necessarily entails and is ordered toward the pursuit of the well-being of one's neighbor and the members of one's community across the varying strata of a society. Virtue is about becoming, collectively, the kind of people who can make the right judgments, prioritize the proper goods, and find a way to flourish, a way to go on, in the world as we find it, even as we hope for its renewal.[94] And this formation is subversive. It rejects the prevailing ideologies our social contexts seek to impress on us and the manner in which these ideologies hope to malform us. Stewart is not asking her listeners merely to see themselves as the audience of the sacred page, to view themselves as image bearers of God, and to recognize their own inherent worth and dignity. Rather, she goes a step further, calling them to resist the manner in which such ideology would instill within them a kind of nihilistic complacency or a desire to pursue fleeting pleasure.[95] This kind of formation in virtue involves a reorientation of the Christian community's imagination and desire so that members are grounded fundamentally in relationship to God.[96] This kind of formation in virtue bears witness in our common life to God's acts in creation and redemption and testifies to the judgments he has and will render upon the sinful ways we have ordered our lives.

Conclusion

Much as we saw in the writing of David Ruggles, Maria Stewart's corpus is more episodic than systematic, kaleidoscopic and dynamic than static. This is to be expected given the nature of the world they inhabited and the difficulties of sustaining a living as an Afro-American writer in the antebellum era. Still, what is valuable about her work is her reminder of the need to become a kind of people capable of enduring and resisting the malformation of the social systems we inhabit. This resistance is not just a resistance of the temptations they have to offer, although it certainly includes that, but also a resistance

94. Waters notes that for Stewart "everyday righteousness is the foundation of moral behavior. . . . Most crucially, a unified community of morally upstanding citizens is a precondition of the successful struggle for political freedom and equality." Waters, *Maria W. Stewart*, 214.

95. Stewart, "Address Delivered at the African Masonic Hall," 60.

96. Cooper sees this explicitly in Stewart's repeated citations of Psalm 68:31, "Let Ethiopia hasten to stretch out its hands to God." Cooper writes, "The Ethiopian prophecy identified Africans as people with a special relationship to God, and as such, a people of promise. The biblical text came to be used as a part of broader themes reaffirming Africa's place among the civilized world and Africans' place within humanity." Cooper, *Word, Like Fire*, 161.

of the way they try to encourage our reimagining of the world around us. Communal formation and cultivation, for Stewart, are essential parts of this resistance. In light of this, Stewart challenges us to pursue the task of cultivation, both of our individual powers and of the powers and capacities of our communities, in order to become people capable of enduring the time between Christ's first and second advents. This call to endurance rejects out of hand the very possibility of any form of triumphalism. We are people who are waiting and who have a calling and a vocation in the waiting. But the city we call home remains just over the horizon. And so we endure the world in hope.

4 ✳ ✳ ✳

William Still

Preserving, Renewing, Anticipating, and Inspiring

Peter Freedman (later renamed Peter Still) was unprepared for the surprise that awaited him that morning as he approached the sharply dressed junior clerk sitting at a desk in front of him. Having purchased his freedom in 1850 at the price of five hundred hard-earned dollars, Peter had made the long journey north from Alabama, leaving his wife and child behind, and arrived in Philadelphia, Pennsylvania. He hoped to be reunited with his mother and father, Levin and Sidney Still, whom he had not seen in over twenty years.[1] After asking around and vainly searching the pockets of African American residents scattered across the city, Peter followed the instructions of some residents and made his way to "the Anti-Slavery Office," where there "were old records of colored Churches."[2] Since his parents were devout, religious people, Peter was told that he might find them there. Upon arriving at the office, he saw a young, colored clerk sitting at a desk, writing. Peter notified the clerk that he was looking for his parents, identifying them by name and describing their flight from Maryland.[3] The clerk's interest was immediately piqued, as the story resonated with his own family history. "Then, looking

---

1. Pickard, *Kidnapped and the Ransomed*, 245.
2. Pickard, *Kidnapped and the Ransomed*, 247.
3. Bordewich, *Bound for Canaan*, 356.

[Peter] in the face, [the junior clerk] said, 'Suppose I should tell you that I am your brother?'"[4] Peter was dumbstruck and terrified, presuming this was a trick of slave catchers intent on selling him back into bondage. Eventually, after a considerable amount of prodding and encouragement, the clerk was able to convince Peter to follow him to a small cottage, and the family was reunited at long last. After over forty years in bondage, Peter met the mother he had lost, the brothers and sisters he had never known.

Peter Still's story is fascinating in its own right, but for the purposes of this chapter, we will turn our attention to his younger brother, that colored clerk he happened upon at the Anti-Slavery Society office: William Still. Abolitionist William Still was born in 1821 to Levin and Sidney Steel, both former slaves. He was the youngest of eighteen children. Although William and thirteen of his siblings were born in New Jersey, a free state, they were technically still classified as "slaves" under federal law because their mother was a fugitive slave. As slaves in Maryland, Still's parents had witnessed firsthand the devastating effects and trauma of chattel slavery. His father, Levin, had earned enough money to purchase his own freedom, but he had been forced to leave his family behind in bondage.[5] Sidney, later renamed Charity, had attempted to run away once before, albeit unsuccessfully.[6] A few months later, she tried again. This time she successfully evaded her captors and escaped her bondage. Yet she was able to take only her youngest two daughters with her, leaving behind her two oldest sons, Levin Jr. and Peter.[7]

William Still, then, was born years later in a free state to a fugitive slave.[8] After he came of age, William moved to Philadelphia in 1844, where he met his wife, Letitia. Eventually, Still found a job working as a clerk for

---

4. Pickard, *Kidnapped and the Ransomed*, 249.

5. Still, preface to *Still's Underground Railroad Records* (1886). Still's work underwent multiple revisions, published under similar but slightly different titles. The first edition of Still's *The Underground Railroad* was released in 1872. A second, expanded edition was released in 1878 with an added preface. A third edition was released in 1883, and a fourth edition was published in 1886. For clarity, I will indicate the year of publication in parentheses.

6. Still writes, "Mother saw no way for herself and children to escape the bondage but by flight. . . . Hardly months had passed ere the keen scent of the slave-hunters had trailed them to where they had fancied themselves secure." Still, preface to *Still's Underground Railroad Records* (1886).

7. Still, preface to *Still's Underground Railroad Records* (1886). As punishment for their mother's escape, Peter and Levin were sold farther south, first to Lexington, Kentucky, and then to Alabama. Peter Still would later purchase his own freedom. After making his way to Philadelphia, he published an autobiography of his own journey toward freedom, having achieved it some forty years after his mother and sisters. Like his father, Peter was forced to leave his wife, Vina, and children behind but would later, after a failed rescue attempt, gather enough funds to buy their freedom as well. Levin Still died in bondage.

8. As Andrew Diemer observes, this complicates Still's civic status. Under New Jersey's gradual abolition law, "the children of slaves would be freed after serving a lengthy apprenticeship,

the Pennsylvania Society for the Abolition of Slavery while working as a stationmaster for the Underground Railroad.[9] He would go on to serve as chairman of the Philadelphia Vigilance Committee and help escaped slaves move through Philadelphia. After the Civil War ended and the United States formally abolished slavery, Still continued his involvement in the public sphere, advocating for civil and voting rights for Afro-Americans, albeit not without significant difficulty and controversy.[10] He formed and helped fund the Social, Civil, and Statistical Association of the Colored People of Pennsylvania (1861), which sought to collect data on Afro-Americans so as to "obtain a mutual recognition of the civil and social rights of man" and improve their social condition.[11] He also was an active participant in the Freedmen's Aid Commission,[12] started an orphanage, served as president of the first black-owned banking institution in Philadelphia, ran a Sunday school, and helped organize one of the first YMCAs for black children.[13] Although he fell out of favor with some of the younger civil rights activists in Philadelphia due in large part to a dispute over the appropriate methods for pursuing the rights of Afro-Americans, Still remained in Philadelphia, where he continued to operate his local coal business and engage in works of philanthropy until his death in 1902.

In this chapter, we will explore the life and work of the last of our three abolitionary figures: William Still. Like Maria Stewart, Still witnessed drastic and sweeping changes take place across the American landscape. His remarkable career as an abolitionist and civil rights activist in Philadelphia

---

a type of pseudo-slavery. Men were bound until their twenty-fifth birthday, women until their twenty-first." Diemer, *Vigilance*, 6.

9. Still was one of two Afro-Americans in Philadelphia who received the privilege and financial stability that clerkship afforded. Brian Luskey writes, "Clerkships connoted respectability among African Americans" albeit at a time when the significance of the position was coming under increased scrutiny (Luskey, *On the Make*, 66). Still's clerkship is all the more exceptional in light of the fact that, when such positions were extended to Afro-Americans, they were normally given to mulattos, Afro-Americans of fairer complexion (Luskey, *On the Make*, 65).

10. Still eventually fell out with younger activists in Philadelphia, such as Octavius Catto and Jacob C. White Jr., over a difference in opinion about how to overturn the segregation of streetcars. See Diemer, *Vigilance*, 229–54.

11. "Good Movement."

12. The Freedmen's Aid Commission was an organization formed after the conclusion of the American Civil War that hoped to provide newly liberated Afro-American citizens with the means of flourishing on the other side of their enslavement, normally in the form of providing educational opportunities. The organization, which sought to pursue the elevation and cultivation of Afro-Americans, "organized to prosecute with unremitting zeal and vigor the education of the freedmen of the South . . . [so as] to see that they are furnished the means with which to secure, maintain, and enjoy the rights belonging to their new condition." *American Freedman's Aid Commission*, 3.

13. Kashatus, *William Still*, 181.

reached from the middle of the antebellum era (1812–61) through the Civil
War (1861–65) and beyond the Reconstruction era (1865–77). From Still, we
learn that public witness takes the form of preservation, renewal, anticipation, and inspiration. In the work of preservation, we seek to ensure that
the goods of the past—namely, goods that have to do with the shape of our
lives, goods that are necessary for the flourishing of human community—
are retained, even as we seek to reform unjust social systems. In the work of
renewal, we seek to take the elements of our common life that are broken or
falling into disrepair and to go about the process of repairing and bolstering them. In the work of anticipation, we look forward to life on the other
side of crisis, asking what possible futures await us and how can we prepare
for them. Regarding inspiration, Still reminds us of the need to remember
the past as a source of encouragement for pressing forward in the midst of
difficulty in the present.

Recording the Underground Railroad

Aiding and Abetting Fugitive Slaves

Throughout the early part of the nineteenth century, Philadelphia was
one of the central hubs for the Underground Railroad, with some historians
estimating that over nine thousand fugitive slaves entered or passed through
the city before the Civil War brought an end to slavery.[14] The city's location
on the Delaware River; its proximity to states such as Maryland, Virginia,
and Delaware, where slavery was still legal; and the influx of traffic due to the
installation of railways all contributed to Philadelphia's status as a frequent
stop for those escaping bondage.[15] Fugitive slaves used any and every means
of transportation available to them, with some stowing away on steamboats,
schooners, and train cars while others traveled over land.[16]

Among the abolitionary community in general and those aiding and abetting runaway slaves along the Underground Railroad in particular, William
Still was somewhat of a unique and exceptional figure. As Andrew Diemer
has noted, while "the vast majority of those who worked on the [Underground

14. Okur, "Underground Railroad in Philadelphia," 537.
15. As Ashley Council notes, "A bustling city with a great rail center and a port busy with
ships from 1830 to 1860, Philadelphia would prove to be a 'natural junction' in the covert
enterprise aimed at aiding those fleeing from bondage. As the Underground Railroad gained
more allies among the free black and white communities, growing numbers of runaways headed
toward the city to either stay or continue their flight further north." Council, "Ringing Liberty's
Bell," 496.
16. Switala, *Underground Railroad in Philadelphia*, 164.

Railroad] did so as volunteers," Still was employed as a clerk for the Anti-Slavery Society and served as the chair of the Acting Committee of the Philadelphia Vigilance Committee.[17] Clerkship was viewed as an entryway into the middle-class lifestyle, but the duties of a clerk in the antebellum era were notoriously vague. As Carole Srole avers, clerks were "supposed to learn skills on the job by gradually learning increasingly complex tasks, from tallying packages to copying letters and invoices to duplicating letters."[18] Clerks were often forced to engage in more mundane tasks, such as delivering packages and transporting goods.[19] Still's clerkship provided him with steady income and allowed him to serve as the face of the Anti-Slavery Society. While his responsibilities were initially limited to managing the office's mail and keeping the office clean, they expanded as the Anti-Slavery Society office became the center of a much larger, informal network that fugitives frequented. As Fergus Bordewich points out, "In the early 1850s Still's office was aiding an average of sixty fugitives per month."[20] Still became responsible for receiving and keeping track of the numerous fugitives who came to the society seeking assistance.

While organizations like the Pennsylvania Abolition Society and the Anti-Slavery Society fought to bring about the abolition of slavery as an institution,[21] a proposal Still ardently supported, the Philadelphia Vigilance Committee sought to provide escaped slaves with safe passage to and through the city of Philadelphia and to protect free blacks and fugitive slaves from slave catchers.[22] As noted above, Philadelphia's proximity to slave states made it a frequent and

17. Diemer, "Business of the Road," 84.

18. Srole, *Transcribing Class and Gender*, 18.

19. Srole, *Transcribing Class and Gender*, 18. Brian Luskey proposes that changes in the economic and demographic landscape of the early nineteenth century changed and expanded the responsibilities of clerks. He writes, "[While] clerks continued to write, copy, and tally, . . . most clerks found their responsibilities expanded. Merchants now expected them to negotiate with and sell goods to wholesale and retail customers and join porters and day laborers in moving goods around stores. Compelled to perform both manual and nonmanual work, the label 'clerk' became a misleading marker, since common labor with porters might be followed by a stint at the cashier's chair, which might precede posting bills, delivering goods to customers, or traveling on behalf of the firm." Luskey, "'What Is My Prospects?,'" 682.

20. Bordewich, *Bound for Canaan*, 356.

21. This is not to suggest that either of these two organizations refrained from addressing the needs of individual runaways and slaves. Rather, while the Vigilance Committee sought to help slaves evade slave catchers and avoid recapture, the Abolition Society's focus and emphasis were on legal transformation. As Beverly Tomek notes, "From the beginning, the society took the leading role in petitioning legislatures to abolish slavery and urging courts to declare slavery illegal. When these efforts failed, the society appealed to individual slaveholders to free their captives. Some members bought enslaved people to free them, and others led fundraising initiatives to help enslaved people buy themselves." Tomek, *Slavery and Abolition in Pennsylvania*, 41.

22. Tomek, *Slavery and Abolition in Pennsylvania*, 89.

natural stop for fugitives seeking freedom. But the presence of so many run-away slaves also made it a haven for slave catchers, who sought to profit from the capture and sale of escapees.[23] When runaways arrived in Philadelphia, they often had slave catchers hot on their heels, and they lacked knowledge of the city's inner workings necessary to navigate and hide within it.[24] As the chair of the Acting Committee of the Philadelphia Vigilance Committee,[25] Still was responsible for organizing and assisting the passage of runaway slaves through Philadelphia. He gathered and dispersed money, arranged transport, and on many occasions found temporary housing for runaway slaves.[26] As Larry Gara notes, "One of the principal activities of the new Philadelphia vigilance was to extend financial aid to fugitives. The committee provided money to board fugitives with the families of free Negroes, sometimes for as long as thirteen days."[27] Andrew Diemer observes that "many [fugitives] had fled with little money and others had spent all they had saved in order to get themselves to Philadelphia. Some fugitives were given small amounts of cash. Others were provided with transportation, clean clothes, new shoes, medi-cine, a haircut: the sorts of things that would help a fugitive move on to a less dangerous place and to blend in while doing so."[28] In addition to providing fleeing slaves with funding, the committee was responsible for arranging legal counsel if arrests were made and suspected fugitives were taken to court.[29]

The Stills appear to have welcomed into their home more than a small num-ber of slaves fleeing recapture, as indicated by the many letters that express

23. Regarding the large number of slave catchers in Philadelphia, William Kashatus writes, "Since Philadelphia was a hotbed of Quaker abolitionism and attracted dozens of fugitives, slave catchers often came to the city searching for runaways. If a slave catcher could not locate the freedom seeker, it was not uncommon for him to kidnap a free black resident as a replace-ment" (Kashatus, *William Still*, 57). The passage of an anti-kidnapping bill in Pennsylvania in 1847 offered significant legal protections for fugitive slaves, even if federal law demanded state cooperation. As Diemer observes, this law imposed harsh fees on those seeking to claim free Afro-Americans as fugitive slaves, outlawed state officials and state jails from participating in the capture of accused fugitives, and repealed an earlier law that allowed slave owners to bring their slaves into the state for up to six months and prevented slaves from testifying in the court of law (Diemer, *Vigilance*, 53–54). The passing of the Fugitive Slave Act of 1850 significantly tempered the hopes and expectations of Afro-Americans within Philadelphia for the legal system to preserve their quests for freedom.

24. Blackett, *Captive's Quest for Freedom*, 273–74.

25. While the race riots of 1842 seem to have tempered the Vigilance Committee's activity within the city for a period of time and led to its dissolution, the committee was eventually revitalized and reorganized in 1852 under the leadership of Robert Purvis and William Still. Switala, *Underground Railroad in Philadelphia*, 160.

26. Still, *Still's Underground Railroad Records* (1886), 611.

27. Gara, "William Still and the Underground Railroad," 35.

28. Diemer, "Business of the Road," 102.

29. Tomek, *Slavery and Abolition in Pennsylvania*, 89.

gratitude to Letitia for her friendship and hospitality.[30] William and Letitia also owned and operated a boardinghouse for Afro-American residents of Philadelphia, enhancing their ability to house and hide fugitive slaves. Much of Still's workdays were consumed with the task of assisting runaway slaves as they attempted to navigate the fraught and treacherous path of the Underground Railroad, traveling from bondage to freedom.

Still's Underground Railroad Records

William Still's contributions to the abolitionary cause and the pursuit of civic renewal come into focus in his *The Underground Railroad*, published originally in 1872. Indeed, much of what we know about the Underground Railroad and its participants comes from Still's records, which include personal interviews with 955 individuals who passed through Philadelphia.[31] Still's work was in large part a work of preservation and history making. He attempted to preserve the memory of the Underground Railroad, its conductors, its passengers, and the slave catchers who sought to undermine its work.[32]

30. Still and his family remain in the background of many of the events recorded in his *Underground Railroad Records*. Yet many of the letters addressed to Still ask him to extend greetings to his wife, Letitia, as well. This certainly seems to lend credence to the idea that the Stills welcomed fugitives into their boardinghouse and home. Other letters are more explicit on this point. For example, Ellen Saunders writes, "Please tell Mrs. Still I have not met any person who has treated me kinder than she did since I left. I consider you both to have been true friends to me." Still, *Still's Underground Railroad Records* (1886), 276.

31. Kashatus, *William Still*, 83.

32. In recent years, the popular conception of the Underground Railroad and the language of "stationmasters" and "conductors" have been subject to some critique. Historian Larry Gara has proposed that current conceptions of the Underground Railroad are indebted more to myth and legend than to reality. He argues, "The legend of the underground railroad rests in part on the propaganda literature of the abolitionists and of their southern opponents" (Gara, *Liberty Line*, 143; see also 1–18). The newspapers and pamphlets of abolitionists portrayed the Underground Railroad and their own efforts to rescue slaves in a certain light so as to sway public opinion to their side (148). Slave owners, on the other hand, used the legend of the Underground Railroad to convince slaves of the near impossibility of escape. This led to a great historical embellishment, the creation of a legend that has limited roots in history (160). Furthermore, Gara worries that the language conceals the active participation of Afro-Americans, both enslaved and free, in the flight from slavery (18). Yet while Gara does highlight the agency and participation of fugitive slaves in the pursuit of their own liberation, a project Still himself would have commended, his analysis may go a bit too far. As Fergus Bordewich has observed, the abolitionary network that is referred to as the Underground Railroad seems to emerge coterminous with the invention of the actual railroad system in the United States (Bordewich, *Bound for Canaan*, 236). Additionally, as Andrew Diemer has pointed out, the language of conductors, stationmasters, and passengers "was not invented by historians after the fact; as early as the 1830s, participants were already adopting the terminology of railroads to describe their efforts to aid fugitives from slavery" (Diemer, "Business of the Road," 87). For example, Still writes in a letter to abolitionist Elijah Pennypacker, "After the middle of this

While the conductors, stationmasters, slave catchers, and slave owners who litter Still's pages receive only a passing description, readers cannot help but notice the attention Still paid to describing the physical features and stories of the more than nine hundred fugitive slaves whose names are recorded. Still described freedom seekers according to their build, their skin color, their height, their former names, the family members they left behind, and, perhaps most curiously, their passionate desire for freedom. He included locations where they were formerly enslaved, their plantations, and the names of their former masters. Put simply, throughout Still's document, he takes a particular interest in the passengers, and he strives to ensure that they are portrayed as active participants in the pursuit of freedom.[33]

Still describes one escapee, Cyrus, as "twenty-six years of age, stout, and unmistakably dark, . . . owned by James K. Lewis, a store-keeper, and would pass for an intelligent farm hand."[34] He describes another fugitive, Harriet, as "a tall, well-made, intelligent young woman, twenty-two years of age."[35] Regarding Silas Long, Still notes that he escaped from Cambridge, Maryland, "leaving his mother, one brother and one cousin" behind.[36] As William Kashatus summarizes, "[Still] recorded their names as well as their age, skin color, and gender and paid careful attention to family information, such as number of siblings and names of parents, spouses, and children. He also recorded details about their bondage, including the owner's name, how they were treated, and their reason for running away."[37] As we will see below, the journey out of slavery often brought along with it a sense of dislocation and relational disintegration. Still's records are a work of preservation, one that seeks to retain for posterity the existence of the individuals who make up a community that sought, fought for, and on many occasions attained freedom.

---

week, I think you might venture to send [the fugitives] to us in 'Small parcels'—that is, not over four or five in a company. If convenient, you will confer a favor by dropping us a few lines of information informing us by what hour & train the arrivals will come" (Still, William Still to Elijah F. Pennypacker, November 2, 1857, in Ripley, *Black Abolitionist*, 333). Here, Still is already referring to fugitives as the kind of cargo carried on a train.

33. Diemer proposes that this emphasis on the agency of the enslaved in their pursuit of freedom throughout the *Underground Railroad Records* is intentional on Still's part. He writes, "For those looking to recover Still's actions this book has sometimes proven frustrating; Still is by no means the center of attention. In fact, for pages at a time it can be difficult to find Still's hand at all. This absence is by design. . . . Still's work . . . shows us that enslaved people were prepared to save themselves—they simply needed a hand." Diemer, *Vigilance*, 8.

34. Still, *Still's Underground Railroad Records* (1886), 286.

35. Still, *Still's Underground Railroad Records* (1886), 306.

36. Still, *Still's Underground Railroad Records* (1886), 394.

37. Kashatus, *William Still*, 83.

In Still's descriptions of slave owners, one cannot help but notice the plurality of Christian traditions that are implicated in the practice of human bondage. Still identifies Methodists, Episcopalians, Presbyterians, and Baptists who own slaves and pursue the fugitives who flee their respective estates.[38] In so doing, Still contrasts a kind of Christianity that is complicit and actively participates in sinful modes of life with that of a "pure philanthropy, that vital Christianity, that True and Undefiled Religion before God and the Father, which is to visit the fatherless and widow in their affliction, and to undo the heavy burden, and let the oppressed go free."[39] In contrast, he laments the involvement of "professed Christians in the city of Brotherly Love" in the kidnapping of Euphemia Williams, who had lived in Philadelphia for many years before being captured under the auspices of the Fugitive Slave Law.[40] Still's not-so-subtle critique of Christian praxis, a failure to exercise "practical Christianity," ebbs and flows throughout his text.[41] As Still puts it, "Slavery exempted from the yoke no man with a colored skin no matter what his faith, talent, genius, or worth might be. The person of Christ in a black skin would scarcely have caused [slavery] to relinquish its tyrannical grasp; neither God nor man was regarded by men who dealt in the bodies and souls of their fellow-men."[42] For Still, slavery's domination and exploitation of the lives and labor of Afro-Americans is due in large part to a failure in Christian witness.

Still raises these critiques not as an outsider but as a committed churchman and Presbyterian.[43] These are not critiques of Christianity as such. Indeed, throughout his *Underground Railroad Records*, Still highlights the belief of many refugees in divine aid in their pursuit of liberty.[44] For example, Still records how one fugitive, Robert Hall, fled his master despite considerable health ailments, noting that "his faith in God afforded him comfort and hope."[45] Instead, these criticisms of Christian participation in the institution

---

38. See, for example, Still, *Still's Underground Rail Road Records* (1883), 378, 483.

39. Still, *Still's Underground Rail Road Records* (1883), 585.

40. Still, *Still's Underground Railroad Records* (1886), 566.

41. Still, *Still's Underground Rail Road Records* (1883), 378.

42. Still, *Still's Underground Railroad Records* (1886), 451.

43. In 1854, Still began to rent a pew in First African Presbyterian Church (Diemer, *Vigilance*, 98). More to the point, the language of the Christian faith is woven throughout many of his texts. For example, Still writes to his daughter, "I would advise you to give more anxiety and consideration to the all important knowledge and studies, which will [ripen?] your mind and strengthen your purposes, not so much to shine in fashionable circlesulars whose reading and delights are more in harmony with this world than they are with Christ & his kingdom." Still, William Still to Caroline Still Anderson, February 1, 1876.

44. See, for example, the letter of John H. Hill in Still, *Still's Underground Rail Road Records* (1883), 194.

45. Still, *Still's Underground Rail Road Records* (1883), 275.

of chattel slavery are emerging from within the ecclesial community—that is, Still is critical of the church's failure to correspond to the reality of the gospel and Christians' numbness to the plight of the enslaved. For Still, God is on the side of the enslaved, and Christian faithfulness demands a participation in what God is doing.[46] Still calls the church to renew its witness and to be faithful to its present task, a task that he believes includes assisting in the liberation of the enslaved and translating "Christian principles into daily deeds."[47] The connection Still seeks to establish between the principles of Christianity and the liberation of the enslaved is all the more telling when the failures of the Christian community are held up against the many faithful allies and witnesses whom Still commends. For example, Still describes Mrs. Geo. S. Hillard, whose house served as an "asylum for fugitive slaves," as possessing the same spirit of "Christian charity" that is evidenced in "the act of the good Samaritan."[48] Still presents her as a contrast to the myriad of Christians who have chosen to turn a blind eye to their brothers and sisters who are in need or, worse yet, those Christians who in one way or another justify the enslavement and reenslavement of other human beings.

The Work of Preservation

Still's *Underground Railroad Records* was updated and rereleased a number of times, yet he consistently demonstrates an interest "in making accessible the histories of the fugitives themselves."[49] In what follows, we'll explore two vectors of Still's work of preservation: the task of remembrance and the task of seeking renewal. In the first instance, Still calls us to remember those who took the fight for freedom into their own hands so we can embody their virtues in the present. In the second, Still hoped that his records

---

46. This reading of divine providence could, of course, be contested. Indeed, this seems to be one of the central issues at stake in Christian understandings of the Civil War. See Noll, *Civil War as a Theological Crisis*, 75–94; and Bender, "American Experience of a Darkening and Receding Providence." Debating the validity of Still's reading of divine providence or the manner in which fugitive slaves saw their pursuit of freedom as undergirded by divine providence would take us too far afield. It is worth noting, as Leon Harris has pointed out, that this is a common theme in the writings of Afro-Americans reflecting on the emancipation and liberation of the slave. He writes, "The Holy Spirit is responsible for granting freedom to the slaves. First, by actively giving enslaved black Christians the drive to participate as a partner with the Spirit to resist slavery and fight for freedom. Second, the Holy Spirit worked passively on the slaves' behalf through the structures of society to move key figures to fight on behalf of the slaves." L. Harris, "Holy Spirit as Liberator," 195.

47. Still, *Still's Underground Rail Road Records* (1883), 652.

48. Still, *Still's Underground Rail Road Records* (1883), 374.

49. Black, "'New Enterprise in Our History,'" 669.

would enable families to reunite so they could flourish in freedom or if slavery was abolished.

Remembering Our Saints

The first aspect of Still's work of preservation is maintaining the memory of the heroes of the past, those who "were determined to have liberty even at the cost of life."[50] On the one hand, Still wants his work to be a historical record.[51] His desire to retain the historicity of these escapees is evidenced in Still's editorial choices. When Still records the letters of former slaves, he retains their spelling, punctuation, and diction, indicating that he is not trying to speak for them as much as he is allowing their words and actions to speak for themselves.[52] Still writes, "The writer is fully conscious of his literary imperfections. . . . Nevertheless, he feels that he owes it to the cause of Freedom, and to the Fugitives and their posterity in particular, to bring the doings of the UGRR before the public in the most truthful manner; not for the purpose of amusing the reader, but to show what efforts were made and what success was gained for Freedom under difficulties."[53]

On the other hand, even as Still attempts to present stories without embellishment or romanticization, his record is not history for history's sake. Indeed, as Alex Black notes, Still refers to his work as a collection of records.[54] In it, he describes the men and women who traversed the Underground Railroad as nothing short of heroes, legends in their own right whose courage and fortitude inspired the abolitionary movement.[55] The language of "courage" and "bravery" appears frequently throughout. For example, Still describes William Jordan as "a brave-hearted young fugitive" who hid in the swamps and caves, enduring the dangers of being "surrounded with bears, wild cats, rattle-snakes, and the like."[56] He states, "The Vigilance Committee of Philadelphia occasionally had the pleasure of receiving some heroes who were worthy to be classed among the bravest

50. Still, *Underground Railroad* (1872), 2.
51. Still, *Underground Railroad* (1872), 6.
52. Still states, "The writer begs to assure his readers that the most scrupulous care has been taken to furnish artless stories, simple facts—to resort to no coloring to make the book seem romantic, as he is fully persuaded that any exaggerations or additions of his own could not possibly equal in surpassing interest, the original and natural tales given under circumstances, when life and death were balanced in the scale, and fugitives in transit were making their way from Slavery to Freedom." Still, *Underground Railroad* (1872), 5.
53. Still, *Underground Railroad* (1872), 5–6.
54. Black, "'New Enterprise in Our History,'" 669.
55. Still, preface to *Still's Underground Railroad Records* (1886).
56. Still, *Still's Underground Railroad Records* (1886), 130.

of the brave."[57] Figures like John Wesley Smith and William Thomas Cope are credited with displaying courage and perseverance as they undertook the daunting road north toward freedom.[58] Isaac White is heralded for his possession of "brains and bravery of a rare order."[59] Through Still's depictions of these figures, we see the virtue of courage and a willingness to suffer for the sake of freedom displayed in vibrant detail. These are people who know the cost of freedom—they "earnestly desire freedom"—and are willing to pay it.[60]

Yet courage is not the only virtue on display in the lives of these former slaves. Still also repeatedly highlights their intelligence, ingenuity, perseverance, and determination. He describes a trio of refugees as "mere lads, not twenty-one years of age, [but] smart enough to outwit the very shrewdest and wisest slave-holders of Virginia."[61] In another example, Still heralds the ingenuity of William and Ellen Craft. Ellen disguised herself as a man and pretended to have a toothache so she could more easily make the long trek to obtain freedom.[62] He records the perseverance of Anthony Blow, who stowed away on a steamboat and hid himself above the ship's boiler in his journey to throw off the shackles of bondage.[63] Still writes, "The hiding place was small and [Blow] was large. A sitting attitude was the only way he could possibly occupy it. He was contented. This place was 'near the range, directly over the boiler,' and of course, was very warm. Nevertheless, Anthony felt that he would not murmur, as he knew what suffering was pretty well, and especially as he took it for granted that he would be free in about a day and a half."[64] Other figures like Washington Somlor, whose journey out of bondage took over eight months, are depicted as paragons of determination in the face of seemingly insurmountable obstacles.[65]

Still frequently employs somewhat chauvinistic language to describe the virtues of the passengers of the Underground Railroad, but he does not believe that such virtues are limited to men alone. In a group of escaping slaves, Maria

---

57. Still, *Still's Underground Railroad Records* (1886), 150.

58. Still, *Still's Underground Rail Road Records* (1883), 481, 508.

59. Still, *Still's Underground Rail Road Records* (1883), 484.

60. As noted above, Still often emphasizes the sacrifices and costs that such a journey out of slavery entailed. For example, he writes of how William Brown leaves "his father, grand-mother, four sisters and two brothers, all living where he fled from" (Still, *Still's Underground Rail Road Records* [1883], 342). This was a common occurrence. Even while many fugitives hoped to be reunited with their loved ones, the flight from slavery forced sacrificial choices to be made.

61. Still, *Still's Underground Railroad Records* (1886), 503.

62. Still, *Still's Underground Rail Road Records* (1883), 368.

63. Still, *Still's Underground Railroad Records* (1886), 61, 67.

64. Still, *Still's Underground Railroad Records* (1886), 63.

65. Still, *Still's Underground Railroad Records* (1886), 304.

Dorsey is lauded as the "heroine of the group," the "heroic female who was willing to endure the most extreme suffering and hardship for freedom [to whom] double honors were due."[66] Indeed, Still is clear that every slave, irrespective of their sex, who undertook the trials of the Underground Railroad in the pursuit of freedom should be admired. He writes, "As the way of travel, *via* the Underground Rail Road, under the most favorable circumstances, even for the sterner sex, was hard enough to test the strongest nerves and to try the faith of the bravest of the brave, every woman, who won her freedom by this perilous undertaking, deserves commemoration."[67] For every Henry Box Brown, who famously stowed away in a shipping crate and mailed himself to freedom, there were countless women who adopted the same drastic measures in the pursuit of freedom.[68] Determination also takes the form of repeatedly striving and pressing through failures in order to obtain liberation.

It bears repeating: Still records the strivings of his saints for a reason. In preserving the memory of the struggles, failures, and triumphs of these men and women who fought so valiantly to attain their freedom, Still hopes to inspire those who follow them to display the same courage, intelligence, ingenuity, perseverance, and determination as an act of paying homage to their ancestors. For Still, "The race must not forget the rock from whence they were hewn, nor the pit from whence they were digged. Like other races, this newly emancipated people will need all the knowledge of their past condition which they can get."[69] Still recognizes that the abolition of slavery does not bring about an end to the troubles of Afro-Americans in the United States, especially during the nineteenth century. He states as much: "In the political struggles, the hopes of the race have been sadly disappointed. From this direction no great advantage is likely to arise very soon."[70] While one immediate obstacle has been surmounted, others remain. Still hopes that in remembering the past, people might be able to appropriate the resources their ancestors have to offer them. He hopes that remembrance will, on the one hand, provide a recognition of the urgency of the present and, on the other hand, provide a source of encouragement in the face of continued oppression. He writes, "Free colored men are as imperatively required now to furnish the same manly testimony in support of the ability of the race to surmount the remaining obstacles growing out of oppression, ignorance, and poverty."[71] In other words, Still hopes that

---

66. Still, *Still's Underground Rail Road Records* (1883), 80.
67. Still, *Still's Underground Railroad Records* (1886), 165.
68. Still, *Still's Underground Railroad Records* (1886), 282.
69. Still, preface to *Still's Underground Railroad Records* (1886).
70. Still, preface to *Still's Underground Railroad Records* (1886).
71. Still, preface to *Still's Underground Railroad Records* (1886).

"the heroism of fugitives" will inspire their descendants to embody the same virtues and deploy them in the pursuit of social change in the same way that their heroism inspired the abolitionists of a previous generation.[72]

Reweaving the Social and Familial Fabric

Second, Still's decision to meticulously record the details, origins, destinations, and physical descriptions of those passing through Philadelphia was undertaken with the intention of reweaving the social fabric that chattel slavery unraveled. Here, it is worth noting that Still began this work in the 1840s and 1850s, long before the Emancipation Proclamation promised the end of the institution of slavery.[73] He writes in 1886, "In 1857, when these remarkable travelers came under the notice of the Vigilance Committee, as Slavery seemed likely to last for generations, and there was but little expectation that these records would ever have the historical value which they now possess, care was not always taken to prepare and preserve them."[74] The implication is that this work was undertaken in anticipation of slavery's eventual abolishment and in recognition that much remained to be done on the other side of emancipation. As an act of anticipation, Still's record, in the words of Oliver O'Donovan, seeks to "[tease] out a future that lurks within the present as a possibility."[75] This future (i.e., the abolition of slavery and the integration of Afro-Americans into common life) was not a present reality. But it was also not completely unimaginable or fantastical. Rather, there were "seeds" that seemed to indicate that the end of slavery was a real possibility, whether they existed in the form of abolitionary movements, shifts in public opinion, or the allegiances of freedom fighters. For Still, the work of recording those who passed through his station was done in the hope that family members who had been separated would one day be able to do what he and his brother eventually did: find one another and become whole. He states as much in the introduction to his first edition of the *Underground Railroad Records*:

> After the restoration of Peter Still, his own brother (the kidnapped and the ransomed), after forty years' cruel separation from his mother, the wonderful discovery and joyful reunion, the idea forced itself upon his mind that all over this wide and extended country thousands of mothers and children, separated

---

72. Still, preface to *Still's Underground Railroad Records* (1886).

73. As mentioned earlier, the first edition of Still's *Underground Railroad Records* was released in 1872. A second, expanded edition was released in 1878 with an added preface. A third edition was released in 1883, and a fourth edition was published in 1886.

74. Still, *Still's Underground Railroad Records* (1886), 132.

75. O'Donovan, *Self, World, and Time*, 121.

by Slavery, were in a similar way living without the slightest knowledge of each other's whereabouts, praying and weeping without ceasing, as did this mother and son. Under these reflections it seemed reasonable to hope that by carefully gathering the narratives of Underground Rail Road passengers, in some way or other some of the bleeding and severed hearts might be united and comforted; and by the use that might be made privately, if not publicly, of just such facts as would naturally be embraced in their brief narratives, re-unions might take place.[76]

Life in the world, on Still's account, is not something to be passively endured. Rather, the Christian community is tasked with striving to preserve and renew elements of social life so that Christians and their neighbors can flourish.[77] In writing his record and hoping to reunite families, Still provides us with a vision of hopeful, communal renewal.

It is important to reiterate that Still was an abolitionist and civil rights activist—that is, he was someone advocating for legal and legislative change in the United States. His preferred mode of activism, moral suasion, was far from a form of Christian quietism in the face of the world's ills. He actively sought to change the minds, behaviors, and political preferences of his fellow citizens so that laws would be supported and passed that would bring about the abolition of slavery. One can hardly read his text without feeling the emotional weight of the horrors of slavery.[78] Yet bringing about the end of slavery would not solve the crisis of displacement, destruction, and disenfranchisement that the institution of slavery had brought into being. Slaves were frequently auctioned off and sold to disparate plantations with little regard for their familial connections. The result was that mothers were separated from their children and husbands from their wives. Still repeatedly describes the effect such trauma has on a person. For instance, he recalls how one fugitive, Mary Epps, "had been the mother of fifteen children, four of whom had been sold away from her; one was still held in slavery in Petersburg; the

---

76. Still, *Underground Railroad* (1872), 4.

77. The concept of human flourishing has birthed a veritable cottage industry of literature in the past few decades. Minimally, we can say with Neil Messer that "to flourish as a human creature is to fulfill the goods, goals, and ends that belong to this kind of creaturely life." Messer, "Human Flourishing," 289.

78. Indeed, as I will note later, this almost does a disservice to the injustice of human bondage. Words on a printed page fail to give an adequate representation of the sweat-stained brows of men and women working in fields, of festering wounds the whip's lash leaves in its wake, of mothers crying as their children are dragged away and sold, and of women left huddled and weeping after they have been sexually assaulted by their masters. Perhaps another option is simply to repeat God's words back to him in lament for the horrors we humans inflict on other image bearers: "How long, O Lord? . . . How long?" (Ps. 13:1).

others were all dead. At the sale of one of her children she was so affected with grief that she was thrown into violent convulsions, which caused the loss of her speech for one entire month."[79] The fact that many slaves felt an urgent need to escape their bondage only heightened this crisis. It was often far easier for men than for women to stow away on ships or run away from their masters, and it was infinitely simpler for adults to undertake the difficulties of life on the Underground Railroad without carrying their children along with them. So the pursuit of freedom not only came at great personal risk but also exacted a familial and relational tax. For example, Still records a letter from Isaac Forman, who had successfully escaped to Canada: "My soul is vexed, my troubles are inexpressible. I often feel as if I were willing to die. I must see my wife in short, if not, I will die. What would I not give no tongue can utter. Just to gaze on her sweet lips one moment I would be willing to die the next. . . . I can say I was once happy, but never will be again, until I see her; because what is freedom to me, when I know that my wife is in slavery?"[80]

If slavery was abolished and slaves were released from bondage, these former slaves would still need to be integrated into society.[81] The social fabric would still need to be repaired. Abolishing slavery, while necessary, would prove rather insufficient to the larger task of bringing black slaves to a place of communal well-being, however we might understand what that entails in a world still beholden to the effects of sin. Still hoped that his records would prove to be an invaluable resource to the men and women who traveled along his route and to their family members and friends who, once freed, hoped to find them again. Stories like that of Eliza and Robert McCoy, a wife and husband whose brother and uncle were both able to escape slavery, are far from incidental or coincidental. Rather, they provide snapshots of what Still and the Vigilance Committee were ultimately hoping for: the reweaving of the bonds of relationship that slavery brought to ruin.

79. Still, *Still's Underground Railroad Records* (1886), 75.
80. Still, *Still's Underground Railroad Records* (1886), 65.
81. As Diemer avers, "The end of slavery in the North would leave free African Americans as second-class citizens: generally denied the right to vote, excluded from most of the best-paying work, segregated in public accommodations and schools. Abolitionism was the beginning, not the end, of the struggle for Black freedom" (Diemer, *Vigilance*, 9). As Benjamin Lynerd and Jack Wartell point out, the abolition of slavery was only part of the Afro-American understanding of the goals of the abolitionary project: "Black abolitionists . . . sought for African Americans a full array of freedoms that included not just a release from the plantation but membership in the body politic, with the rights to vote, serve on juries, give testimony under oath, and serve in the military." Lynerd and Wartell, "'Natural Right to the Soil,'" 72.

Retrieving William Still's Vision of Public Witness

As inspiring as Still's stories and depictions may be—and it bears repeating that they *are* in fact inspiring—the objective of this current project is not to re-present the past. The goal is retrieval. So what goods does Still's work provide us with as we seek to construct an evangelical account of public witness? How might the meticulous work of his *Underground Railroad Records* provide tools for conceiving of an evangelical approach to public witness? I suggest that Still's work provides two key resources that will prove vital as we transition from retrieval to construction in this project's final chapters.

Preservation and Renewal

Still's work is a helpful reminder that the church's task in public life depends to a large degree on the presence of particular forms of life that must be preserved and renewed. These are necessary for navigating the saeculum, which I have referred to throughout this work as the era of "futility and decay," following the text of Romans 8:20–21. If it is indeed the case that some of our forms of action will fail and that our institutions will continually decline, that we are in the "long defeat," as J. R. R. Tolkien affectionately puts it, and that we are called to pursue the good of our neighbors, then there must be an active attempt to continually preserve and renew forms of life that promote the common good.[82] In times of crisis, it is almost natural that these networks of relationships and the institutions that support them will be strained to the point of breaking and, invariably, crumble. Still's own life bears witness to this, as his father left his family behind in pursuit of freedom, and his mother followed a similar course of action a few years later. In times of crisis, a certain kind of calculus is impressed upon the conscience, one that requires sacrifices that would otherwise be unthinkable. This, unfortunately, is part and parcel of life in a postlapsum world that awaits a renewal and a transformation that are yet to come.

The church's acts of public witness within this context must strive to preserve what is worth saving and renew what is decaying. In part, this is an act

---

82. Tolkien writes in a letter, "I am a Christian, and indeed a Roman Catholic, so that I do not expect 'history' to be anything but a 'long defeat'—though it contains (and in a legend may contain more clearly and movingly) some samples or glimpses of final victory" (Tolkien, "From a Letter to Amy Ronald," 273). As George Hunsinger astutely observes, this is not to say that this long defeat will have the final or ultimate word. But, as Hunsinger goes on to note, it is the realization of the time we inhabit, a realization that ought to chasten and serve as a corrective "to any ill-considered talk in Christian circles (whether academic or ecclesial) about 'human flourishing' or 'thriving.'" Hunsinger, "Barth and Tolkien," 699–700.

of bearing witness to God's resounding "nevertheless" to his created order. God remains committed to the world he made and established the church as "first fruits" of creation's subsequent renewal (James 1:18). This future is absolute in that God has promised to bring it about. The church's task is not to realize this future through its actions and political involvements, for it can do nothing of the sort. Rather, its task is to bear witness to what God has promised to do in his world. Preservation is one of the forms this witness takes insofar as God has made known to his people that he will not abandon his world, even as he is committed to making all things new (Rev. 21:1–5). Admittedly, preservation as an act of public witness requires a great deal of wisdom and the ability to exercise practical reason. The church finds itself ever tempted by various forms of ecclesial triumphalism, on the one hand, and a naive progressivism, on the other. We all too often become wedded to forms and institutions that are culturally and temporally specific, thinking that various common goods and the realization of human flourishing are contingent on the preservation of some way of life that is merely a reflection of convenience, preference, or custom. What has worked in the past is not always fitting for the present. Yet equally as perilous is the temptation to jettison the past in the allure of the new and novel. Not only must we allow the past to speak to and inform our action in the present, but we must also be attentive to the ways that we are called to build on the foundation that our ancestors have established.

Still is helpful here. Recall that he strives to preserve both institutions (e.g., familial relationships) and the memories of particular heroes (e.g., fugitive slaves and their helpers). But he does this not for the sake of nostalgia or in an attempt to lionize his ancestors. Indeed, preservation as a vocation (preserving the goods of the past) should be disconnected from any ideology that seeks to repristinate or idealize the past. For someone like Still, the "good ol' days" simply do not exist. Rather, Still views this collection of memories as a resource for navigating the challenges that exist in *the present*. He argues, "In looking back now over these strange and eventful Providences, in the light of the wonderful changes wrought by Emancipation, I am more and more constrained to believe that the reasons, which years ago led me to aid the bondman and preserve the records of his sufferings, are to-day quite as potent in convincing me that the necessity of the times requires this testimony."[83] Memory is a resource for addressing, responding to, and overcoming the obstacles that lie strewn across the path to communal well-being. Still desires change, but it is important to note that this change is not a wholesale revision of the social

---

83. Still, preface to *Still's Underground Railroad Records* (1886).

order, even while it would bring about a considerable reorientation of society's present construction. As noted in chapter 1, the emancipation of slaves and their enfranchisement ostensibly led to drastic changes in American life. Newly freed slaves were released without land or capital, without access to public works, and without knowledge of the forms of politics they were now inhabiting. Still seeks to preserve the goods they do possess, both in terms of communal memories and in terms of communal bonds.

The work of preservation, then, is deeply intertwined with the work of renewal. In attempting to preserve the names, identities, and legacies of the past, Still is also hoping to provide resources for building for the future. Recognizing that his newly emancipated readers will face a new set of challenges in the present, Still seeks not only to preserve these bonds but to provide the resources and institutional forms that will enable his audience to navigate their present circumstances. In other words, Still's work of preservation is an attempt to build and establish roots for Afro-Americans on the other side of slavery. Here I borrow and apply a concept from Simone Weil. Weil writes, "To be rooted is perhaps the most important and least recognized need of the human soul. It is one of the hardest to define. A human being has roots by virtue of his real, active and natural participation in the life of a community which preserves in living shape certain particular treasures of the past and certain particular expectations of the future."[84] Still's work attempts to preserve familial bonds and communal memories for the sake of renewing the relational and societal bonds that slavery has eroded. Recall that Still himself experienced this very thing. His mother made the heart-wrenching choice to leave his brothers behind in bondage. His father was forced to abandon his family. And here, as his *Underground Railroad Records* indicate, his family is far from exceptional. His father and mother made a choice that millions of other slaves were also confronted with, and this does not even take into account the dissolution of relational bonds that occurred when slaveholders bought or sold their slaves from one plantation to another. All of these are clear indications of relational bonds and nexuses that have become disordered and stand in need of renewal. Still's work of preservation attempts to provide the requisite resources for navigating the challenges of the present and rebuilding the forms of common life that chattel slavery has effectively dissolved. He tells his readers where their family members are, how earnestly they fought and desired freedom, and what drastic steps they were willing to take to attain it. As we have noted, Still does this so as to provide the Afro-American community with its own source of treasured memories from the past, its own

84. Weil, *Need for Roots*, 43.

history, and to cultivate a certain ethos that will inspire this community to unite and work in the present.

In retrieving his work, the church would do well to think deeply about how it too can reweave social fabric in times of unraveling. In the work of preservation as a means of bearing witness to the gospel, the church must continually ask what goods are at risk of being lost, what values must be retained, and what resources are available for preserving the past and renewing forms of common life that have fallen into disarray. In short, the church must position itself retrospectively for the sake of the present.

Anticipation and Inspiration

While Still provides us with resources for how we ought to orient ourselves to the past and the present (namely, in the forms of preservation and renewal), he also provides us with tools for positioning ourselves with regard to the future (namely, how to act and improvise as our social contexts invariably shift and change). In short, Still reminds us that much of the work of public witness consists of anticipating the needs, challenges, and opportunities of the present and motivating social actors to respond to them with the resources intrinsic to the logics of the gospel.

First, the church, in its vocation of public witness, attempts to respond not only to the needs of today but also to the needs of tomorrow. It plans so as to respond appropriately. This involves anticipation. Oliver O'Donovan observes, "Anticipations are based on tendencies and tendencies are aspects of *present* regularities."[85] Identifying and responding to tendencies and regularities requires a great deal of wisdom. Christians must be able to sense and ascertain the potentialities that exist within the present order of things. Consider a handful of kiwi seeds. These seeds have the potential to one day clamber up a lattice and, Texas summers and hungry snails notwithstanding, sprout flowers and produce kiwis. But this is not the only potentiality. Some of the seeds are inert; others are viable. Some of the seeds are male and will produce pollen; others are female and will not.[86] Nurturing these seeds into a viable crop requires the recognition of a possible future that might arise and the conditions necessary to bring about that future. For example, in central Texas one does not typically assume that it will rain every other day or that the temperature will remain below 100 degrees Fahrenheit for any extended

---

85. O'Donovan, *Finding and Seeking*, 157.

86. It is of course possible that all the seeds are viable, inert, female, or male. For the sake of my readers, I have opted not to exhaust all the possibilities, but the very fact that there are a number of possibilities perhaps is part and parcel of my point.

period of time. Certain precautions need to be taken for the sake of the kiwi crop if it is to survive. Of course, as O'Donovan warns us, there is no definiteness or "factual knowledge" of the future at work here.[87] We are dealing with tendencies and possibilities within the present. Accordingly, the work of anticipating the needs of the future must be supplemented with a hope rooted in the resurrection of Jesus Christ from the dead and the fullness of the eschatological kingdom that God will bring about.[88] O'Donovan writes, "Hope will focus our deliberation, showing us ways of action that had apparently had no prospects but now seem to have them in the light shed by the promise [of God]."[89] And so the individual social agent, or better yet the community of social agents if we are to keep Ruggles's insights in view, requires a kind of insight and wisdom in order to look into that pile of seeds, care for them appropriately, and nurture the various vines that grow from them. Similarly, in the contexts in which the church finds itself, there are various possible futures and crises that could arise from the present moment. Christians must recognize the potentialities of a given moment and refine their powers of practical reason to respond appropriately.

But a second step is required: inspiring a community to act. A kind of catalyzing force is required to motivate the people of God to bear witness to the resurrection of Jesus Christ in public, a task the church is called to embrace again and again, even when rejection and failure seem all but certain. This too can be attributed to life in "the present age." As we will see in the next chapter, inhabiting the time of futility and decay implies that our actions will often fall short and fail. Still, it is in this time that we are called to bear witness. It is in this time that we are called to hear the Lord's voice again in the wilderness, to refuse to harden our hearts and become callous to the suffering and despair that surrounds us. Today is the day to take action; today is the day to act. But social actors need to be continually motivated to press forward through discouragement.

Rightly or wrongly, William Still is concerned that the realization of some semblance of liberty has dampened the continued fight for freedom. He writes to his daughter, "The great majority of our young people are carried away with dress & show—love pleasure, music & light studies—but I hope you will go in for solid worth. Aim for a high moral character, superior knowledge and a marked love for justice & right."[90] He worries that access to some "temporal goods" has disinclined the youth of his day to pursue goods of greater value,

---

87. O'Donovan, *Finding and Seeking*, 156.
88. O'Donovan, *Finding and Seeking*, 162.
89. O'Donovan, *Finding and Seeking*, 163.
90. Still, William Still to Caroline Still Anderson, April 30, 1866.

such as virtue, justice, and self-improvement. Still himself was not immune to this kind of despair. He lamented some six years after the end of the Civil War, "'The future looks very dark to me for the colored man both North & South.' This had been my notion for a long time."[91] But Still's outlook on the future of black people in the United States did not lessen his social action. Instead, it inspired him to continue pressing forward.

Still reminds us that our motivations for action need to be renewed and refreshed. Here, the lives of our ancestors provide us with the necessary although perhaps not sufficient resources for imagining new possibilities for our actions. The church's public witness requires energy and exertion. We must "make every effort" to do good in the present age and in the face of impending forces of futility and decay (2 Pet. 1:3, 5, 10–11). The spiral of sin seems interminable. The destruction that evil leaves in its wake appears unending. It is almost natural to become weary in light of our neighbor's need and the brokenness of the world, especially given that the church cannot transform the present age into the fullness of the kingdom of God. It is almost natural to want to retreat from the brokenness of the world and the distress such brokenness can cause us. Still is not unaware of the difficulty. He writes, "Too much pains cannot be taken by the unimproved to gain improvement; nor can too much pains be taken by the improved to aid and encourage the unimproved."[92] But just as hearing the story of Washington Somlor's "sufferings and experience had a very inspiring affect [on those] who had the pleasure of seeing [him] in Philadelphia," so the stories of our ancestors can inspire us to continue in our vocation of bearing witness to the gospel in public and shared life.[93]

Conclusion

In this final descriptive chapter, we canvased the life and work of William Still, the famed angel of Philadelphia. Still reminds us that we need to be people who continually look backward in remembrance, understanding memory as a necessary resource for navigating life in the present. We need to remember our ancestors and saints so that we can embody their virtues and live in a manner that is faithful to their legacy. Additionally, Still's work in the Underground Railroad and in Philadelphia more broadly encourages us to think of public witness as an act of preservation and renewal. In the saeculum, things fall into

---

91. Still, William Still to Edward A. Wiley, October 13, 1873.
92. Still, "Self-Improvement."
93. Still, *Still's Underground Railroad Records* (1886), 304.

disrepair. And it is the church's task to bear witness to God's commitment to this world and the things of this world by striving to preserve and renew those forms of life that are indeed good. Still also shows us that public witness is an act of anticipation and inspiration. The church seeks to peer, ever so tentatively, into the future and anticipate the needs the church might meet, even as it recognizes that it cannot transform this world into a facsimile of the fullness of the kingdom of God. The church inspires its members to act in such a way as to indicate what God has done and is doing in Christ. As I will demonstrate in the final chapters, this public witness takes the forms primarily of speaking the truth about the world as it is and bearing the world's burdens.

PART 2

The TWOFOLD WORK *of* PUBLIC WITNESS

5

Lament as Public Witness

As noted in the introduction, the goal of this book is to construct an evangelical account of public witness with the help of Afro-American abolitionary figures. In each of the previous chapters, I sought advice from our ancestors, canvasing the lives of David Ruggles, Maria W. Stewart, and William Still, hoping to glean from them specific ways in which the gospel fueled their participation in the abolitionary cause. The degree to which these figures were steeped in the language and logics of evangelical thought should be obvious to readers at this point. Still's felt need for a distinct and personal encounter with God, Stewart's prayers and devotionals as well as her commitment to working across denominational boundaries to provide educational opportunities for Afro-American children in Washington, DC, and Ruggles's repeated appeals to the text and norms of Holy Scripture reveal that each of these figures sits beneath the evangelical umbrella, however nebulously defined. And it is worth noting, as we have in previous chapters, the way their evangelical commitments engendered a particular ethos, one in which the life of faith and the good news of the gospel called them and motivated them to bear witness in public.[1] In other words, they were motivated from within a distinctively

1. In this chapter and the following, I am using the idea of "public," somewhat loosely, to indicate the areas in which the shared nature of a community's common life is more or less visible. So, for example, when I choose not to cut my grass or trim the hedges by my house, this decision is not a "private" one that does not affect the lives of those around me. Such a decision has ramifications not only for the property values of my neighbors' properties but

evangelical framework to pursue the good of their neighbors and loved ones who remained enslaved.

The burden of this book is not to provide an explicitly "evangelical" account of political theology or the church/state relationship. Such a project would be contingent to a large degree on which subset of the evangelical community one lives in and where that particular community is located in space-time. Nor is the focus of this project on statecraft per se—that is, on how governments should function, be organized, and maintain themselves. Rather, the goal is to situate the church's very nature as being "of the gospel" within the task of bearing witness in public space. The church is inescapably public and so too are its practices, as we have already noted.[2] And the life the church enjoys is inseparably bound up with the nexus of relationships that it participates with believing and nonbelieving neighbors. The Christian community shares in a host of spaces that constitute our common life, ranging from the concrete realities of public works, such as water treatment plants, roads, and parks, to the grocery stores we frequent and the schools our children attend. In short, the church's existence is public and its life is shared, held in common with the other. So what shape does Christian witness take in light of this fact? How does the church's inescapable participation in these networks of relationships bear witness to and attest to what God has done and is doing in Christ?

To move toward an answer, it is important that we return to where we first began. If we are seeking an evangelical account of public witness, it is worth returning to what is (and is not) meant by the term "evangelical" and what this account seeks to bear witness to. Earlier in this volume, I appealed to Kevin Vanhoozer and Daniel Treier's prescription of evangelical theology as a particular theological vision. We can revisit this vision again now, as it provides a helpful dialogue partner for what follows. Vanhoozer and Treier propose that the theological vision of evangelical theology seeks "to say, on the basis of the Scriptures, what God is doing *in* Christ, and then to indicate how to live it *out*. Stated differently: the purpose of evangelical theology is to help make communities of disciples who come to understand and correspond to the reality of the gospel."[3] An evangelical account of public witness will extend this vision to the various "publics" that evangelicals inhabit—shared spaces, relationships, and commitments—where we not only seek to correspond as a community to what God has done in Christ and live out the logics of the gospel but also strive to bear witness to this reality to, with,

---

also for the perception of the neighborhood and the manner in which children and adults alike relate to the neighborhood.

2. K. Johnson, *Theology, Political Theory, and Pluralism*, 242.

3. Vanhoozer and Treier, *Theology and the Mirror of Scripture*, 45, emphasis original.

and for the sake of our neighbors. Yet we have also seen in the work of both Stewart and Ruggles a commitment to bringing the logics and text of Holy Scripture to bear on the concerns of our common life, particularly as it relates to the issue of slavery. So, in following their lead, we too will examine the work of public witness through a series of sustained interactions with and interpretations of Holy Writ. In this chapter, I will argue that the church is a community situated within two contexts, one ultimate and one penultimate, and that the task of bearing witness to what God has done and is doing in Christ involves speaking the truth about current realities and lifting up the laments of the world to God.

Seeing the World (and the Church) in the Light of God

In chapter 1, we began our foray back into the abolitionary era by taking stock of the time in which our ancestors operated. There, we all too briefly met figures like the abolitionist Daniel Coker and investigated the landscape of American slavery. Recognizing that the past is not so foreign as to avoid our grasp entirely, we saw how drastic changes took place in the nineteenth century in the United States and how numerous enslaved peoples tried to realize their long-hoped-for freedom. We noted the exodus of slaves that took place as the American War of Independence concluded; the trends of abolition in Europe, England, and the Caribbean; and the manner in which abolitionists in the United States attempted to respond to the crisis of slavery in light of these shifting currents. Some abolitionary figures, like Henry Highland Garnet and David Walker, championing the legacy of successful slave revolts in places like Haiti, called for slaves to arm themselves and participate in violent uprisings to secure their own freedom. Others, doubting the ability of former slaves to coexist peacefully alongside their former masters or despairing over the continued disenfranchisement of Afro-Americans writ large, advocated for Afro-Americans to emigrate to places like Liberia or Canada. Yet many blacks in the United States bristled at the notion that their future lay elsewhere and sought to form a life in the nation they helped build.

Canvasing the history of American slavery and taking stock of the time in which our three abolitionary figures lived and the crises to which they responded provide us with some guidance for understanding the church's task of public witness: it consists of taking stock and telling time. For the church, this task is twofold. First, it consists of remembering where the church sits in the plan of God. We might refer to this as its ultimate context. Second, it consists of remembering the nature of life here, in the saeculum, in the time of hoping, waiting, and longing for the promise of cosmic renewal. Created by

God, the church exists in the here and now. But God has also given his people the promise that he will make all things new in the end. He has promised this community that it is destined for a new city, a better country, one that God has prepared for it (Heb. 11:16). And it is this promise that enables the church to see the present afresh. So the first element of the church's public witness is keeping track of time in a way that avoids optimistic triumphalism on the one hand and a debilitating despair on the other. The church must see the world for what it is but also for what it will be in the ultimate plan of God.

The Church's Ultimate Context: Created by God for a Life with God

To understand the church, we must first see it in light of its origin and destiny. Created by God, the church is a community "of the gospel" that is destined for a life with God, a life God himself has made possible. The Christian community is not a community like any other.[4] It is a community founded by God and sent forth by God for a particular purpose. To understand the shape and scope of the church's task to bear witness to what God has done in Christ, we must begin with the God who makes the church's life possible, the God who forms the church, loves it, and calls it to himself. And so we will all too briefly situate the church and its life in the light of the God of the gospel, the one who provides the church with its ultimate context and horizons.

The God of the gospel is the living God, the maker of heaven and earth (Neh. 9:6). As the Spirit attests, this God—Father, Son, and Holy Spirit—is "the true God . . . the living God and the everlasting king" (Jer. 10:10), a predication that sets the God of Abraham, Isaac, and Jacob in contradistinction to the gods of the other nations. This is perhaps the starkest contrast between the God of Israel and the gods of the nations. The Lord God is *the* living God; the gods of the nations are merely idols or no-things. Christian doctrine frequently associates this "living-ness" or "life-full-ness" of God with the doctrines of divine freedom and/or aseity. As the living God, God possesses life in and from himself, life underived and self-sufficient.[5] The freedom and aseity of God are bound up with each other.[6] And, as Paul reminds the Athenians, this God is not "served by human hands, as though he needed anything" (Acts 17:25a). Possessing the fullness of life, he is free to give life to whom or what he pleases, creating and sustaining creaturely being as a gift of his grace (17:25b).

4. Radner, *Church*, 65–67.
5. Bavinck, *God and Creation*, 151.
6. Sonderegger, *Doctrine of God*, 481.

Yet God's freedom *from* the creature is also a freedom he chooses to exercise *for* the creature. Indeed, the Father, out of his freedom and love for a world he does not need, sends the Son and the Spirit into the world to reconcile and perfect it, to offer the world a creaturely share in his own life.[7] Christian doctrine refers to this movement of the Son and the Spirit into creaturely space-time with the language of "mission," a term that highlights the communicative purpose these two persons of the Trinity intend to accomplish in the economy and the resultant created effect.[8] The Son takes on human flesh in the incarnation; the Spirit, poured out at Pentecost, creates a community whom he indwells.[9] As the Spirit and very presence of Christ, the Holy Spirit reminds the church of all that Christ taught, leading and guiding the church into all truth as he cultivates within Christians' hearts a love for God, one another, and the world (John 14:26; 16:13). In so doing, he reveals the face of the Father shining in the face of the Son and nurtures an attendant love for God and all things in relation to God within the hearts of the redeemed.[10] More of course could and should be said here, but space precludes an extensive or exhaustive treatment. The name for the community of those bound together in the Spirit around the glory of Christ in the fellowship with the Father that Christ has made possible is "the church."

The church, then, is a people, a creature of the Word operating in the power of the Spirit, sent forth by the Lord of life into the world for the sake of the world.[11] God does not need the world (God also does not need the church or this particular theologian, which is perhaps a healthy thing to keep in mind). Yet God in his freedom has chosen to love the world and has chosen to gather this community and transform it into a particular people marked by his promise and presence. Additionally, God has given this people, the church, the promise that he will bring them into the fullness of eschatological

---

7. Webster, *Holiness*, 40.

8. Vidu, *Divine Missions*, 16. See also Sanders, *Triune God*, 69. D. Glenn Butner Jr. gives a helpful summary of the relationship between the divine processions and the divine missions, writing, "The missions are constituted by the processions, ensuring a connection between the Trinity *ad intra* and the divine economy." Butner, *Trinitarian Dogmatics*, 170.

9. Butner, *Trinitarian Dogmatics*, 170.

10. T. F. Torrance writes, "The Paraclete is the living and life-giving Spirit of God who mediates to us the life of God, glorifies Christ as the Son of the Father, by throwing his radiance upon him, who thus actualized among us the self-giving of God to us in his Son, and resonates and makes fruitful within us the intervening, atoning and intercessory activity of Christ on our behalf." Torrance, *Trinitarian Faith*, 249.

11. Christoph Schwöbel, in a celebrated essay, summarizes the matter succinctly: "The Church is *creatura veribi divini*: the creature of the divine word. The Church is constituted by God's action and not by any human action." Schwöbel, "Creature of the Word," 122.

communion with him (Eph. 1:13–14).[12] A significant portion of this promise lies in the eschatological future. It is this community's destiny, a redemption it awaits. In the present, God has graciously given the church a task: to bear witness to what God has done in Christ in the power of the Spirit. John writes, "When the Advocate comes, whom I will send to you from the Father, the Spirit of truth who comes from the Father, he will testify on my behalf. You also are to testify because you have been with me from the beginning" (John 15:26–27). The church, animated by the Spirit, is given the privilege of sharing in the announcement to the world of the world's redemption, echoing the judgment of God that the new creation has begun and all things have been reconciled to God in Christ Jesus (Col. 1:20).[13]

And so the church is a witness to the gospel in two senses. On the one hand, it is a witness to the gospel by virtue of its very existence. As a creature God brings into being, the church is a sign that God has acted and spoken. On the other hand, the church is a community that is called to correspond to and order its life in accordance with what God has done in Christ. Accordingly, the church's life should mirror the character of its God and the gratuitous nature of his actions on its behalf, albeit in a creaturely manner. Freely the followers of Christ have received life from the Lord of life, and freely they might expend their lives for the sake of their neighbors (Matt. 10:8). It is this secondary element of bearing witness that we might identify as the church's vocation, a vocation we will turn our attention to in what follows, particularly as it relates to the church's penultimate context and the task of public witness.

The Church's Penultimate Context: The Present Age of Suffering, Futility, and Decay

Having established the church's life and origin in the plan of God, we can turn to how its vocation relates to its particular context—namely, the penultimate context in which it exists: the era of suffering, futility, and decay. To do so, we will first turn to Paul and his magisterial letter to the Romans. Here, Paul highlights the tension that exists between navigating life in the world in light of the work of God in Christ and awaiting the renewal of all things. He is worth quoting at length:

> I consider that the sufferings of this present time are not worth comparing with the glory about to be revealed to us. For the creation waits with eager longing for the revealing of the children of God; for the creation was subjected to futility,

---

12. Hill, *Gathered on the Road to Zion*, 179.
13. Webster, "Christ, Church, and Reconciliation," 221.

not of its own will but by the will of the one who subjected it, in hope that the creation itself will be set free from its bondage to decay and will obtain the freedom of the glory of the children of God. We know that the whole creation has been groaning in labor pains until now; and not only the creation, but we ourselves, who have the first fruits of the Spirit, groan inwardly while we wait for adoption, the redemption of our bodies. For in hope we were saved. (Rom. 8:18–24)

Much could be and indeed has been said about this important passage. Yet a few things merit commentary for what follows. First, Paul is not unaware that present existence in the world is one of suffering (παθήματα). There is no looking past this present suffering, no amount of promise or wishful thinking that can cause it to fade from view.[14] Our abolitionary friends from the previous three chapters were all too familiar with this reality. It is heard in the voice of the mother screaming as her child is torn from her breast and sold deeper into the swirling abyss of slavery. It is heard in the trembling sobs of the father and mother as they trek through marshes and hide away on steamboats, the faces of their children and loved ones preserved only in the hallowed halls of memory. More recently in our day, it is heard in the sighs of a sweat-soaked inmate seeking some form of respite in an unair-conditioned prison cell while the sweltering, ever-rising summer heat rages on. There is no escaping, no way of overlooking the suffering of the present age.

But Paul situates and relativizes this suffering in light of the promise of eschatological inbreaking.[15] Through "the eyes of faith," as C. E. B. Cranfield notes, "Paul is convinced that the sufferings of the present time are only a very slight thing in comparison with the glory which is to be revealed."[16] And Paul will remind his readers in a few short verses that they inhabit this time of suffering "in hope" and that "in hope" they were saved (Rom. 8:20, 24). Indeed, this language of hope punctuates these verses like a trumpet blast, appearing five times in verses 24 and 25 alone. Such language indicates that there is a unique orientation or mode that describes the Christian's navigation of the present age. We will return to the implications of this in a moment.

14. Karl Barth writes, "There is here no exuberant stretching of our normal observation upwards or downwards. There is here no overlooking or toning down of human suffering in order to offer some more solid consolation. . . . No careless attitude to present tribulation can stand even before the aching of a tooth, and still less before the brutal realities of birth, sickness, and death, before the iron reality which governs the broad motions of the lives of men." Barth, *Epistle to the Romans*, 302.

15. Moo, *Epistle to the Romans*, 511.

16. Cranfield, *Critical and Exegetical Commentary*, 408. Robert Jewett writes, "For Paul, the sufferings experienced by the believers 'are not equivalent in comparison with the glory' yet to be revealed, for the weight of such glory is incalculably immense." Jewett, *Romans*, 508.

But for now, we must sit in something akin to a caesura, for both Paul and his readers inhabit the present age, recognizing its incongruence with the reality of new creation realized in the work of God in Christ. And this is a time of suffering, groaning, and longing. We would do well to heed Karl Barth's reminder: "The time in which we live and suffer is the *present time*, the time when glory is made manifest in suffering. So clearly does God manifest his glory in the secret of suffering, that, so far from shrinking for His sake from the contemplation of suffering, it is for His sake that we are bound to gaze upon it, to see in it the step, the movement, the turning-point from death to life, and to apprehend it as the place where Christ is to be seen. To overlook suffering is to overlook Christ."[17]

The time in which we exist is indeed a time of suffering, but this suffering is not unique to the human person or the believing community, as Paul makes clear. Rather, it is a suffering that all of the created order shares in, albeit not in the same way. There has been considerable debate in New Testament studies on what Paul means by "the creation" (κτίσις) and what it means for creation to be in bondage to decay.[18] It is reasonable to suppose that "the creation" refers specifically to the nonhuman elements of the created order, at least in no small part because Paul distinguishes "the creation's" subjugation to bondage and decay from that of those rational animals who are his readers and hearers.[19] The former is not subjugated to bondage of its own choice (Rom. 8:20), a description that distinguishes this group from the angelic and human members of the created order.[20] The fall brings about a cosmic disordering, what Paul Griffiths refers to as "the devastation."[21] He writes, "To observe any creature for long . . . is to observe its decay, its ineluctable loss of goods it has now as it approaches its last loss, which is of life if it is animate, and of continued existence if it is inanimate."[22] This descent into decay is true not only of human creatures and living things, like slugs and

---

17. Barth, *Epistle to the Romans*, 305.

18. Richard Longenecker notes at least eight interpretive options for "the creation" in Romans 8 popular among modern commentators, ranging from all of humanity to believers in Christ to the angels (Longenecker, *Epistle to the Romans*, 720). See also Fewster, *Creation Language in Romans 8*; and Kruse, *Paul's Letter to the Romans*, 347.

19. Siu Fung Wu notes that interpreting *ktisis* as referring to nonhuman creation is the near consensus among recent scholars because Rom. 8:23 makes a distinction between "creation" and "human beings" (Wu, *Suffering in Romans*, 138). As Wu goes on to note, "It is important to remember that the ancients did not partition the components of the cosmos in clearly identifiable terms like moderns do. . . . For sure, the human and non-human components are distinguishable, but they are considered to be integral parts of the whole" (138–39).

20. Schreiner, *Romans*, 426.

21. Griffiths, *Decreation*, 4.

22. Griffiths, *Decreation*, 91.

kunekunes, but also of inanimate creatures such as mountains and rivers.[23] Accordingly, there is a kind of solidarity that exists among the members of the whole creation insofar as we all suffer, groan, and long for liberation and reconciliation together. So, Yoonjong Kim insightfully concludes, "Believers are not alone in experiencing and enduring sufferings but all of creation also participates in such endurance through suffering."[24]

To describe the present age as one that is marked by suffering is to describe not only how the devastation affects creation on a broad scale but also the manner in which life in the devastation affects the human subject and the communities we construct and inhabit.[25] Much could be said about what suffering is and what does or does not constitute suffering.[26] Minimally, we might say that suffering occurs when something impedes our well-being or our access to the things that we desire.[27] Paul's description of creation's suffering is something of an anthropomorphism, employing metaphorical language to illustrate a particular underlying reality. This underlying reality, as far as the whole creation is concerned, is the constant threat to its well-being and its inability to realize its telos. Of course, some individual creatures, those possessing more or less rationality, may also "suffer" the frustration of their desires. To say that these more or less rational creatures suffer is to say that they experience a kind of distress in response to the perceived badness and wrongness of a situation they inhabit.[28] The lonely orca wants to be reunited with its pod. The sea lion does not want to experience dismemberment and mastication at the hands of the aforementioned orca pod. And insofar as the lonely orca and terrified sea lion experience this perceived badness, they experience it as a kind of pain. "Pain is," in the words of Robert Spaemann, "essentially and immediately what we do not want."[29] We suffer when we do not get what we want or lose the things we care about.[30] Yet the concept of suffering is applied to the human person in light of the frustration of their desires, not merely desires for food, shelter, and community but also desires for the transcendent, for the ideal that we perceive as good. The grieving widow may desire reunion with her spouse, but this desire is often not reducible to

23. Griffiths, *Decreation*, 311.

24. Kim, *Divine-Human Relationship in Romans 1–8*, 145.

25. Schreiner, *Romans*, 425.

26. Daniel Castelo writes, "The issue of what constitutes 'suffering' itself is another deeply contested matter. . . . Most people seem to assume that suffering is something that needs no explanation: when one is in pain, one suffers." Castelo, *Apathetic God*, 17–18.

27. Stump, *Atonement*, 182.

28. Hector, *Christianity as a Way of Life*, 187.

29. Spaemann, *Persons*, 46.

30. Stump, *Atonement*, 182.

proximal or conjugal presence. In many ways, the grieving widow longs for a specific kind of reunion with the person lost and also the ideal that dissolved with his demise. She desires not just presence but the particular forms of union that bodily presence affords. To live in the present age of suffering is to inhabit a world where the dissonance between reality and our ideals and aspirations impinges on us time and time again.

But to describe the present age as one of suffering is not merely to make a comment about how the devastation affects the individual desires of a particular human subject. It is also to describe the manner in which the devastation impinges on communal life. Affirming the suffering of communities or an entire community, let alone an era, is of course not without its difficulties. There is a kind of first-person subjectivity to suffering that at times can seem to render the phenomenon almost incommunicable, as Karen Kilby has observed.[31] Yet the word "almost" must be pressed a bit,[32] for it seems that the thoughts and emotions of others can be, at least to some degree, accessible to us and present in us as theirs.[33] And it also seems that there is a degree to which we share in the sufferings of others when "something *importantly* bad happens to something [or someone] we care about."[34] If a family member or close friend were to fall ill or face a terminal diagnosis, I would experience profound suffering and feelings of loss, feelings that may be shared with my spouse. Indeed, my wife may even grieve *because* I am suffering beneath the weight of tragic loss. If the illness were miraculously and instantaneously healed, we would share feelings of relief. So at least in some sense, it can be said that we are beneath the same weight, together. Insofar as suffering happens to those I love and desire good things for, when they suffer, I too can be said to suffer, albeit not in the same sense. "If one member suffers, all suffer together with it" (1 Cor. 12:26).

---

31. Kilby writes, "It is clear that it makes a vital difference in any talk about suffering, whether I am talking about my suffering, or yours, or theirs—whether I am in a first- or second- or third-person relation to suffering. It is not always easy to find the right stance toward someone else's suffering. . . . This is at least partly because there are certain types of things that can be said in relation to *my* suffering . . . that usually can*not* be said in relation to yours or to theirs." Kilby, "Seductions of Kenosis," 169, emphasis original.

32. Kilby notes as much in another place, writing, "It is not absolutely impossible to talk about pain, but it is difficult. . . . Serious suffering is often associated with a difficulty of speech, and of thought. It is likely to disrupt a person's projects, to interfere with their sense of themselves, with their ability to narrate their life, either forward or backward. . . . In many contexts it seems to be the case that suffering comes with an element of disruption to the understanding." Kilby, "Negative Theology and Meaningless Suffering," 96.

33. Stump, *Atonement*, 128–33. Stump's work builds on recent developments in neuroscience with regard to empathy and "mind-reading." For an overview of these developments, see Goldman, *Joint Ventures*.

34. Hector, *Christianity as a Way of Life*, 58, emphasis original.

So, on the one hand, describing the present age as an age of communal suffering can indicate the manner in which the suffering of others crosses over and reaches into us and becomes our suffering as well. But on the other hand, describing the present age as an age of communal suffering can also refer to the "brokenness" of the world and the subsequent disorientation that suffering can bring about with regard to "one's self-relationship and one's relationship to others."[35] Kevin Hector notes that suffering can lead to disorientation precisely because of the way that suffering can seem so all-encompassing, can undermine our ability to find stability, can lead to self-isolation, and can disrupt our ability to make sense of our lives.[36] To describe the present age as one of suffering is, then, to recognize that there are goods we desire and aspire to attain that are necessary for our well-being of which we will be deprived. But at the same time, given that we are enmeshed in communities and relations with others, describing the present age as one of suffering also refers to the deprivation of the goods that we desire *for others* and *for our communities* that are necessary for their well-being, flourishing, and integration. It refers to the personal and the communal disorientation that life in the devastation brings about.

But we inhabit an era not only of suffering. It is also an era characterized by futility and decay. If suffering describes the manner in which the present age presses in on the self and our communities, then futility (ματαιότης, Rom. 8:20) and decay (φθορά, 8:21) describe how the present age affects our actions and the various forms of life we try to build in the postlapsum world. We will briefly deal with each in turn.

Describing the creation as subject to futility means, minimally, that "the sub-human creation has been subjected to the frustration of not being able properly to fulfill the purpose of its existence."[37] Some commentators see here a reference to the cursing of the ground in Genesis 3:17–19,[38] but there also may be an allusion to the "vanity" of life that the author of Ecclesiastes takes pains to note (Eccles. 1:1–10).[39] Perhaps a decision between the two is not necessary.[40] Insofar as creation is unable to fulfill its purposes and we children of the dust are tethered to it, the futility that infects creation imposes itself upon our actions and our intentions as well, rendering many of them vain. The sky will, on occasion, turn to bronze, and all our agricultural

---

35. Hector, *Christianity as a Way of Life*, 187.
36. Hector, *Christianity as a Way of Life*, 187.
37. Cranfield, *Critical and Exegetical Commentary*, 413.
38. Schreiner, *Romans*, 427. See also Longenecker, *Epistle to the Romans*, 722.
39. Jewett, *Romans*, 513. See also Hultgren, *Paul's Letter to the Romans*, 322–23.
40. Thiselton, *Discovering Romans*, 174.

endeavors will be for naught. The sky will, on other occasions, fall down on us and return our roads, buildings, homes, and construction projects to dust. To describe the present age as one of futility is to make a specific claim about the nature and limits of human agency and human action. It means that there are ends we desire—some good, some ignoble, some suboptimal— that we will fail to bring into being. Individual as well as collective action will unravel and fail to achieve our desired ends. It is for reasons such as this that William Still can stand on the other side of emancipation and wonder about the progress of his people.[41] Even we, those of us united to Christ by the Spirit of love whose agency has been invigorated by the power of God (2 Pet. 1:3), cannot transform the time of futility in which we live into one of effectivity and triumph. Indeed, doing so would be nothing less than a form of ecclesial or national triumphalism, both of which are ultimately failures of Christian witness.

But the creation is subject not merely to futility. It is also enslaved to decay and longing for liberation, to "be set free [ἐλευθερωθήσεται]" so as to "obtain the freedom [ἐλευθερίαν] of the glory of the children of God" (Rom. 8:21). We will return to the notion of creation's longing and groaning, but here again the text alludes to something like a cosmic fall—that is, that the fall of humanity as recorded in Genesis "brought condemnation and harmful consequences for the creation as a whole."[42] Not only are our actions bound by futility, but the continual process of decay or corruption also affects the totality of created existence in the devastation. Barth describes this enslavement as "the perpetual interaction of energy and matter, of coming into being and passing to corruption, of organization and decomposition, of thirst for life and the necessity of death."[43] This of course is a feature not of creation as such but of creation qua the devastation—that is, creation in a postlapsum world.[44] Insofar as the artifacts and institutions that we build have their roots in a world that is bound to decay, the very lives we build are "*fleeting* in a temporal sense," a fate we share with the rest of the creation.[45] And if it is indeed the case that "the whole creation" is in bondage to decay, of which humanity is also numbered and from which humanity constructs its institutions and artifacts, then many of the forms of life and "the judgments about

41. As noted in chapter 4, Still writes, "'The future looks very dark to me for the colored man both North & South.' This had been my notion for a long time." Still, William Still to Edward A. Wiley, October 13, 1873.

42. Hultgren, *Paul's Letter to the Romans*, 323.

43. Barth, *Epistle to the Romans*, 308.

44. Jewett, *Paul's Anthropological Terms*, 298.

45. Burroughs, *Creation's Slavery and Liberation*, 165, emphasis original.

how to live together" will also be "frail and contingent, subject to dissolution and revision through time."[46]

In chapter 4, when discussing William Still's life and work and bringing him into conversation with the writing of Simeon Weil, I argued that Still attempts to establish roots of various sorts for those recently released from bondage. But here an essential caveat and amendment are required. The present time in which we live renders all such action temporary and penultimate. Ultimately, the Christian community is still longing for "the city that has foundations, whose architect and builder is God" (Heb. 11:10), and for the cosmos to be made new. The roots we establish and the institutions we build are all, then, penultimate, suitable for life in the world and good in just that sense. Yet there must also be an attendant recognition that they will not, nay cannot, endure, *even in this life*. These roots and institutions are temporal and, as creaturely things of the present age, still subject to bondage and the perpetual process of decay.

An evangelical account of public life must begin here, with the recognition that things are not as they are supposed to be and that we, both individually and collectively, are longing and hoping for something greater. "Here and now," of course, is not the whole of it. The light of Christ has broken into the present and brought with it the promise that all things are being and will be made new (Isa. 43:19; Rev. 21:4). But we begin here in the present age precisely because of the fact that what God has done in Christ he has done in "the fullness of time" (Gal. 4:4) and in the midst of this current desolation. As Holy Writ continually reminds us, God sends his Son "into the world" (e.g., John 1:10, 14; 3:17), and in so doing, the Father sends the beloved Son into an epoch that is characterized by suffering, futility, groaning, and decay. It is into this world, the world as it is, that the Son is sent, and it is this world that the Son has come to redeem.[47] The world is fractured and groaning under the weight of sin, a splintering that permeates the whole of the created order. There is no escaping it, and there is no ignoring it. Indeed, the Christian, evangelical or otherwise, should have no desire to do so.[48]

---

46. Bretherton, *Christ and the Common Life*, 7.

47. There are a number of ways that the term "world" is used in the Scriptures, and the limits of space preclude an exhaustive delineation. At times, "world" is used merely to refer to the cosmos or sphere of creaturely space we inhabit. So James 2:5 states, "Has not God chosen the poor in the world [τῷ κόσμῳ] to be rich in faith and to be heirs of the kingdom that he has promised to those who love him?" Here, "world" is theologically neutral and is used as something of a synonym for "earth." At other times, "world" is used to refer to a way of being or system that is opposed to the things of God. Indeed, just a few verses earlier James states, "Religion that is pure and undefiled before God, the Father, is this: to care for orphans and widows in their distress, and to keep oneself unstained by the world [τοῦ κόσμου]" (1:27).

48. Hauerwas, "How to Tell Time Theologically," 94.

Part of the burden, then, of bearing witness to the God of the gospel and what he has done in Christ is declaring the world to be as and what it is: a place staggering beneath the weight of suffering—a place God has sent the Son to redeem. Christians must not run from suffering, nor should they attempt to insulate themselves from the suffering of others.[49] Rather, they should seek to bear witness to the good news of God's reign in Christ in the midst of a world of suffering. More concretely, this means that, for the Christian, attempts to build a life here and now, attempts to carry on, are all conditioned by the reality that things must be changed and that it is only through a radical interruption of the present that the world will be as it ought to be. "We will be changed" applies to the present created order as well as time itself, when the "perishable body puts on imperishability" and the sting of death is removed at last (1 Cor. 15:52, 54, 56). But here and now, we must speak the truth about the world as it is while clinging to and declaring the hope of what it one day will be. The form this truth telling takes is one of hopeful lament.

Hopeful, Truthful Speech and Lament

Recall that in chapter 2 David Ruggles asked us to reimagine the possibilities for communal and political action. Ruggles's appeal took on two valences. First, he invites the church to reexamine the world and its communities with what I referred to as a kind of retrospective analysis. Here, the church analyzes the degree to which its own witness and calling have been compromised as it continually seeks the renewal and purity of its life as it navigates its place in the world. We will return to this in the next chapter when we focus on the church's need to become a particular kind of community for the sake of bearing burdens. At the same time, and more important for the task at hand, Ruggles calls us to reimagine the ways in which we can act in the present for the sake of our neighbors. As Ruggles puts it poignantly, "It is clear to my imperfect vision that we shall never arrive to that equality which you so ardently desire until we know our condition and feel ourselves as a disfranchised and enslaved people whose condition is a great remove below that of our *enfranchised* countrymen. . . . In America our complexions furnish a badge to our condition as *disenfranchised and enslaved* Americans."[50] Notice here the kind of solidarity

49. This is a claim made less about particular forms that suffering may take (e.g., the suffering that can be alleviated through medical treatment or the alleviation of potential suffering brought about by avoiding an oncoming tsunami or typhoon) and more about suffering on a general level. The Christian recognizes that to inhabit the postlapsum world *just is* to negotiate between and with various instantiations of the phenomenon of suffering.

50. Ruggles, "David Ruggles' Letter in Reply to Wm. Whipper and Robert Purvis."

Ruggles envisions between free and disenfranchised Afro-Americans. As an abolitionist, he is calling his readers to take on the concerns of their enslaved brethren *as their concerns*. From there, men and women, free and slave, can all meaningfully contribute to the pursuit of freedom for the enslaved. Yet Ruggles also asks his *free* readers to reimagine their agency and ability to act, believing that there are avenues through which they can meaningfully pursue the goods of their neighbors who are in bondage. "It is nugatory to ask what can a small number of women do? *What cannot they do?*"[51] Actions *are* available to them, irrespective of where they sit in the strata of society. But perhaps more than anything else, the public witness Ruggles envisions involves seeing the concerns of our neighbors *as our concerns* and taking the burden of those concerns upon ourselves. And then, from there, viewing the practices that make up the church's life as venues and instruments of seeking the good of our neighbors. Two particular practices Ruggles highlights are the celebration of the Eucharist and the ban. Taking heed of his counsel, we will head in a different direction and examine the practice of lament.

If the church inhabits the present age of suffering, futility, and decay but was created by God for a life with God, then it stands to reason that its navigation of this age will be informed by who God is and what God is doing. The church knows that pain and suffering will mark its life, a fact it shares with the world. The reality of hardship in its inevitable and variegated forms is not something the church can or should try to escape. But the church also knows that God loves the world and, accordingly, can adopt a disposition of solidarity, sharing in the world's concerns, needs, and cries as if they were its own. Yet the church's hope in God and its intimacy with God make available particular forms of action and life that are not bound by the horizons of the present age. And if it is indeed the case, as I have argued above, that the church is sent from God, exists for God, is destined for a life with God, and is set free to serve the world God loves, then the church is able to see its actions, even the seemingly insignificant action of crying out to God for aid, as pregnant with power. The church is capable of *meaningful* action. And perhaps one of the powerful tools the church has at its disposal is the practice of lament, wherein it picks up the cries and concerns of the world and offers them to God as if they were its own.

Paul describes not only the time in which we exist but also our disposition within it: it is a time of groaning, it is a time of waiting, and insofar as it is the Lord of heaven and earth on whom we wait, it is a time of hope.[52] Paul

---

51. Ruggles, *Abrogation of the Seventh Commandment*, 16–17, emphasis original.

52. William Campbell notes that Paul's language here "indicates the non-arrival as yet of the *fulfillment* of hope. . . . Present lack of fulfillment does not denote failure or annulment,

says, "The whole creation has been groaning in labor pains until now; and not only the creation, but we ourselves, who have the first fruits of the Spirit, groan inwardly while we wait for adoption, the redemption of our bodies. For in hope we were saved" (Rom. 8:22–24). Christians inhabit the present age as those who simultaneously exist in the new reality brought about by the resurrection of Jesus Christ from the dead.[53]

Yet this groaning is not something we do apart from the rest of the created order. As noted above, we groan with and alongside the whole of creation, forming something of a chorus of lamentation.[54] Kim rightly notes that Paul seems to portray the broader groaning of creation (συστενάζω in Rom. 8:22) as an activity that is linked to and bound up with the groanings of the believer (στενάζω in 8:23).[55] The time in which we exist, then, is a time not of suffering in isolation, as isolated as the sufferer may feel and be, but of groaning *with*, an experience of solidarity that unites us with the desperate flora and fauna of creation. All of creation has been subjected to a "deathlike condition" as a result of human sin and the concomitant act of divine punishment.[56] Groaning, then, is a mode of inhabiting the present age of suffering in lament with the knowledge and recognition that a future redemption is coming.[57] And it is a mode that is characterized by the hope that makes enduring the devastation possible (8:24). Both the believer and creation as a whole are yearning for the time of victory, joy, and fulfillment, the time when the eschatological promises of God will be realized in their resplendent glory.[58]

Hope, then, conditions and motivates Christian witness and public life in the devastation. Not to be confused with either blind optimism or wishful thinking, given that neither's existence is conditioned upon truth, the Christian's hope is rooted in the gospel.[59] Hope is a kind of confidence that is rooted

---

rather it denotes the need to wait in eager expectation (8:19)." W. Campbell, *Romans*, 234–35, emphasis original.

53. As Stanley Hauerwas puts it, "Christians believe they exist in the time God enacted in the Son. Accordingly Christians tell time on the basis of that enactment. They may not know what time is but they know it is Advent." Hauerwas, "How to Tell Time Theologically," 100.

54. Laurie Braaten notes that "in the LXX, στενάζειν and its cognates are often employed in mourning contexts, including psalms of lament. The word group can connote mourning, or groaning due to deaths or community crises. It characterizes the inarticulate sighing, or groaning expressed in psalms of lament or thanksgiving, which accompanies petitionary mourning." Braaten, "All Creation Groans," 138.

55. Kim, *Divine-Human Relationship in Romans 1–8*, 144. Kim goes on to note that Paul's use of the expression οὐ μόνον δέ, ἀλλά "emphasizes the fact that the activity of believers in 8:23 is closely related to the creation's activity in 8:19–22" (145).

56. Braaten, "All Creation Groans," 144–45.

57. Moo, *Epistle to the Romans*, 518.

58. Jewett, *Romans*, 517.

59. Hauerwas, *Christian Existence Today*, 200, 214.

and grounded in the promises of God.[60] And as far as participation in common life is concerned, hope is the mode of life that distinctively marks the Christian community's inhabitation of the time of suffering, futility, and decay.[61] Hope describes a way of life that is anchored in God's absolute promise and future, revealed in the person and work of Jesus Christ. Attendant to this anchoring is a set of necessary "moral activities and moral judgments"—that is, hope is bound up with and made visible in "the particular activities and abstentions by which members of Christ's fellowship dispose themselves in the world."[62] The promise of God in the gospel and this hope order us in a particular way to the world around us and to those with whom we share a common life.

Yet knowing how to navigate the time of suffering in a manner that is ordered by hope in God's promised future is far from obvious. Here, the Christian community has consistently found it helpful to depict and describe what it means to be a people of hope through the lives of others—namely, our flawed heroes and saints. Stanley Hauerwas writes, "We are not likely to learn enough about how to hope by reflecting abstractly on what hope is or on how hope relates to other virtues (such as faith and love). We can learn—we do learn—more when we look to those whose lives were helpful; we learn not whether to hope but how to hope."[63] The depictions of the lives of these heroes and saints are intended to stir within us a certain kind of admiration so that we might creatively emulate and imitate them.[64] The words of William Still to newly emancipated slaves apply to the people of God as well: they "must not forget the rock from whence they were hewn, nor the pit from whence they were digged. Like other races . . . [they] will need all the knowledge of their past condition which they can get."[65] The Christian community must also look back to their exodus, to the act of God in Christ that sets them free from bondage to the past. This act of remembrance fuels our action in an ever-changing world, for we know what God has done and what he will do. It is here again that our abolitionary friends prove helpful. For William Still, inhabiting the time of suffering "in hope" took the form of ferrying

60. O'Donovan, *Self, World, and Time*, 121.
61. John Webster writes, "[Christian hope] finds itself in the time of grace, in that space in human history which follows the death and resurrection of Jesus Christ and the outpouring of the Spirit. . . . This is not to dismiss the reality of sin and suffering, nor to turn from its victims: to wait in hope is to groan (Rom 8:22). But the situation in which hope finds itself remains—solely by the merciful judgment of God—one in which grace is superabundant, and therefore one in which the possibility of a tragic reading of our history has been taken away." Webster, "Hope," 204.
62. Webster, "Hope," 195.
63. Hauerwas, *Christian Existence Today*, 200.
64. Hector, *Christianity as a Way of Life*, 138.
65. Still, preface to *Still's Underground Railroad Records* (1886).

men and women in and out of Philadelphia, providing them with funds for transport, and recording their stories so that their liberated progeny might read them. Even when the din of slavery was at its loudest, even as the Dredd Scott decision threatened to slacken abolitionary sails, Still committed to doing the work, to going on about the process of assisting fugitive slaves and recording and preserving their lives. Recall that Still, after years of working on the Underground Railroad, was less than optimistic about the future of Afro-Americans in America. Yet this perspective of the immediate future did not restrain his commitment to pursuing various goods for his fellow citizens. The Christian community bears witness to the suffering of the world in part by suffering with the world *in hope* and speaking truthfully about the time in which it exists. Again, the form this witness takes is one of hopeful lament.

In lament, the church confesses aloud that the world and its own life within it are not the way things ought to be. Lament is a kind of communal address to God, asking him to bring resolution to a real or perceived form of suffering.[66] In so doing, the church echoes the words of the psalmist, crying out to God, "Rouse yourself! Why do you sleep, O Lord? Awake, do not cast us off forever!" (Ps. 44:23). In lament, we offer up the groanings and longings of our hearts and our communities to God with the expectation that he will hear us and that he can and will act to bring about redemption.[67] This cry is not just in response to the suffering that an individual or a particular Christian community experiences; it is a plea voiced on behalf of the world. Here, the issue at stake is not necessarily who is at fault or who is morally culpable, points that may differentiate lament from the jeremiad. Rather, lament ultimately trusts that God loves the world he has made and will take responsibility for righting its wrongs and bringing about the future he has promised. Robin Parry observes that "the biblical God allows sufferers to voice their pain to him with brutal honesty. Such prayer takes place within the covenant relationship of God and Israel."[68] And so lament is fundamentally ordered by faith and hope. In faith, lament reaches out to God knowing *that* he is and *who* he is. In hope, lament expects the God of our ancestors to continue to be faithful to who he has revealed himself to be for the sake of those he loves. As Hector avers, "By bringing our suffering to God . . . we can see it in light of God's love and power and can thus resist the message that suffering conveys to us,

---

66. Building on the work of Hermann Gunkel and Claus Westermann, D. Keith Campbell writes, "An OT lament is a distressful complaint/question/appeal directed toward God (a prayer) in order to work change for a real or perceived problem." D. Campbell, "NT Scholars' Use of OT Lament Terminology," 217.

67. Hector, *Christianity as a Way of Life*, 188.

68. Parry, *Lamentations*, 22.

namely, that it has the final word on our existence."[69] Lament names the problems, hurt, and damage of the devastation as real and true sufferings that matter to God and in so doing refuses to turn a blind eye to the present age.

As far as public witness is concerned, lament also operates on a horizontal axis—that is, with respect to creation and those outside the walls of the Christian community. This is alluded to in Romans 8:22–23, as the groaning of the Christian is bound up with the lamentation of creation as a whole. The lamenting Christian *listens to* and *joins in with* the laments of the world but directs these groans and utterances to the God of Abraham, Isaac, and Jacob. And so, again, the church voices not only its pain and suffering in lament but also the pain and suffering of the communities it shares life with. As W. Derek Suderman points out, "Because biblical lament rhetorically reflects the presence of a listening community, the church has the challenge to consciously step into this role of being a social audience that hears, discerns, and responds appropriately."[70] The church turns its ear to hear the sobs echoing off the alleyways and from behind closed doors, refusing to allow such pain to be relegated to the realm of the private. In lamenting on behalf of the world, the Christian community bears witness to the cosmos as it truly is, as presently bound to futility and decay but loved by God and destined for reconciliation with God.

Conclusion

In this chapter, I have argued that the church's task is to bear witness to the time in which it exists but to do so with a disposition that is marked and ordered by hope. The present time in which the church exists is an age of suffering, futility, and decay. Accordingly, the church's task of public witness takes the shape of speaking the truth about the world as it is. Yet God loves the world deeply and promises to bring about the world's transformation at the return of Christ. Therefore, the church is to lift up the cries of the world to God in *hopeful* lament. It is called to "pour out [its] heart like water before the presence of the Lord! Lift [its] hands to him for the lives of [its] children, who faint for hunger at the head of every street" (Lam. 2:19).

As we will see in the next chapter, it is into this time that the Spirit sends the church to "fulfill the law of Christ" by becoming the kind of people capable of bearing the burdens of the world (Gal. 6:2), the second form that Christian witness takes in the present age. This need not result in a kind of progressive

---

69. Hector, *Christianity as a Way of Life*, 189.
70. Suderman, "Cost of Losing Lament," 214.

utopianism. The time in which we exist is and remains the time of the devastation. Only the act of God in Christ can change that. Still, the church's task is to bear witness to what God has done in Christ through its service to the law of Christ. And one of the primary ways it does this, as we will see in the chapter that follows, is through bearing the burdens of the world.

6

Burden Bearing as Public Witness

In the previous chapter, I argued that the Christian community inhabits the time of suffering, futility, and decay in hope, a hope that characterizes its action in the present. Attendant to a commitment to the gospel of God is the assurance of God's acting presence in and among his people and his promise to bring about the world's transformation at the return of Christ. Yet Christians do not inhabit this world as people who merely daydream about the arrival of a better city, although we do indeed desire that. The church is called to bear witness to the time in which it exists: the time of the devastation, the time in need of a cosmic renewal still to come. This first element of public witness is speaking the truth about the world as it is and as it will be in the plan of God, a witness that is characterized by hopeful lament.

There is a second component of public witness that we turn our attention to now. Liberated by the work of God in Christ, the church is set free to become a particular type of people and to bear witness to the Christ whose law it serves through the perpetual act of burden bearing (Gal. 6:2). While there are a number of ways that Christians might attest to the work of Christ—namely, in the central practices of the church—in what follows I will focus specifically on the act of bearing the world's burdens in dialogue with Galatians 5 and 6. In short, I will argue that the church bears witness to the good news of the gospel by extending, preserving, and cultivating shared, temporal goods as a distant echo of the truth that God in Christ bore our burdens in his body on the cross.

On Being Set Free (Galatians 5:1, 13–15; 6:1–2)

In chapter 3, we engaged the work of Maria Stewart and her injunction for Afro-American women to cultivate communities of virtue and character, an act that may in fact require the formation of new institutions and relational networks. For Stewart, this call to become a community of character was not set up as a mode of political quietism or erected in opposition to pursuing legislative changes that would lead to the abolition of slavery. Rather, Stewart viewed the cultivation of virtue within the communities as itself an act of bearing witness, both to the fullness of Afro-Americans' humanity and to the beauty of the Christian way of life. She longed for the day when "the professing followers of Christ arise and shine forth, and prove to the world that there is a reality in religion, and a beauty in the fear of the Lord."[1] Similarly, in chapter 2 we highlighted David Ruggles's call for retrospective analysis, through which the church reevaluates its life and witness in light of how it actively compromises the call of the gospel. For Ruggles, this takes the form of emphasizing the language of the Ten Commandments or the institutions God approves of and then contrasting that with the manner in which the church lives in the world. His goal in doing this is that the church will see the manner in which it has failed to measure up to the life God has called it to and seek renewal. For both Ruggles and Stewart, the pursuit of communal character, morality, and virtue is intrinsically political in nature. Wherever and whenever the church finds itself, it must attend to its life as a witness to the good news that Christ has liberated it from bondage to sin, death, and the self.

Part and parcel of the church's vocation of bearing witness to the resurrection of Jesus Christ is engaging in the ongoing work of becoming the kind of people who correspond to this reality. In other words, the Christian community bears witness to the gospel in its continual commitment to pursue the virtues that show the beauty of "the fear of the Lord," to borrow the language of Stewart, in how they live their lives. "Never; no, never will the chains of slavery and ignorance burst till we become united as one and cultivate among ourselves the pure principles of piety, morality, and virtue."[2] While Stewart is perhaps a bit overly optimistic about the possibilities of positive social change, her intuition appears to be correct that the cultivation of character is a political and public act that attests to whom the Christian community serves, the goods it pursues, and the conditions that make its life possible.

1. Stewart, introduction to *Spiritual Narratives*, by Stewart, Lee, Foote, and Broughton, 24.
2. Stewart, "Religion and the Pure Principles of Morality," 30.

Freed to Become Free

Keeping Stewart's and Ruggles's insights in mind, we now turn to the words of Holy Scripture, which remind us of the life we have been liberated to enjoy on account of the work of God in Christ. Paul writes:

> For freedom Christ has set us free. Stand firm, therefore, and do not submit again to a yoke of slavery. . . . For you were called to freedom, brothers and sisters; only do not use your freedom as an opportunity for self-indulgence, but through love become slaves to one another. For the whole law is summed up in a single commandment, "You shall love your neighbor as yourself." If, however, you bite and devour one another, take care that you are not consumed by one another. . . . My friends, if anyone is detected in a transgression, you who have received the Spirit should restore such a one in a spirit of gentleness. Take care that you yourselves are not tempted. Bear one another's burdens, and in this way you will fulfill the law of Christ. (Gal. 5:1, 13–15; 6:1–2)

Paul's letter to the Galatians repeatedly summarizes the gospel with a word: freedom (ἐλευθερία).[3] Two things are worth noting. First, the freedom of the gospel is a summons to become. It is a freedom to enjoy and inhabit a particular kind of life with God. Yet there is a priority to the liberating work of Christ. Christ "has set us free [ἠλευθέρωσεν]," a liberation that while telic in nature chronologically and logically precedes the works of love that flow from it. Paul is explicit that it is the action of this singular subject, the Messiah, that enables the life the Christian community is called to live and enjoy.[4] Paul's emphasis seems to be on the rite that enables entrance into the people of God (circumcision) and whether or not gentiles must enter through this gate to access the salvific benefits of the Jewish Messiah.[5] The aorist tense here indicates that whatever these benefits may be, they have already been communicated to and received by the community, a freedom in which they are now told to "stand firm" (στήκετε). A distinction is present here between the state of being Christ's work has realized and the purposes to which the

---

3. Commentators note that Paul uses an abrupt transition to draw attention to and emphasize the word "freedom." See Keener, *Galatians*, 439; and Oakes, *Galatians*, 159. James Dunn comments on Galatians 5:1, "'Freedom' had been the word which encapsulated the gospel for Paul in 2:4 (see on 2:4). There he had spoken of 'our freedom in Christ.' Here he speaks of the freedom which Christ had achieved . . . freedom given the place of emphasis ('for freedom'), freedom as characterizing the gospel from beginning to end, freedom as the goal of the divine act of liberation. . . . It is a striking fact that Paul can thus sum up the goal of God's saving act and call (5:13) in the one word 'freedom.'" Dunn, *Epistle to the Galatians*, 261.

4. De Boer, *Galatians*, 309.

5. Watson, *Paul, Judaism, and the Gentiles*, 353.

beneficiaries of said work are directed. And it is a distinction that must be maintained. Eberhard Jüngel is surely right in stating, "Being born, like being raised from the dead, is a process in which the human participates only as all his or her own activity is excluded. One cannot call oneself to life. Just as one cannot beget oneself, neither can sinners do anything to become righteous before God and thereby share in the relationally rich life of God. God alone can make the new beginning which comes with the joyful exchange from death to life. We can only receive it."[6] This is one of the reasons I have opted to speak of the ways that we *witness* to the gospel, language that attempts to preserve the difference in kind that exists between God's act of liberation in the work of Christ and the effect that liberation has upon those on whom the Spirit rests.

The phrase "for freedom" (τῇ ἐλευθερίᾳ) indicates the purpose of the Christian's liberation, both from the jurisdiction of the law and from the life of the flesh.[7] Freedom is not a state merely to enjoy and certainly not an occasion for various forms of self-indulgence. Rather, Galatians portrays freedom as something that "must be lived out in slavery to the body of Christ."[8] As John Webster puts it, "Evangelical freedom, emerging from our being put to death and made alive in Christ and the Spirit, is thus freedom from the *care of self* which so harasses and afflicts the lost creatures of God. My freedom is in part my freedom from final responsibility for maintaining my self, a freedom which is the fruit of my having been liberated from the anxious toil of having to be my own creator and preserver."[9] The Christian is set free by the Spirit *for freedom.*[10] It is possible that the text is evoking the image of pre-sacral manumission inscriptions, wherein a slave is set free "for freedom" and service to the deity.[11] Yet as Craig Keener points out, it is more pressing, and possibly a more appropriate reading of the noun's dative case, that a liberated slave could be reenslaved under certain conditions.[12] It is imperative, then, that

6. Jüngel, "Living Out Righteousness," 254.

7. As Matthew Thiessen has noted, this freedom from the law does not necessarily entail a particular degeneration of the merits or goodness of Torah. Rather, Paul's proclamation that the gentile Christian is free from particular uses of the Mosaic law is predicated upon the conviction that it was never intended to apply to gentiles. "Throughout his letters, [Paul] resisted the application of the law to gentiles, not because he was the apostle of freedom, but because he believed that the Jewish law did not apply to gentiles. Paul opposed gentile judaizing because it was a misappropriation of the holy law" (Thiessen, *Paul and the Gentile Problem*, 162). See also Hayes, *What's Divine about Divine Law?*, 151.

8. Greene-McCreight, *Galatians*, 162.

9. Webster, "Evangelical Freedom," 225, emphasis original.

10. Bryant, *Risen Crucified Christ*, 217.

11. Longenecker, *Galatians*, 224; and Witherington, *Grace in Galatia*, 340.

12. Keener, *Galatians*, 441–42.

those set free "stand firm" in freedom and resist the gravitational pull to the ways of life that are devoid of God.

The Spirit works to form and fashion this community in and for freedom—that is, in a particular way that corresponds to the work of God in Christ. Their freedom is a freedom to *become* a community marked by wisdom and love. The immediate list of virtues and vices that follows serves as a means of contrasting the life "of the flesh" with that "of the Spirit." This list provides an outline for what this form of becoming entails (see Gal. 5:16–26). The life of the Spirit is *distinct* with regard to its animating principle, as it is the action of God himself that enables the possibility of the life of grace (5:25).[13] Again, there is a logical priority here, in that the Spirit of freedom communicates the gift of freedom that thereby enables the believing community to *live* as those who are set free. Yet the communal life the Spirit brings into being and makes possible is also unique with regard to its form and shape. The life of the flesh is characterized by conflict, disunity, self-aggrandizement, and discord (5:17–21). In contrast, the life of the Spirit is one of harmony, love, and peace (5:22–23). And so the injunction to "stand firm in freedom" serves as a clarion call for the believing community to conform to the liberation that has been achieved on its behalf and to the character of its Liberator. Christian theology has, traditionally, described this process of becoming with the language of the virtues or the doctrine of sanctification. While this language is not without its difficulties and complications,[14] the emphasis here is on the power of God the Spirit to produce within the believing community a character that serves as a distant, creaturely echo of the character of its God.[15] And it bears repeating that this freedom that the gospel enables is intended to germinate in a particular kind of *communal* life.[16]

Freed to Bear Burdens

Second, the gospel of freedom is also a summons to serve another law: "the law of Christ" (Gal. 6:2). The Christian has been liberated not only *from* the tyranny of sin, death, and the passions but also *for* a particular kind of life in the world. This, fundamentally, is a freedom to serve the other in and

---

13. John Owen writes, "God himself is the absolute infinite *fountain*, the supreme efficient *cause*, of all grace and holiness; for he alone is originally and essentially holy, as he only is good, and so the first cause of holiness and goodness to others." Owen, *Works of John Owen*, 514–15.

14. See Zahl, "Non-Competitive Agency."

15. Gordon Fee argues that the contrast between "*works* of the flesh" and "*fruit* of the Spirit" intentionally highlights the divine empowerment that is required to produce the character of God in the believer. Fee, *God's Empowering Presence*, 443–44.

16. Hays, *Faith of Jesus Christ*, 224.

with the love of Christ.[17] Here, Paul returns to the motif of enslavement with a slight modification. Whereas in chapter 4 Paul argued that the Galatians were children of the "free woman" set free for freedom (4:31), here he depicts them as engaging in servile work for the sake of one another.[18] This reinforces the fact that freedom is not autonomy or self-determination. Rather, as John Barclay notes, "'Freedom' is here given a distinctive shape: opposed to (and threatened by) 'the flesh,' it entails a new allegiance (paradoxically, a form of 'enslavement'), whose hallmark is love."[19] And so the gospel of freedom is one that sets us free to act on and within the world, even as we recognize the limitations of those actions as well as the inevitable frustrations and disappointments pertaining thereto.

Paul proceeds to describe this life of the Spirit with concrete specifics, ranging from avoiding conceit and envy (Gal. 5:26) to having an appropriate view of self (6:3). We will focus our attention on one specific injunction: "bear one another's burdens, and in this way you will fulfill the law of Christ" (6:2). This seems, at least in part, to be a reiteration of the commandment to "love your neighbor as yourself" in 5:14.[20] Yet here the point of emphasis is on the christological shape that such love must take.[21] In the immediate context, as David deSilva avers, the bearing of burdens (ἀλλήλων τὰ βάρη βαστάζετε) "refers metaphorically to the moral and personal failures from which individual disciples need restoration. . . . Each disciple will at some point rely upon others to help him or her carry this weight in order to remain in the Spirit's path."[22] But deSilva goes on to note that this command invariably extends to the physical, psychological, and personal burdens of life. He writes, "Paul would no doubt also understand this injunction to extend to include all burdensome experiences of life, all the trials that life simply sends a person's way. Believers are to extend love, kindness, support, and, as needed, material help toward those experiencing such burdens so as to make them easier to bear."[23] In so doing, the Christian community here too provides a distant, creaturely echo of the burden-bearing work of God in Christ.

17. Wolter, *Paul*, 365.
18. De Boer, *Galatians*, 376.
19. Barclay, *Paul and the Gift*, 425. Similarly, Robert Bryant writes, "To be in Christ is to be free from the yoke of the law (5:1) but it is also to be free for serving one another through love (5:13; cf. 5:6)." Bryant, *Risen Crucified Christ*, 216.
20. Lührmann, *Continental Commentary*, 116.
21. Greene-McCreight, *Galatians*, 176.
22. DeSilva, *Letter to the Galatians*, 482.
23. DeSilva, *Letter to the Galatians*, 482–83. See also Burton, *Critical and Exegetical Commentary*, 329.

The foregoing provides the grounds for articulating a secondary aspect of Christian public witness: bearing witness to the work that Christ has accomplished for us. The Christian community is tasked with bearing burdens and becoming a particular kind of people, both of which are actions and processes that fulfill "the law of Christ." Insofar as they do so, they indicate and bear witness to that law. Just as the law of God is a reflection of the character and nature of the one who gave it, God himself,[24] so too when the ecclesial community fulfills the law of Christ, it provides a creaturely reflection of the character and nature of the one to whom this law belongs.[25] As Brian Rosner argues, in line with the work of Richard Hays, "the law of Christ" (τὸν νόμον τοῦ Χριστοῦ) in Galatians 6 refers to the pattern Christ sets on the road to Golgotha of carrying our burdens.[26] Paul calls his readers to follow Christ's self-sacrificial example of burden bearing and allow this example to serve as the normative pattern for their relationships with others.[27] The law of Christ is then, paradigmatically, a reference to the sacrificial act of Christ exhibited in the carrying of our burdens in his passion. And again, perhaps more importantly, insofar as they fulfill this law, the members of the Christian community point to the one from whom this law originates: Christ himself.

The task of bearing one another's burdens is one that is given to each and every member of the Christian community. There is a form of reciprocity built into the "one another's" in Paul's letter. Accordingly, we would do well to remember C. René Padilla's injunction that "life in community cannot be conceived in terms of a situation in which one section of the church is always on the giving end while another is always on the receiving end."[28] While Padilla's focus seems to be on the interaction of ecclesial communities around the globe, it seems that we can apply it as well to members within the same community. The reciprocity of the command and the fact that this command is tethered to a life in the Spirit seem to indicate that this injunction is one given to Christians for the governing of Christian life together. What implications does this have on public witness? Here it is worth remembering three things. First, as I have stated already, the Christian community's life is invariably and irrevocably public in nature. It is a shared life, one held in common with the nonbeliever, the invisible other, and the outsider. Second, while there are necessary distinctions between Christian and non-Christian

24. Bavinck, *Sin and Salvation in Christ*, 141–42. See also McCall, *Against God and Nature*, 242–43.

25. Bruce, *Epistle to the Galatians*, 26.

26. See Hays, *Faith of Jesus Christ*, 225.

27. Rosner, *Paul and the Law*, 117.

28. Padilla, "Fullness of Mission," 153.

communities, the membrane between them is semipermeable and somewhat fluid.[29] Ecclesial spaces are filled with non-Christians and Christians alike, as the tradition has widely attested. So while it may be the case that only the "spiritual" can fulfill the law of Christ, this is an injunction given to the church as a whole. It then does not delimit *whose* burdens the church bears, since even if it bears only the burdens of other members of its community, this will invariably include non-Christians. Third and finally, if this bearing of burdens is a "good," then it is a good the church works to share with all, even those outside the household of faith (Gal. 6:10). The gifts and practices of the church are not given merely for the believing community's enjoyment and sustenance. Practices like forgiveness, hospitality, truth telling, and so on are gifts God gives his church to share with and extend to its neighbors.

The Common Good and Temporal Goods

One of the primary ways that Christians attest to the freedom that God has opened up for them in the person of Christ is by seeking their neighbor's "good." Christian freedom is a freedom for a life with God, but it's also a freedom to pursue the interests of the other. As Holy Writ reminds us, "Do not seek your own advantage, but that of the other [τοῦ ἑτέρου]" (1 Cor. 10:24). "The other" seems to signify those outside the ecclesial community, as Paul seems to indicate later on (10:31–11:1). Commenting on 1 Corinthians 10:24, Webster proposes that "to seek that which is one's neighbour's is . . . to be free for life. Looking to the neighbor's cause is not mere self-abandonment; it is rather to exist in the human fellowship by which, precisely by not striving to realize ourselves, we attain to the liberty of the children of God."[30] A similar sentiment is found in the epistle to the Galatians: "So then, whenever we have an opportunity, let us work for the good of all, and especially for those of the family of faith" (Gal. 6:10). And insofar as we attain and realize a good (e.g., liberty or freedom in the case of our abolitionary friends) in and through a form of life that is shared with other human beings, it is a good we hold in common with them, a good that is bound up in the life that we share with them.

29. Karl Barth writes, "Between the community and Christians on the one side and the rest of the world on the other, there is a distinct yet not absolute, but only fluid and changing frontier" (Barth, *Church Dogmatics* IV/3, 192). Barth's point echoes a sentiment that is common throughout the Christian tradition—namely, the manner in which the church on earth is filled with sinners and saints, wheat and tares. Minimally, we might say that the church is not only the community of the saints but also one of sinners *and* one in which sinners consistently transition into being full members of the community of the saints.

30. Webster, "Evangelical Freedom," 226.

The notion of the "common good" has given birth to a veritable cottage industry of work and debates in the past few years.[31] I will not rehearse them here. Given the limits of space, I am precluded from engaging in a thorough investigation into the various articulations, revisions, and criticisms of the notion. With Oliver O'Donovan, we might say that "'the' common good is the good of the community *of* communicating members, consisting in their capacity to realize fulfillment *through* living together."[32] What O'Donovan seems to mean is that particular human creatures exist in networks of relations and meanings—that is, the individual is enmeshed within a community.[33] Indeed, the very notion of communication carries with it a commitment to shared meanings, understandings, and goods, material and otherwise. "'Community' means a sphere in which things are held in common rather than in private, as 'ours' rather than as 'yours' or 'mine.' The essence of community is 'communication,' the exercise of sharing things or transmitting them among two or more people."[34] The members of these communities communicate meanings and goods to one another in order to realize particular ends and forms of *shared* life. The common good, then, refers to a community's good and the forms of fulfillment its members attain through sharing in a common life. Appeals to "the" common good are made by a particular, concrete, existing community "to which the obligation we owe can be specified."[35] As a communal notion, it draws on the wide range of communities in which we find ourselves but stops short of evoking some notion of universal humanity.[36]

This limitation of the common good to particular communities while it is still tethered to the larger networks in which we are enmeshed may help alleviate Luke Bretherton's legitimate concern that appeals to the common good as an all-encompassing vision of national or human life is fundamentally anti-democratic. For Bretherton, these appeals to the common good deny "the plurality and contestability of moral vision in complex societies and the conflicts that arise in pursuit of divergent moral goods, all of which must be negotiated through politics."[37] But even this concern does not negate the need

---

31. See, for example, Volf, *Public Faith*; and O'Neill, *Reimaging Human Rights*. These publications are not limited to the realms of theology and Christian ethics but include works ranging from discussions of economics (e.g., Tirole, *Economics for the Common Good*) to issues pertaining to ecology and the environment (e.g., Gorringe, *Common Good and the Global Emergency*).

32. O'Donovan, *Entering into Rest*, 54, emphasis original.

33. O'Donovan, *Entering into Rest*, 48.

34. O'Donovan, *Common Objects of Love*, 26.

35. O'Donovan, *Entering into Rest*, 55.

36. O'Donovan, *Entering into Rest*, 55.

37. Bretherton, *Christ and the Common Life*, 32–33n13.

to appeal to "common goods" for communities on a much smaller scale. As Bretherton notes, "Arguably, a notion of the common good understood as an ever-deferred horizon of possibility can still operate as a helpful regulative ideal or guiding point of reference for large-scale social formations."[38] This resonates well with the appeal in Galatians 6. We should always, ever work *for the good of all* as the opportunity arises, pursuing the sharing of this good with all irrespective of their relationship to the family of faith (Gal. 6:10). Our relations to and communications with our neighbors (and the other) cannot be conceived as so irrevocably and irreconcilably competitive that our flourishing and "carrying on" can come only at their expense.[39]

So we might distinguish between the common good and the various common temporal goods that, when bound together, serve as the constitutive basis from which a community's vision of *the*, singular, common good might emerge. By "temporal good," I mean any of those goods that are necessary for the continuation of life in the world.[40] Some of these goods are material (e.g., food, clothing, shelter), and others are not (e.g., education, friendships). In theory, the possession of *all* these temporal goods would lead to human flourishing, although in a postlapsum world such aspirations should surely be tempered. Of course, admittedly there may be additional goods we require to thrive or flourish of which we do not know.[41] At minimum, the possession of a small number of these temporal goods enables us to carry on.[42]

A few things are worth noting about the nature of temporal goods. First, temporal goods are instrumental in nature—that is, they are goods that are in service of and ordered to a higher good, which is our common life. The consumption of the fiber inherent to blanched kale is good for a person insofar as it helps, among other things, with the proper growth, animation, and function of that person's body.[43] If I were to somehow lose the ability to digest and break down kale, its fiber would be inaccessible to me and it would cease to be good for me. Second, the value of temporal goods is in many ways related to their spatiotemporal contexts in which we find ourselves. Literacy was, ostensibly, somewhat less important in Susa during

---

38. Bretherton, *Christ and the Common Life*, 32–33n13.

39. Adams, *Finite and Infinite Goods*, 378.

40. Wolterstorff, *Justice*, 222–25.

41. Wolterstorff, *Justice*, 226.

42. An example of this might be food and shelter. Minimally, if one possesses only the goods of food and shelter, which are necessary for realizing the goods of communication and community, one can continue living or "carrying on," as I have put it. But neither the possession of the goods of food and shelter nor the possession of the goods of communication and community are enough to constitute a human creature's flourishing or thriving.

43. Adams, *Finite and Infinite Goods*, 93.

the years leading up to the tenth century BCE before the invention of token-based writing systems. The adequate insulation of pipes may be a necessary good in Ypsilanti, Michigan, with its frigid, sunless, arctic winters. But one probably would not need such insulation in San Diego, California, where the weather is perpetually 72.3 degrees and sunny. Thus, the value of insulated pipes as a good would be significantly undermined in this latter context. Third, some of these goods are more public in nature, like air and water quality or access to forms of education. Others are somewhat less public in nature, like those of the existential variety—namely, the absence of shame or fear.[44] And finally, fourth, insofar as these goods are "good," they are so because we view them as essential for living and forming a certain kind of life together. Temporal goods are not individual goods, even when "possessed" and held by individuals. Our life together is irrevocably social, as I have stressed. The attainment and enjoyment of temporal goods always takes place within the networks of relationships and communications that make up a community.

I will refer to these goods from which the common good emerges as temporal goods because they are related to and contingent on the existence of certain spatiotemporal conditions and are, in many cases, subject to dissolution and decay in the present age. And insofar as the common good emerges from these temporal goods and the pursuit of the common good bears witness to the ultimate transformation and redemption of the created order at the return of Christ, the extension, preservation, and cultivation of these temporal goods are vital elements of bearing witness to the gospel of God. As Bretherton puts it, the "pursuit of the kingdom of God is inseparable from the pursuit of penultimate goods in common."[45] More to the point, to follow the language of this chapter, the act of bearing witness to the kingdom of God and to the God of that kingdom is tethered to extending, preserving, and cultivating the temporal goods held in common with the other.

44. To say that these goods are *less* public is not to suggest that there are some goods that are public and others that are private, which has been a maxim of liberalism. The scale is, rather, from more to less public. For example, the shame I feel with regard to my coffee "dependence" is less public than, say, my failure to abide by city water restrictions during a drought. But that is not to say that this shame is *wholly* or even *primarily* private, insofar as it affects the goods I purchase (namely, coffee and coffee filters) and the manner in which I use them, all of which are interwoven with a whole host of other persons and parties, ranging from coffee farmers in Uganda, Ethiopia, and Columbia to the trash collectors and neighbors whose property value is affected by my compost pile.

45. Bretherton, *Christ and the Common Life*, 23. Bretherton appears to be borrowing the distinction between penultimate and ultimate goods that is found in Dietrich Bonhoeffer's *Ethics*. In what follows, I will use the language of "temporal goods," simply because the locution is somewhat less cumbersome.

Public Witness as Extending, Preserving, and Cultivating Temporal Goods

Returning to the work of Maria Stewart, we saw in chapter 3 how she not only called for the cultivation of character on a personal and communal level for the sake of public witness but also urged her listeners to create new institutions and renew old ones for the sake of social change. If there was no place in antebellum society for women to nurture their intellectual gifts, then they needed to pool their resources and create their own spaces. "Let every female heart become united and let us raise a fund ourselves; and at the end of one year and a half, we might be able to lay the corner-stone for the building of a High School, that the higher branches of knowledge might be enjoyed by us."[46] If life in the world of slavery did not afford Afro-Americans access to forms of capital, such as education and the like, then they needed to take matters into their own hands and form their own institutions that would provide them with the ability to obtain these goods. Stewart recognized that there were certain social goods that women and Afro-Americans did not have access to, and she wished to create modes of extending those goods to them. But the formation of new institutions was only half of the equation for Stewart. Stewart consistently advised parents to tend to the intellectual, religious, and moral formation of their children, viewing their formation as an investment in the younger generation so that the entire community might become "a thriving and flourishing people."[47] We might view this as a form of renewing and reviving institutions that already exist to preserve the temporal goods these institutions communicate.

A similar point of emphasis is present in the work of William Still, particularly with his meticulous note taking and record keeping of those who passed through Philadelphia via the Underground Railroad. Still recognized that the institution of slavery disrupted vital family and social relations, especially if slaves sought to escape their enslavement or were sold to distant plantations. Still strove to provide the resources that would enable fugitives to reconnect with their loved ones if either slavery came to a close or their still-enslaved friends and family members found their way to freedom. He writes, "It seemed reasonable to hope that by carefully gathering the narratives of Underground Rail Road passengers, in some way or other some of the bleeding and severed hearts might be united and comforted; and by the use that might be made privately, if not publicly, of

46. Stewart, "Religion and the Pure Principles of Morality," 37.
47. Stewart, "Address Delivered at the African Masonic Hall," 62.

just such facts as would naturally be embraced in their brief narratives, re-unions might take place."[48]

In each of these instances, Stewart and Still are seeking to create and preserve institutions so that the disenfranchised can receive particular temporal, social goods (e.g., the goods of education or familial relationships). For both of them, this work of extension, preservation, and cultivation is principally a task and extension of Christian witness—that is, the church's vocation of bearing witness in a shared, common life involves the work of finding ways to ensure that the people living on the margins of society have access to the goods necessary for carrying on in the world.

Christian life is a life of freedom lived in the present age of suffering, futility, and decay as an act of hopeful attestation to God's eternal promise to be with and for his creatures, reconciling them to himself through the work of his Son. Insofar as the Christian faith is inexorably public in nature, the Christian community's life is a sign of the work of God in Christ, both corporately and individually.[49] Again, it bears repeating that by the term "witness" I do not mean exclusively or even primarily the task of evangelism, as pressing and imperative as that task might be. Rather, the church indicates in its words, its practices, and the very definitive shape that its life takes that the world belongs to God and that Jesus Christ is Lord.[50] In essence, the church's life ought to be a sign of the gospel, a life that points back to what God has done in Christ (John 17:21).

Extending Temporal Goods

First, the Christian community strives to bear witness to the gospel of salvation and the law of Christ in its common life through the extension of temporal goods to the other. We start here because, invariably, we enter a world we did not form or fashion, and there are already goods present within it, goods given to us, inherited by us, and shared with us by the communities we inhabit. But as we noted above, this present world we enter is also a world of suffering. And insofar as suffering pertains to individuals and communities, it also pertains to the goods our neighbor (the other) desires, wants, and lacks. The task of the Christian community is to bear witness to the gospel by extending the temporal goods it has access to and possesses to those within its context.

---

48. Still, *Underground Railroad* (1872), 4.
49. Greggs, *Priestly Catholicity of the Church*, 163.
50. Hauerwas, *Approaching the End*, 42. See also Hill, *Gathered on the Road to Zion*, 86–88.

Seeking the good of the other involves, minimally, extending the gift of social goods to them and inviting them to share in their goodness. The manner in which we engage in this act of witness is necessarily multivalent. As our contexts differ with regard to time and place, so too will our capacity to share with those who are in need and extend the gift of hospitality (Rom. 12:13). But this requires the Christian community to consistently seek its own renewal so that it might cultivate the habits that are necessary for doing this well, consistently, and faithfully. For example, we must develop habits of attentiveness so that we might see and recognize those within our communities who are precluded from enjoying the goods we have. It is often the case that the suffering of the present age is felt most acutely by those existing on the margins of society. The church's gaze is outward, to the need of its neighbor, whether it is stable housing for those recently released from prison or access to grocery stores in food deserts.

Additionally, we must cultivate habits of creativity and discernment so that we can identify the appropriate means of sharing access to these goods. Much of the manner in which we extend these goods will depend on the spatiotemporal conditions in which we find ourselves, and so here discernment is necessary. The Christian community hiding from a totalitarian regime may find itself with less political agency, although Still, Ruggles, and Stewart all serve as challenging reminders of the ways we can and must imagine possibilities for action.[51] Discernment is necessary so that we might adjudicate between needs and preferences, between the different courses of action available to us, between the different routes we might take to achieve a particular end.[52] Creativity ought to flow naturally out of our collective attempt to discern the mind of Christ in our midst.[53] We will return to creativity as it pertains to public witness below, but for now suffice it to say that the Christian community's task to inhabit the present age of suffering in hope calls it again and again to reimagine the possibilities of its action, the shape its witness can take, and the ways it might extend goods to its neighbors. Insofar as we see these goods as goods, they are goods we are called to share with the other as we seek their interest.

Yet there are some teeth lurking in this injunction. The church's task is to extend goods, but this does not mean the church is to do so in the pursuit of profit. It does so with an explicit eye toward the interest of the other, the neighbor. The extension of social goods may cost it something, and it must

---

51. See especially chap. 4.
52. O'Donovan, *Entering into Rest*, 29.
53. On this, see Hill, *Gathered on the Road to Zion*, 174–77.

be prepared to pay that cost: "You received without payment; give without payment" (Matt. 10:8). Here, perhaps an example will suffice. It has become customary to decry the state of Christian education, particularly as it relates to issues of diversity and inclusion. It may seem appropriate, therefore, to increase the enrollment of "ethnic minorities." Given the rising costs of college tuition and disparities in income levels, these aforementioned ethnic minorities will most likely be encouraged to take out loans to procure their entrance into these halls of higher learning. But it is unclear to me how this aspiration is fundamentally about the good of the other (i.e., the previously excluded neighbor). It seems to me that they are being included in service of the institution and the assuaging of its conflicted conscience or perhaps, worse yet, cultivating a particular public image for the sake of prospective donors. A so-called Christian college that wants to increase the diversity of its student body without attending to the material conditions of poor, under-resourced communities that prohibit their involvement in such forms of common life in the first place and seeks merely to profit off the presence of minorities does not deserve to be taken seriously.

The extension of temporal goods to the other bears witness to the gospel insofar as it provides a distant, creaturely echo of the act of God in Christ when he bore our burdens "in his body on the cross" and extended ultimate goods of friendship and fellowship with God to us (1 Pet. 2:24; see also Rom. 5:10). As we extend temporal goods to the other, we declare their status as creatures situated in a particular relationship to God, creatures whom God loves and stooped low to receive. Simply put, we recognize that the Lord of life has set his love on them in Christ, and so we strive to treat them in a way that is commensurate with their status as honored by God. We do this by extending the goods we have in our possession to them. As Martin Luther famously puts it, "The Christian thinks in the following way: 'Although I am an unworthy and condemned person, my God has given me in Christ all riches of righteousness and salvation without merit on my part. . . . I will therefore give myself as a Christ to my neighbor, just as Christ offered himself to me. I will do nothing in this life except what is profitable, necessary, and life-giving to my neighbor, since through faith I have an abundance of all good things in Christ.'"[54] The Christian community recognizes that the present age is an age of suffering. This suffering, among other things, denotes the pressure that the devastation impresses on the individual and their community as well as the absence of particular goods conducive to communal well-being. Within this context the Christian community seeks

---

54. Luther, *Freedom of the Christian*, 82.

to bear the burden of this suffering with and for the world as a testimony to the law of Christ.

Preserving Temporal Goods

Second, the Christian community bears witness to the work of God in Christ not only through the extension of temporal goods but also through the preservation of temporal goods. By preservation, I mean the act of attempting to ensure that appropriate modes and means of communicating temporal goods remain intact. Preservation is an act of repairing that which will inevitably fall into disrepair. The objects of such efforts at repair can vary, ranging from inefficient public works to corrupted and decaying institutions, from individuals to entire communities and cultures. The preservation of temporal goods is imperative because, as I outlined in the previous chapter, the Christian community inhabits the present age, which is not only a time of suffering and futility but also a time of decay. Institutions and the modes of life we construct are inevitably trapped in a spiral of dissolution and fall into disrepair. A political representative may find ways around a law that bans the ownership and trading of stocks while serving in office, obtaining handshake agreements and the promise of future compensation from a pharmaceutical company that stands to benefit from certain policies. A public-school leader, held accountable by certain laws for the reading and mathematical performance of their students, may find ways to encourage teachers to "teach the test," avoiding the need to cultivate the cognitive and artistic capacities of students in an effort to avoid the state's ire. Here, certain social goods, such as integrity in office and basic competency in educational pedagogy, stand at risk of being lost, and the absence of these goods causes suffering. Often we find ourselves echoing the words of Obierika that life in the present age has "put a knife on the things that held us together and we have fallen apart."[55] In the present age, the institutions we create, the ideals we aspire to, and the means we appropriate for sharing social goods do indeed fall apart over time, standing in need of constant efforts of preservation and renewal. Insofar as this is the case and the church seeks to bear the burdens of the world, the church is almost necessarily interested in the process of preservation, whether it is the preservation of forms of life, creation itself, or memories and lessons of the past.

Yet this preservation need not be restricted to particular modes of life, although the church may do well to consider how to do this. Preservation

---

55. Achebe, *Things Fall Apart*, 176.

can also extend to the preservation of the goods themselves. For example, it may be the case that marriage is necessary for human flourishing and that the relational nexuses contained therein are optimal for the right cultivation of the potentiality of young children. Indeed, some social scientists have suggested as much.[56] But insofar as the church recognizes this, it may strive to preserve marriage as an institution and to look for ways of extending the goods of marriage to children in single-parent households. Instead of merely trying to think of ways to incentivize the next generation to commit to one another, a quest that may teeter on the brink of statecraft, the church might ask how it can extend the goods that familial life contains (e.g., financial stability, adult supervision) to the children in single-parent homes and what kinds of sacrifices would make this extension possible. So, for example, the Homewood Children's Village (HCV) in Pittsburgh, Pennsylvania, seeks to extend and preserve the goods family life affords to children in low-income communities by connecting children and families with advocates who commit to at least a two-year period of assisting students and their families so that they might "succeed in school and life." They do this "by connecting them to high quality programs and services to support their well-being and stability."[57] These advocates consistently track a student's academic progress, regularly contact their stakeholders, and connect the family with tools and resources that will support their development on a holistic level.[58] In collaboration with local partners, such as Bible Center Church, HCV provides goods such as food, rental assistance, winter clothing, and college and career preparation for residents of the Homewood neighborhood.

The preservation of temporal goods bears witness to the gospel insofar as it declares that the world is both one of suffering and one in perennial bondage to decay. In striving to preserve particular temporal goods, the church confesses that this is in fact the time of the devastation, when things fall into disrepair and ruin. Yet with its attempts at preservation, the church not only indicates the way things are but also testifies to the fact that this is not the way things are supposed to be. God is in fact making all things new (Rev. 21:5). And insofar as the church strives to preserve temporal goods and the modes through which these goods are communicated, it refuses to separate itself from the fate of the world or quarantine itself from the world's ills. Furthermore, in so doing it provides a distant, creaturely echo of the God who stooped low, in the fullness of time, to bear our burdens in his body on

56. See, for example, Kearney and Levine, "Economics of Nonmarital Childbearing."
57. Homewood Children's Village, "Annual Report 2019–2020," 4.
58. Homewood Children's Village, "Impact Report 2020–2021," 7.

the tree (1 Pet. 2:24). There can be no running away from the suffering of the present age. God in Christ did not do so, and neither can his church.

Cultivating Temporal Goods

Third and finally, Christians bear witness to the resurrection of Jesus Christ in public life through the work of cultivating temporal goods.[59] Kevin Hector writes, "When God gives a vocation, God is calling us to care for and cultivate specific goods."[60] While Hector's emphasis seems to be on the *individual's* vocation and calling, it seems to me that it can be extended outward to encompass a community or a network of communities joining together in the cultivation of particular goods and forms of life that will enable the enjoyment of these goods. Here, the eye is turned to what is lacking and what is needed. Because the present age is one not only of suffering and decay but also of futility, the Christian community recognizes that its attempts to extend temporal goods to the other will often fail to realize their respective ends. The same holds true for the states we inhabit and the various spheres we live within. For example, given the pressures and nature of the housing market, particularly the needs to secure loans and sign leases, it is common for citizens released from incarceration to struggle to find stable housing. This is all the more the case in the current housing shortage that many inhabitants of the United States find themselves navigating. Christians may choose to extend the good of housing by opening up their own homes or providing access to forms of capital that they possess. But they may also need to cultivate forms of life or institutions that enable this good to be shared and enjoyed.[61] If shelter is a good, then how can we establish communities, institutions, forms of life, and so on that ensure that this good will be extended to the neighbors with whom we share a common life? If the aim of preservation is renewal in the face of decay, then cultivation focuses on the futility of our actions. In recognition of the fact that many of our actions will fail to achieve their desired ends, cultivation seeks to create alternative, newly imagined ways of realizing them. In this way, we seek to take what is present, what is given in the world, and remake it with an eye toward the needs of our neighbors.

Two caveats are necessary here. Because we inhabit the time of futility and decay, many of our attempts at cultivating temporal goods and modes

---

59. Oliver O'Donovan writes, "The church renews society by renewing possibilities for work. . . . There is in principle no limit to the forms in which Christians may discover opportunities to use their material resources as a medium of communication that opens up a sphere of work for them to do." O'Donovan, *Ways of Judgment*, 280.

60. Hector, *Christianity as a Way of Life*, 176.

61. Benac, *Adaptive Church*, 106.

of extending them will ultimately fall short and fail. This is to be expected. As stated above, we cannot change the present age from one of suffering, futility, and decay into a facsimile of the eschatological kingdom. To do so would be to fall captive to ecclesial triumphalism. Additionally, in speaking of the cultivation of temporal goods, we do not necessarily intend to say that all technological developments are necessarily beneficial and good. Nor are we indicating that it is the task of the Christian community to extend these "technological" programs and processes to the other. Our technological developments are not achieved in sealed bubbles, kept free from the contaminating effects of our own vices. Here too discernment is required. To borrow again from Kevin Hector, "We cannot care well for certain goods without a diachronically stable commitment to them and, so, a commitment to prioritizing them and becoming good at caring for them. . . . Answering God's calling requires that we learn how to care well for the goods that God has entrusted to us, and that we organize our lives so as to ensure that these goods can receive the care they deserve."[62]

The cultivation of temporal goods bears witness to the gospel insofar as it strives to attest to the goodness of the created order and the hope of creation's transformation and as it follows the pattern of Christ's burden bearing on the road to Golgotha. To take on the work of cultivation for the sake of doing good to all is, in a real sense, to take on their burdens as our own. Cultivation takes time, patience, and energy. It does not happen on its own. So when the Christian community takes on the burdens of its neighbors, it does so knowing full well that such an endeavor will not come easily. Yet the Christian community does this precisely because such burden bearing attests to what Christ has done on its behalf. Christians follow in the burden-bearing way of Christ, alleviating forms of suffering in the present age when possible. Additionally, in a way not dissimilar from that which we delineated with respect to the extension of temporal goods, the cultivation of temporal goods serves as a reminder that those on the margins, those who most acutely feel the pressures of the present age, matter to God. And because they matter to God, they matter especially to those who claim to be God's kin. So whether it is purifying polluted water systems or addressing the air quality concerns that plague low-income communities, Christians seek to cultivate temporal goods for these communities as a way of indicating that the members of these marginalized and ignored populations are treasured in the sight of their God. In so doing, Christians testify not only to what God has done for them but also to the love God has for them. They strive to provide for them a distant,

---

62. Hector, *Christianity as a Way of Life*, 176.

creaturely echo of what God's love in Christ looks like. Hector states, "If I love God, . . . I will want to love those whom God loves, such that my love for them can be an expression of my love for God."[63]

It is worth noting that proclaiming the church's task as one of bearing witness to the good news of the gospel through the extension, preservation, and cultivation of temporal goods does not mean that the world will hold the church in high esteem. Broadly, the followers of Christ are promised that they too will be hated by the world, just as their Lord was before them (John 15:18, 20). There may be times when subsets of the world or peoples of the world look favorably on the church for the burdens that it bears as a testimony to the gospel. The unbelieving, runaway slave may indeed be grateful to the AME pastor who hid them and the Christian who fed them. This is well and good. But in the extension, preservation, and cultivation of temporal goods, the church is ultimately pointing to a greater good—*the* greater good—as the necessary and sufficient condition for human happiness. Insofar as it does this, the church confronts the world with its Lord and the claims and judgments this Lord sees fit to render. There is in a sense a Good hidden behind the goods we extend, preserve, and cultivate, "the greater communication offered us by God with himself and with one another."[64]

Creative Improvisation in Changing Times

Changing Times

I have argued that it is within and from the devastation—that is, this post-lapsum world of suffering, futility, and decay—that evangelical public witness bears witness to the world as it is. Yet I have also argued that the world as it is, in bondage to decay, is not the whole of the story. Rather, the Christian inhabits this place in hope and with freedom, bearing witness to the resurrection of Christ through the extension, preservation, and cultivation of temporal goods. Freedom describes not merely a release from bondage to sin, death, the law, and Satan but also a freedom to serve the other in love.

---

63. Hector, *Christianity as a Way of Life*, 206. Earlier, Hector writes, "The idea here . . . is that when we love people, we become invested in them to such an extent that their well-being is included in our own well-being" (Hector, *Christianity as a Way of Life*, 71). He refers to this as the "transitive property of love" and goes on to note that this parallel applies to the relationship between humanity and God as well. "If God loves people and is therefore invested in them to such an extent that their well-being is included in God's own, then it follows that if we do something good (or bad) for them, we are likewise doing something good (or bad) for God" (71).

64. O'Donovan, *Entering into Rest*, 51.

Here, we must return again to our ancestors from the abolitionary era: Ruggles, Stewart, and Still. It is worth noting that in addition to their evangelical ethos there is a consistent dependence in each of these figures on a particular form of life that is commonly referred to as the "voluntary society."[65] This was a reconstitution of civic life, one that occurred in the early years of the nation, when a clear distinction was created between the spheres of the church and the state. Whereas much of life in the colonial era centered on the parish, this changed after the formation of the United States and the resultant separation of church and state. From that point on, if societal ills were to be programmatically addressed, this would need to happen through like-minded individuals coming together to form a common cause. A plethora of benevolence societies sprang up throughout the United States, addressing issues such as alcoholism (e.g., the American Temperance Society, which was formed in 1826) and the proliferation of orphans (e.g., the Orphan Society of Philadelphia, which was formed in 1814). It must be noted that these are broad, sweeping generalizations. Still, the organizations we discussed in the previous chapters, ranging from the American Colonization Society to the Anti-Slavery Society, were not sponsored or supported by the state. Instead, they depended on the raising of funds and the voluntary participation of fellow community members in the pursuit of a common cause. Yet it was not only that these societies provided a means of addressing societal ills. They also performed an important social function. As Mary Ryan observes, "Much of community life seemed organized around these associations."[66] In the decades leading up to the Civil War, many Americans found themselves actively participating in the plethora of Bible, tract, missionary, temperance, and benevolent societies that littered the American landscape.[67]

Ted Smith, in his work on theological education, refers to this organization of civic life as a particular form of the "social imaginary," one that is passing away in our current day and age.[68] The term "social imaginary" refers to the way large groups of ordinary people imagine their social settings and surroundings, as carried along in stories, images, and legends.[69] It is a common way of seeing and being in the world that "makes possible common

---

65. Noting that definitions for this society vary, Don Doyle identifies three primary characteristics of voluntary associations. They are (1) "formally organized social groups" that are (2) "formed to serve specified goals" and that are upheld by means of (3) voluntary forms of organization and inclusion. Doyle, "Social Functions of Voluntary Associations," 333.

66. M. Ryan, *Cradle of the Middle Class*, 105.

67. Blumin, *Emergence of the Middle Class*, 192.

68. T. Smith, *End of Theological Education*, 29. This language is, notably, borrowed from Charles Taylor. See Taylor, *Modern Social Imaginaries*, 3–23.

69. Taylor, *Modern Social Imaginaries*, 23.

practices."[70] Smith argues that we live in a time of transition, a time of the "unraveling" of the predominant social imaginary that has animated American public life (i.e., the voluntary associations). Whereas in the past Americans broadly viewed participation in ecclesial, communal life or voluntary associations as a means of identity and agency, this no longer seems to be the case.[71] In the present era, Smith argues, "the consolidations of the age of voluntary associations are coming undone. Space is opening between the institutions, individuals, and ideals woven so tightly together."[72] For Smith, this means that the voluntary societies are being stripped of much of their social significance. And if that is the case, and I suspect that Smith may be right on this score, then we might see the voluntary societies of yesteryear cease to be the primary means through which the church might engage in public space. We may need to retrieve the spirit and aspirations of our ancestors while recognizing that the means they used no longer prove viable.

While the focus of Smith's book is theological education, his remarks about the current unraveling of our social imaginary are helpful and necessary when attempting to retrieve the insights of our abolitionary friends. Still's work in large part depended on donations and allegiance to the Anti-Slavery Society of Philadelphia. The same holds true for Ruggles's Committee of Vigilance and Stewart's involvement in urban education in Washington, DC. Our abolitionary friends' appropriation and utilization of these voluntary societies made the Underground Railroad and its attendant forms of resistance possible. If the age in which we exist is indeed undergoing transition, we would do well to think of the means we have used in the past for extending temporal goods and to consider creative, improvisational ways of doing so in new circumstances and settings.

Creative Improvisation

If the time in which we exist is indeed one of futility and decay, a present age of suffering, and if the social forms we create and construct as well as the social imaginary that accompanies them are continually and presently unraveling, how do we determine the concrete shape that the church's public witness should take in the present? Here, we might again return to the work of William Still. Recall in chapter 4 how Still attempted to preserve the memory of freedom seekers so as to inspire his readers to continue their legacy and

---

70. Taylor, *Modern Social Imaginaries*, 23.
71. Smith is reticent to identify this as a narrative of decline. See T. Smith, *End of Theological Education*, 23.
72. T. Smith, *End of Theological Education*, 97.

their cause in the face of whatever obstacles they encountered. Still writes as much in the preface to his 1872 *The Underground Railroad*, where he states that his goal is "to show what efforts were made and what success was gained for Freedom under difficulties."[73] For Still, portraying the saintly and heroic character of the individuals who sought to realize their desire for freedom is imperative for their descendants, who must carry on their legacy. The past is a resource, an inspiration that motivates us to remember the kind of people we have been so that we might be inspired to address the needs of the present. According to Still, "Free colored men are as imperatively required now to furnish the same manly testimony in support of the ability of the race to surmount the remaining obstacles growing out of oppression, ignorance, and poverty."[74]

Needless to say, the transformation of one form of life into another does not delimit or invalidate the Christian's summons to bear witness to all that God has done in Christ through the work of bearing the other's burdens and seeking their good. It merely calls for a continual process of creative improvisation and a renewal of the church's imagination for how to act meaningfully and faithfully in the present. In short, the director has made clear where the play is headed, and now his cast is called to act on the world stage.

Earlier, in chapter 1, I referred to Afro-American resistance to fugitive slave laws, kidnappers, and the American Colonization Society as forms of improvisation, borrowing language from Samuel Wells. For Wells, the redemptive story is a five-act play consisting of creation (act 1), Israel (act 2), Jesus (act 3), the church (act 4), and the eschaton (act 5).[75] The Christian community currently inhabits act 4, awaiting the dramatic resolution that God himself will bring about.[76] Clothed in the power of the Spirit and gifted with practices for sustaining its life, the church is called to follow Christ in the present. To do so, creative improvisation is necessary because the church inevitably encounters new situations and contexts. To my knowledge, there is no explicit teaching within Holy Writ on how to deal with issues like chattel slavery, redlining, artificial intelligence, or whether to install air conditioners in Texas prisons and at whose cost. But this does not mean there is no guidance from the Spirit regarding how the church might navigate these issues. Rather, its navigation will have to be an improvisation that is governed by the good news of what God has done in Christ, an improvisation that must cohere and be congruent with the story of redemption thus far and the final act of God's reconciliation of the

73. Still, *Underground Railroad* (1872), 5–6.
74. Still, preface to *Still's Underground Railroad Records* (1886).
75. S. Wells, *Improvisation*, 53.
76. S. Wells, *Improvisation*, 55.

cosmos. The gospel both liberates and constrains the church's improvisational witness. Wells writes, "When improvisers are trained to work in the theater, they are schooled in a tradition so thoroughly that they learn to act from habit in ways appropriate to the circumstance. This is exactly the goal of theological ethics."[77] According to Wells, the church's task is not to be original, clever, or witty but to apprentice itself in the school of Christ so that it might form the requisite habits for navigating the present faithfully.[78] Here again it is worth stressing the importance of becoming the kind of people who can do this well. In short, Christians must cultivate the requisite virtues that will enable them to carry out this task, virtues that will enable them to feel and follow the "hermeneutical pressure" of the script in a way that is faithful to the preceding acts.[79]

For our purposes, we might say that improvisational witness is bound to the gospel and its God. Christians are free to act in the world in endlessly creative and imaginative ways that attest to the reign of God in Christ. If we learn anything from our abolitionary friends, it is that in dealing with the world as it is, we are given the opportunity to take the "raw materials" of the spatiotemporal contexts in which we find ourselves and leverage them in pursuit of the good of others. Smith refers to these materials as "affordances," which he defines as "concrete, historically contingent, morally ambivalent forms that can make possible a range of actions."[80] As Smith goes on to note, "To see something as an affordance, then, does not require seeing it as good or useful. It simply involves seeing it in the light of redemption."[81] For figures like Ruggles, Stewart, and Still, the free press and the voluntary societies of the nineteenth century were affordances that they creatively appropriated in their fight against slavery. But if Smith is right that we inhabit a time of unraveling, then we must avoid repristinating the forms their witness took. Indeed, the church will have to continue to think creatively about what raw materials are at its disposal and how it might appropriate them wisely, creatively, and humbly as it seeks to follow in the footsteps of its Lord.

Conclusion

The Christian community is a community that is "of the gospel" in its very bones. While it cannot complete, perpetuate, or extend the work of Christ,

---

77. S. Wells, *Improvisation*, 65.
78. S. Wells, *Improvisation*, 213.
79. Here I am borrowing language from Rowe, "Biblical Pressure and Trinitarian Hermeneutics."
80. T. Smith, *End of Theological Education*, 169.
81. T. Smith, *End of Theological Education*, 170.

the church is sent forth into the world to "be [Christ's] witnesses" (Acts 1:8). In this chapter and the previous one, I argued that this act of witnessing requires determining particular points on the redemptive plotline—namely, where we are, where the whole creation is headed, and what God has done and is doing in Christ. Because the present age is characterized by suffering and is bound to futility and decay, the Christian community's task here and now is to speak the truth about the world as it is. But the church inhabits the time of the devastation in hope, a hope that is rooted in the promises of God and what this God will do. And it is a hope that moves the church to act— that is, Christian hope engenders Christian action in the present. It enables the Christian community to be and act in endlessly creative ways that attest to the work of God in Christ, the one who has surely carried our afflictions, sorrows, and, yes, burdens (Isa. 53:4).

In this chapter, I have attempted to extend the logic of this injunction to the pursuit of the common good(s) through the extension, preservation, and cultivation of temporal goods. While this is not the only way the church bears witness to the gospel of God—indeed, the church's proclamation, sacramental life, and ordinances all point to the God who calls this community into being—the extension, preservation, and cultivation of temporal goods for the sake of the world is an essential element of the church's *public* witness. And insofar as the church does this, it serves the state by reminding it of its limits, of its needs, and of its own inability to transform the present age of suffering into a utopian ideal.[82]

82. Barth, "Church and State," 136.

Conclusion

Remembering the Dead

Over the course of the past few years, it has become commonplace to criticize and decry the state of the evangelical community, lamenting its support of particular political candidates or its failure to advocate on behalf of the marginalized. This has been all the more the case since the rise of the religious right and the progression of the internet age. But irrespective of how we might view the present moment and those evangelicals who live within it, the burden of this book has been to retrieve voices from the past to construct an evangelical account of bearing witness to God's work in Christ in our common life. Figures such as David Ruggles, Maria W. Stewart, and William Still should have a voice in determining what this community has been and, more to the point, what this community can be, particularly in relation to the life we share with others. Yet it is important to notice that another argument in this book has been that Ruggles, Stewart, and Still are not merely *my* ancestors; they are *our* ancestors. As no less than Karl Barth has put it, "In order to serve the community of today, theology itself must be rooted in the community of yesterday."[1] And this community includes the Stewarts and Stills of the nineteenth century just as much as it includes the Edwards and Whitefields of the eighteenth century. Or so I have argued. To better bear witness to God's work in Christ today, we must root ourselves in and learn from them how to improvise on the logics of the gospel in a way that is faithful to what God has done and is doing in Christ.

1. Barth, *Evangelical Theology*, 42.

The Work Thus Far

After examining the historical context in which the three abolitionary figures operated (chap. 1), we turned our attention to David Ruggles (chap. 2). The famed abolitionist and founder of the New York Committee of Vigilance provides us with resources for reading the world at large and reimagining social agency. According to Ruggles, we might see something of the vicious, and perhaps virtuous, nature of a given social structure by considering how it shapes human participants in accordance with the law of God. His analysis focuses primarily on the church, since it is an institution called to mirror God's ways to the world, and how participation in chattel slavery led to the compromise of the church's Christian witness. From Ruggles, we also see that figures on the margins, such as women in the nineteenth century, freeborn blacks, and runaway slaves, possess the capacity for communal agency, contribute their resources, and employ ecclesial practices for the sake of social change.

In chapter 3, we turned to the work and speeches of Maria W. Stewart, focusing predominantly on her career in Boston. Although her public-speaking career was short-lived, Stewart's fiery speeches display an urgency to read the world in light of divine revelation and the impending judgment of God on our wicked ways of living in the world. Similar to Ruggles, she calls for us to appropriate the goods of the present in order to create new institutions and reform old ones as we seek a better life for our community members. Stewart also encourages us to view the cultivation of communities of character as a means for social and political engagement.

In chapter 4, we canvased the thought of William Still. Born to a fugitive slave, Still is referred to as the father of the Underground Railroad for good reason, helping almost a thousand slaves pass through the city of Philadelphia. From Still, we learned that we must remember our saints, our heroes, so that we might emulate their character and carry on their legacy. Moreover, Still reminds us that we need to preserve and renew certain institutions, even if they are bound up with the minutia of life in the saeculum. Things like familial relations, communities, memories, and so on can be viewed as necessary for "carrying on" in the world and enabling us to act well in the immediate future, even while we look forward in hope for the new city to come (Heb. 11:16).

Having articulated key insights from Ruggles, Stewart, and Still, I then made a series of constructive arguments in this book's final two chapters on the shape of the church's public witness. Grounding the possibility for the church's life in the missions of the Son and the Spirit *ad extra*, I argued that the church's public witness takes two vectors. First, the church is called to speak truthfully about the world as it is: a present time of suffering, futility, and decay that stands in need of renewal. Of course, to say that the present age is one of suffering is not to exclude the world as it is from the love of God. Quite the contrary, it is this world, this present world, that God loves and into which he sent the beloved Son. Yet the church's task in this world is to bear witness to the world as it is, groaning and hoping for its ultimate redemption and transformation.

The second vector that public witness takes is bearing witness to what God has done in Christ through carrying the world's burdens. This is one of the good gifts the church seeks to share with the world, albeit in a way that does not deny the world's need for eschatological transformation or try to "save" the world from its present suffering. The shape of this burden bearing takes the form of extending, preserving, and cultivating temporal goods to meet temporal needs. Again, it is worth repeating that the church must ever resist the temptation of triumphalism. We cannot convert the present age into the fullness of the kingdom. Only God himself can do that. And he will. Our task in the meantime is to bear witness in the life we (the church) share with others to what God has done and will do in Christ.

Learning to Live and Die Well

Frederick Douglass, lamenting the death of David Ruggles, writes, "The memory of the just will live, and thousands who have escaped the yoke of slavery by his aid (we among the number) will never cease to remember this faithful friend of the slave, and lover of mankind."[2] The same might have been written of William Still or Maria Stewart, both of whom were friends of the fugitive, lovers of humanity, and willing to risk their lives in defense of the downtrodden. And to some degree, this project has been an attempt to honor Douglass's wish, to keep the memory of these abolitionary figures alive and to assert their value for an evangelical account of public witness. Our ancestors have a great deal to teach us about how to live in times of crisis, about how to live and die well as we seek the good of our neighbors. If the evangelical community, however nebulously defined, is in a crisis of definition, as is almost perennially the case, the dead should have a vote on the kind of community we will be and become. In the foregoing chapters, I sought to exposit and extend the insights of some of our faithful dead. In so doing, I argued that the Christian community, liberated from the laws of consumption and self-preservation, is set free to pursue the interests, goods, and well-being of its neighbors as a witness to the resurrection of Jesus Christ from the dead,

2. Douglass, "David Ruggles."

lamenting the world's suffering and joyously bearing the world's burdens in fulfillment of the law of Christ. And I suppose, if the church takes up its cross and follows its Savior on the road to Golgotha, it will be a church that mirrors the distant, creaturely echo of the love of God in Christ found in the lives of William Still, Maria Stewart, and David Ruggles. It will be a church that finds in them a testimony worth preserving, even if it costs its power, privilege, and prestige, even if it forces it to loosen its grip on the halls of legislative and political power.

Accordingly, the church might love and serve the world in general and the communities in which individual churches exist in particular, knowing that together they share a common life. The church might give this love freely, having received freely and without cost from its Lord. The life we share with our neighbors is a gift from God that the church has not earned and does not deserve. The church does not choose its neighbors, nor does it choose its mission. It accepts both as a gift from the Lord of life. Irrespective of its neighbors' immigration status, religion, incarceration record, political affiliation, and so on, the church is called to bear witness to the resurrection of Christ through lifting up its neighbors' laments and bearing its neighbors' burdens. And if the world hates the church, as it is wont to do on more than one occasion, a church set free by the gospel of God can still go forth in its service, knowing that it is following in the footsteps of its ancestors and holding fast to the promises of its Lord, its North Star and Drinking Gourd, whom the world hated first (John 15:18–20). And I suppose there may in fact be worse ways to spend a life.

Works Cited

Achebe, Chinua. *Things Fall Apart*. New York: Anchor Books, 1994.

Adams, Robert Merrihew. *Finite and Infinite Goods: A Framework for Ethics*. Oxford: Oxford University Press, 1999.

Allen, Richard. "Letter from Bishop Allen." *Freedom's Journal* 1, no. 34 (November 2, 1827): 134.

The American Freedman's Aid Commission. African American Pamphlet Collection (Library of Congress). New York: n.p., 1865. https://www.loc.gov/item/12003486/.

Anizor, Uche, Rob Price, and Hank Voss. *Evangelical Theology*. Doing Theology. London: T&T Clark, 2021.

Bailey, Henry. "Letter from Henry Bailey." In Richardson, *Maria W. Stewart*, 96–97.

Bambara, Toni Cade. *The Salt Eaters*. New York: Penguin Random House, 1980.

Bantum, Brian. *Redeeming Mulatto: A Theology of Race and Christian Hybridity*. Waco: Baylor University Press, 2010.

Barclay, John. *Paul and the Gift*. Grand Rapids: Eerdmans, 2015.

Barth, Karl. "Church and State." In *Community, State, and Church: Three Essays*. Eugene, OR: Wipf & Stock, 2004.

———. *Church Dogmatics*. Vol. IV/3, edited by G. W. Bromley and T. F. Torrance. Edinburgh: T&T Clark, 1962.

———. *The Epistle to the Romans*. Translated by Edwyn C. Hoskyns. 6th ed. Oxford: Oxford University Press, 1968.

———. *Evangelical Theology: An Introduction*. Grand Rapids: Eerdmans, 1979.

Bavinck, Herman. *God and Creation*. Vol. 2 of *Reformed Dogmatics*. Edited by John Bolt. Translated by John Vriend. Grand Rapids: Baker Academic, 2004.

———. *Sin and Salvation in Christ*. Vol. 3 of *Reformed Dogmatics*. Edited by John Bolt. Translated by John Vriend. Grand Rapids: Baker Academic, 2006.

Bebbington, David W. *Evangelicalism in Modern Britain: A History from the 1730s to the 1980s.* London: Routledge, 1989.

Bell, Richard. "Counterfeit Kin: Kidnappers of Color, the Reverse Underground Railroad, and the Origins of Practical Abolition." *Journal of the Early Republic* 38, no. 2 (Summer 2018): 199–230.

———. "'Thence to Patty Cannon's': Gender, Family, and the Reverse Underground Railroad." *Slavery and Abolition* 37, no. 1 (2016): 661–79.

Benac, Dustin D. *Adaptive Church: Collaboration and Community in a Changing World.* Waco: Baylor University Press, 2022.

Bender, Kimlyn J. "The American Experience of a Darkening and Receding Providence: The Civil War and the Unmaking of an American Religious Synthesis." In *Reflections on Reformational Theology: Studies in the Theology of the Reformation, Karl Barth, and the Evangelical Tradition,* 263–80. London: Bloomsbury, 2021.

Black, Alex W. "'A New Enterprise in Our History': William Still, Conductor of the Underground Rail Road (1872)." *American Literary History* 32, no. 4 (2020): 668–90.

Blackburn, Robin. "Haiti, Slavery, and the Age of the Democratic Revolution." *William and Mary Quarterly* 63, no. 4 (2006): 643–74.

Blackett, R. J. M. *The Captive's Quest for Freedom: Fugitive Slaves, the 1850 Fugitive Slave Law, and the Politics of Slavery.* Cambridge: Cambridge University Press, 2018.

———. "The Underground Railroad and the Struggle against Slavery." *History Workshop Journal* 78, no. 1 (2014): 274–86.

Blumin, Stuart M. *The Emergence of the Middle Class: Social Experience in the American City, 1760–1900.* Cambridge: Cambridge University Press, 1989.

Bonhoeffer, Dietrich. *Ethics.* Edited by Victoria J. Barnett. Translated by Reinhard Krauss, Charles C. West, and Thomas H. West. Minneapolis: Fortress, 2015.

Bordewich, Fergus M. *Bound for Canaan: The Underground Railroad and the War for the Soul of America.* New York: Amistad, 2005.

Boring, M. Eugene. *Mark: A Commentary.* New Testament Library. Louisville: Westminster John Knox, 2012.

Bowens, Lisa M. *African American Readings of Paul: Reception, Resistance, and Transformation.* Grand Rapids: Eerdmans, 2020.

Braaten, Laurie J. "All Creation Groans: Romans 8:22 in Light of the Biblical Sources." *Horizons in Biblical Theology* 28 (2006): 131–59.

Bretherton, Luke. *Christ and the Common Life: Political Theology and the Case for Democracy.* Grand Rapids: Eerdmans, 2019.

Briggs, Richard S. "The Bible before Us: Evangelical Possibilities for Taking Scripture Seriously." In *New Perspectives for Evangelical Theology: Engaging with God, Scripture, and the World,* edited by Tom Greggs, 14–28. Oxford: Routledge, 2010.

Brown, David, and Clive Webb. *Race in the American South: From Slavery to Civil Rights*. Edinburgh: Edinburgh University Press, 2007.

Brown, Isaac V. *Biography of the Reverend Robert Finley, D. D., of Basking Ridge, N.J.* 2nd ed. Philadelphia: John W. Moore, 1857.

Bruce, F. F. *The Epistle to the Galatians: A Commentary on the Greek Text*. New International Greek Testament Commentary. Grand Rapids: Eerdmans, 1982.

Bryant, Robert A. *The Risen Crucified Christ in Galatians*. SBL Dissertation Series. Atlanta: Society of Biblical Literature, 2001.

Burin, Eric. *Slavery and the Peculiar Solution: A History of the American Colonization Society*. Gainesville: University Press of Florida, 2005.

Burroughs, Presian Renee. *Creation's Slavery and Liberation: Paul's Letter to Rome in the Face of Imperial and Industrial Agriculture*. Cascade Library of Pauline Studies. Eugene, OR: Cascade Books, 2022.

Burton, Ernest De Witt. *A Critical and Exegetical Commentary on the Epistle to the Galatians*. International Critical Commentary. New York: Scribner's Sons, 1920.

Butner, D. Glenn, Jr. *Trinitarian Dogmatics: Exploring the Grammar of the Christian Doctrine of God*. Grand Rapids: Baker Academic, 2022.

Campbell, D. Keith. "NT Scholars' Use of OT Lament Terminology and Its Theological and Interdisciplinary Implications." *Bulletin for Biblical Research* 21, nos. 1–4 (2011): 213–25.

Campbell, William S. *Romans: A Social Identity Commentary*. London: Bloomsbury, 2023.

Carwardine, Richard J. "Antebellum Reform." In *Turning Points in the History of American Evangelicalism*, edited by Heath W. Carter and Laura Rominger Porter, 65–83. Grand Rapids: Eerdmans, 2017.

———. *Evangelicals and Politics in Antebellum America*. Knoxville: University of Tennessee Press, 1997.

Castelo, Daniel. *The Apathetic God: Exploring Contemporary Relevance of Divine Impassibility*. Eugene, OR: Wipf & Stock, 2009.

Chesterton, G. K. *Orthodoxy*. New York: John Lane Company, 1909.

Coker, Daniel. "A Dialogue between a Virginian and an African Minister." In Newman, Rael, and Lapsansky, *Pamphlets of Protest*, 52–65.

Cooper, Valerie C. *Word, Like Fire: Maria Stewart, the Bible and the Rights of African Americans*. Charlottesville: University of Virginia Press, 2011.

Couenhoven, Jesse. *Stricken by Sin, Cured by Christ: Agency, Necessity, and Culpability in Augustinian Theology*. Oxford: Oxford University Press, 2013.

Council, Ashley. "Ringing Liberty's Bell: African American Women, Gender, and the Underground Railroad in Philadelphia." *Pennsylvania History: A Journal of Mid-Atlantic Studies* 87, no. 3 (Summer 2020): 494–531.

Cranfield, C. E. B. *A Critical and Exegetical Commentary on the Epistle to the Romans*. Vol. 1. International Critical Commentary. New York: T&T Clark International, 2004.

Daly, Daniel J. "Structures of Virtue and Vice." *New Blackfriars* 92, no. 1039 (2011): 341–57.

Davis, David Brion. *Challenging the Boundaries of Slavery*. Cambridge, MA: Harvard University Press, 2006.

———. *Inhuman Bondage: The Rise and Fall of Slavery in the New World*. Oxford: Oxford University Press, 2006.

de Boer, Martinus C. *Galatians: A Commentary*. New Testament Library. Louisville: Westminster John Knox, 2013.

deSilva, David A. *The Letter to the Galatians*. New International Commentary on the New Testament. Grand Rapids: Eerdmans, 2018.

Deyle, Steven. *Carry Me Back: The Domestic Slave Trade in American Life*. Oxford: Oxford University Press, 2005.

Diemer, Andrew K. "The Business of the Road: William Still, the Vigilance Committee, and the Management of the Underground Railroad." *Journal of the Early Republic* 42 (Spring 2022): 83–113.

———. *Vigilance: The Life of William Still, Father of the Underground Railroad*. New York: Knopf, 2022.

Douglass, Frederick. "David Ruggles." *The North Star* (Rochester, NY) 3, no. 6, February 1, 1850.

———. *My Bondage and My Freedom*. New Haven: Yale University Press, 2014.

———. *Narrative of the Life of Frederick Douglass: An American Slave, Written by Himself*. John Harvard Library. Cambridge, MA: Belknap, 2009.

———. "Speech at Rochester, July 5, 1852." In Woodson, *Negro Orators and Their Orations*, 185–208.

Doyle, Don H. "The Social Functions of Voluntary Associations in a Nineteenth-Century American Town." *Social Science History* 1, no. 3 (1977): 333–55.

Drescher, Seymour. "Whose Abolition? Popular Pressure and the Ending of the British Slave Trade." *Past and Present* 143 (1994): 136–66.

Dunn, James D. G. *The Epistle to the Galatians*. Black's New Testament Commentary. London: Continuum, 1993.

Ellison, Ralph. "What America Would Be Like without Blacks." In *The Collected Essays of Ralph Ellison*, edited by John F. Callahan, 581–88. Modern Library. New York: Modern Library, 2003.

Ericson, David F. "The American Colonization Society's Not-So-Private Colonization Project." In *New Directions in the Study of African American Recolonization*, edited by Beverly Tomek and Matthew J. Hetrick, 111–28. Gainesville: University Press of Florida, 2017.

————. "Slave Smugglers, Slave Catchers, and Slave Rebels: Slavery and American State Development, 1787–1842." In Hammond and Mason, *Contesting Slavery*, 183–206.

"Examination of the Black Man, Ruggles." *Morning Herald* (New York) 4, no. 101, September 10, 1838.

Fee, Gordon D. *God's Empowering Presence: The Holy Spirit in the Letters of Paul.* Grand Rapids: Baker Academic, 2011.

Fewster, Gregory P. *Creation Language in Romans 8: A Study in Monosemy.* Linguistic Biblical Studies 8. Leiden: Brill, 2013.

Finn, Daniel K. "What Is a Sinful Social Structure?" *Theological Studies* 77, no. 1 (2016): 136–64.

Forten, James. "Series of Letters by a Man of Colour." In Newman, Rael, and Lapsansky, *Pamphlets of Protest*, 66–73.

Gara, Larry. *The Liberty Line: The Legend of the Underground Railroad.* Lexington: University Press of Kentucky, 1961.

————. "William Still and the Underground Railroad." *Pennsylvania History: A Journal of Mid-Atlantic Studies* 28, no. 1 (1961): 33–44.

Gardner, Eric. "Introduction." *Publications of the Modern Language Association* 123, no. 1 (2008): 156–58.

Garnet, Henry Highland. "An Address to the Slaves of the United States of America." In Woodson, *Negro Orators and Their Orations*, 142–49.

Garrison, William Lloyd. "Thomas Paine." *The Liberator* 15, no. 46 (November 21, 1845): 186.

Garrison, William Lloyd, and Isaac Knapp. "Death of David Ruggles." *The Liberator* 19, no. 51 (December 21, 1849): 202.

————. "Meeting for David Ruggles." *The Liberator* 14, no. 35 (August 30, 1844): 139.

Gilroy, Paul. *The Black Atlantic: Modernity and Double Consciousness.* London: Verso, 1993.

Goldman, Alvin. *Joint Ventures: Mind-Reading, Mirroring, and Embodied Cognition.* Oxford: Oxford University Press, 2013.

González, Justo L. *Mañana: Christian Theology from a Hispanic Perspective.* Nashville: Abingdon, 1990.

————. *The Mestizo Augustine: A Theologian between Two Cultures.* Downers Grove, IL: IVP Academic, 2016.

Goodman, Paul. *Of One Blood: Abolitionism and the Origins of Racial Equality.* Berkeley: University of California Press, 1998.

"A Good Movement." *Weekly Anglo-African* 2, no. 36 (March 23, 1861).

Goring, Darlene C. "The History of Slave Marriage in the United States." *John Marshall Law Review* 39, no. 2 (2006): 299–347.

Gorringe, Timothy. *The Common Good and the Global Emergency: God and the Built Environment*. Cambridge: Cambridge University Press, 2011.

Greene-McCreight, Kathryn. *Galatians*. Brazos Theological Commentary on the Bible. Grand Rapids: Brazos, 2023.

Greggs, Tom. *The Priestly Catholicity of the Church*. Vol. 1 of *Dogmatic Ecclesiology*. Grand Rapids: Baker Academic, 2019.

Gregory, Eric. *Politics and the Order of Love: An Augustinian Ethic of Democratic Citizenship*. Chicago: University of Chicago Press, 2010.

Grenz, Stanley J. *Renewing the Center: Evangelical Theology in a Post-Theological Era*. Grand Rapids: Baker Academic, 2000.

Griffiths, Paul. *Decreation: The Last Things of All Creatures*. Waco: Baylor University Press, 2016.

H., Z. W. "David Ruggles." *North Star* (Rochester, NY) 3, no. 7, February 1, 1850.

Hahn, Steven. *The Political Worlds of Slavery and Freedom*. Cambridge, MA: Harvard University Press, 2009.

Hall, Prince. "A Charge." In Newman, Rael, and Lapsansky, *Pamphlets of Protest*, 44–51.

Hamilton, William. "Address to the National Convention of 1834." In Newman, Rael, and Lapsansky, *Pamphlets of Protest*, 110–13.

Hammond, John Craig, and Matthew Mason, eds. *Contesting Slavery: The Politics of Bondage and Freedom in the New American Nation*. Charlottesville: University of Virginia Press, 2011.

Harris, Leon. "The Holy Spirit as Liberator: An Exploration of a Black American Pneumatology of Freedom." In *The Third Person of the Trinity*, edited by Oliver D. Crisp and Fred Sanders, 179–95. Explorations in Constructive Dogmatics. Grand Rapids: Zondervan, 2020.

Harris, Leslie M. *In the Shadow of Slavery: African Americans in New York City, 1626–1863*. Historical Studies of Urban America. Chicago: University of Chicago Press, 2003.

Harrold, Stanley. *The Abolitionists and the South, 1831–1861*. Lexington: University Press of Kentucky, 1995.

Hauerwas, Stanley. *Approaching the End: Eschatological Reflections on Church, Politics, and Life*. Grand Rapids: Eerdmans, 2013.

———. *Christian Existence Today: Essays on Church, World, and Living in Between*. Grand Rapids: Eerdmans, 1988.

———. "How to Tell Time Theologically." In *The Work of Theology*, 90–102. Grand Rapids: Eerdmans, 2015.

Hayes, Christine. *What's Divine about Divine Law? Early Perspectives*. Princeton: Princeton University Press, 2015.

Hays, Richard B. *The Faith of Jesus Christ: The Narrative Substructure of Galatians 3:1–4:11.* 2nd ed. Biblical Resource Series. Grand Rapids: Eerdmans, 2002.

Hector, Kevin W. *Christianity as a Way of Life: A Systematic Theology.* New Haven: Yale University Press, 2023.

Hill, Daniel Lee. "Bound Together in the Holy Fire: The Holiness of the Church and Ecclesial Sin." In *Confessing the Church*, edited by Oliver D. Crisp and Fred Sanders, 183–98. Explorations in Constructive Dogmatics. Grand Rapids: Zondervan Academic, 2024.

———. *Gathered on the Road to Zion: Toward a Free Church Ecclesio-Anthropology.* Eugene, OR: Pickwick, 2021.

Hill, Daniel Lee, and Ty Kieser. "Social Sin and the Sinless Savior: Delineating Supra-Personal Sin in Continuity with Conciliar Christology." *Modern Theology* 38, no. 3 (2022): 568–91.

Hodges, Graham Russell Gao. *David Ruggles: A Radical Black Abolitionist and the Underground Railroad in New York City.* John Hope Franklin Series in African American History and Culture. Chapel Hill: University of North Carolina Press, 2010.

———. *Root and Branch: African Americans in New York and East Jersey, 1613–1863.* Chapel Hill: University of North Carolina Press, 1999.

Homewood Children's Village. 2020. "Annual Report 2019–2020." Accessed July 7, 2024. https://hcvpgh.org/impact/.

Homewood Children's Village. 2021. "Impact Report 2020–2021." Accessed July 7, 2024. https://hcvpgh.org/impact/.

Hultgren, Arland J. *Paul's Letter to the Romans.* Grand Rapids: Eerdmans, 2011.

Hunsinger, George. "Barth and Tolkien." In *The Wiley Blackwell Companion to Karl Barth*, edited by George Hunsinger and Keith L. Johnson, 693–700. Vol. 2. Hoboken, NJ: Wiley & Sons, 2000.

Hutchinson, Mark, and John Wolffe. *A Short History of Global Evangelicalism.* Cambridge: Cambridge University Press, 2012.

Jasanoff, Maya. *Liberty's Exiles: American Loyalists in the Revolutionary World.* New York: Knopf, 2011.

Jefferson, Thomas. *Notes on the State of Virginia: An Annotated Edition.* New Haven: Yale University Press, 2022.

Jefferson, William B. "Letter from William B. Jefferson." In Richardson, *Maria W. Stewart*, 95.

Jenson, Matt. *Theology in the Democracy of the Dead: A Dialogue with the Living Tradition.* Grand Rapids: Baker Academic, 2019.

Jewett, Robert. *Paul's Anthropological Terms: A Study of Their Use in Conflict Settings.* Leiden: Brill, 1971.

———. *Romans: A Commentary*. Vol. 1. Edited by Eldon Jay Epp. Hermeneia. Minneapolis: Fortress, 2006.

Johnson, Adam J. *Atonement: A Guide for the Perplexed*. Guides for the Perplexed. London: Bloomsbury T&T Clark, 2015.

Johnson, Kristen Deede. *Theology, Political Theory, and Pluralism*. Cambridge Studies in Christian Doctrine. Cambridge: Cambridge University Press, 2007.

Jones, Absalom. "The Petition of the People of Colour, Free Men, within the City and Suburbs of Philadelphia." In *Early Negro Writing, 1760–1837*, edited by Dorothy Porter, 330–32. Baltimore: Black Classics, 1995.

Jüngel, Eberhard. "Living Out Righteousness: God's Action—Human Agency." In *Theological Essays II*, 241–63. Translated by Arnold Neufeldt-Fast and J. B. Webster. London: T&T Clark, 2014.

Kalantzis, George. *Caesar and the Lamb: Early Christian Attitudes on War and Military Service*. Eugene, OR: Cascade Books, 2012.

Kant, Immanuel. "*Menschenkunde* [1781–82?]." In *Lectures on Anthropology*, edited by Robert B. Louden and Allen W. Wood, 281–334. Translated by Robert B. Louden. Cambridge Edition of the Works of Immanuel Kant. Cambridge: Cambridge University Press, 2012.

Kashatus, William C. *William Still: The Underground Railroad and the Angel at Philadelphia*. Notre Dame, IN: University of Notre Dame Press, 2021.

Kearney, Melissa S., and Phillip B. Levine. "The Economics of Nonmarital Childbearing and the Marriage Premium for Children." *Annual Review of Economics* 9 (2017): 327–52.

Keener, Craig S. *Galatians: A Commentary*. Grand Rapids: Baker Academic, 2019.

Kilby, Karen. "Negative Theology and Meaningless Suffering." *Modern Theology* 36, no. 1 (2020): 92–104.

———. "The Seductions of Kenosis." In *Suffering and the Christian Life*, edited by Karen Kilby and Rachel Davies, 163–74. London: T&T Clark, 2020.

Kim, Yoonjong. *The Divine-Human Relationship in Romans 1–8 in Light of Interdependence Theory*. Library of New Testament Studies 635. London: T&T Clark, 2020.

Kirkland, Frank M. "Enslavement, Moral Suasion, and Struggles for Recognition: Frederick Douglass's Answer to the Question—'What Is Enlightenment?'" In *Frederick Douglass Critical Reader*, edited by Bill E. Lawson and Frank M. Kirkland, 243–310. Malden, MA: Blackwell, 1999.

Knight, Franklin. "The Haitian Revolution." *American Historical Review* 105, no. 1 (2000): 103–15.

Kruse, Colin G. *Paul's Letter to the Romans*. Nottingham: Apollos, 2012.

LaRoche, Cheryl Janifer. *Free Black Communities and the Underground Railroad: The Geography of Resistance*. Urbana: University of Illinois Press, 2014.

Larsen, Timothy. "Defining and Locating Evangelicalism." In *The Cambridge Companion to Evangelical Theology*, edited by Timothy Larsen and Daniel J. Treier, 1–14. Cambridge: Cambridge University Press, 2007.

Lee, Hak Joon. *God and Community Organizing: A Covenantal Approach*. Waco: Baylor University Press, 2020.

Legates, Marlene. "The Cult of Womanhood in Eighteenth-Century Thought." *Eighteenth-Century Studies* 10, no. 1 (1976): 21–39.

Levine, Robert S. "Frederick Douglass, War, Haiti." *Publications of the Modern Language Association* 124, no. 5 (2009): 1864–68.

Longenecker, Richard N. *The Epistle to the Romans: A Commentary on the Greek Text*. New International Greek Testament Commentary. Grand Rapids: Eerdmans, 2016.

———. *Galatians*. Word Biblical Commentary 41. Grand Rapids: Zondervan, 1990.

Lührmann, Dieter. *A Continental Commentary: Galatians*. Minneapolis: Fortress, 1992.

Luskey, Brian P. *On the Make: Clerks and the Quest for Capital in Nineteenth-Century America*. New York: New York University Press, 2010.

———. "'What Is My Prospects?': The Contours of Mercantile Apprenticeship, Ambition, and Advancement in Early American Economy." *Business History Review* 78, no. 4 (2004): 665–702.

Luther, Martin. *The Freedom of the Christian*. Translated by Mark D. Tranvik. Luther Study Edition. Minneapolis: Fortress, 2008.

Lynch, James V. "The Limits of Revolutionary Radicalism: Tom Paine and Slavery." *Pennsylvania Magazine of History and Biography* 123, no. 3 (1999): 177–200.

Lynerd, Benjamin T., and Jack Wartell. "'A Natural Right to the Soil': Black Abolitionists and the Meaning of Freedom." *Journal of Black Studies* 54, no. 1 (2022): 62–82.

MacIntyre, Alasdair. *After Virtue: A Study of Moral Theory*. 3rd ed. Notre Dame, IN: University of Notre Dame Press, 2015.

Malcomson, Thomas. "Freedom by Reaching the Wooden World: American Slaves and the British Navy during the War of 1812." *Northern Mariner* 22, no. 4 (2012): 361–92.

Mason, Matthew. "Necessary but Not Sufficient: Revolutionary Ideology and Antislavery Action in the Early Republic." In Hammond and Mason, *Contesting Slavery*, 11–31.

———. *Slavery and Politics in the Early American Republic*. Chapel Hill: University of North Carolina Press, 2006.

Mathewes, Charles. *A Theology of Public Life*. Cambridge Studies in Christian Doctrine. Cambridge: Cambridge University Press, 2007.

McBride, Jennifer M. *The Church for the World: A Theology of Public Witness*. Oxford: Oxford University Press, 2012.

McCall, Thomas H. *Against God and Nature: The Doctrine of Sin*. Foundations of Evangelical Theology. Wheaton: Crossway, 2019.

Menschel, David. "Abolition without Deliverance: The Law of Connecticut Slavery 1784–1848." *Yale Law Journal* 111, no. 1 (2001): 183–222.

Messer, Neil G. "Human Flourishing: A Christian Theological Perspective." In *Measuring Well-Being: Interdisciplinary Perspectives from the Social Sciences and the Humanities*, edited by Matthew T. Lee, Laura D. Kubzansky, and Tyler J. Vander-Weele, 285–305. Oxford: Oxford University Press, 2021.

Moo, Douglas J. *The Epistle to the Romans*. New International Commentary on the New Testament. Grand Rapids: Eerdmans, 1996.

Moses, William Jeremiah. *Black Messiahs and Uncle Toms: Social and Literary Manipulation of a Religious Myth*. Rev. ed. University Park: Pennsylvania State University Press, 2010.

———. *Creative Conflict in African American Thought: Frederick Douglass, Alexander Crummell, Booker T. Washington, W. E. B. Du Bois, and Marcus Garvey*. Cambridge: Cambridge University Press, 2004.

Murray, Albert. *The Omni-Americans: Some Alternatives to the Folklore of White Supremacy*. 15th anniv. ed. New York: Literary Classics of the United States, 2020.

Nash, Gary B. *Forging Freedom: The Formation of Philadelphia's Black Community, 1720–1840*. Cambridge, MA: Harvard University Press, 1988.

———. *Race and Revolution*. Lanham, MD: Rowman & Littlefield, 2001.

Nell, William C. "Letter from William C. Nell." *The Liberator* 22, no. 10 (March 5, 1852): 39.

Newman, Richard, Patrick Rael, and Phillip Lapsansky, eds. *Pamphlets of Protest: An Anthology of Early African-American Protest Literature, 1790–1860*. New York: Routledge, 2001.

Noll, Mark A. *The Civil War as a Theological Crisis*. Chapel Hill: University of North Carolina Press, 2006.

———. *A History of Christianity in the United States and Canada*. Grand Rapids: Eerdmans, 1992.

Oakes, Peter. *Galatians*. Paideia Commentaries on the New Testament. Grand Rapids: Baker Academic, 2015.

O'Donovan, Oliver. *Common Objects of Love: Moral Reflection and the Shaping of Community*. Grand Rapids: Eerdmans, 2002.

———. *Entering into Rest*. Vol. 3 of *Ethics as Theology*. Grand Rapids: Eerdmans, 2017.

———. *Finding and Seeking*. Vol. 2 of *Ethics as Theology*. Grand Rapids: Eerdmans, 2014.

———. *Self, World, and Time*. Vol. 1 of *Ethics as Theology*. Grand Rapids: Eerdmans, 2013.

———. *The Ways of Judgment*. Grand Rapids: Eerdmans, 2005.

Okur, Nilgun Anadolu. "Underground Railroad in Philadelphia, 1830–1860." *Journal of Black Studies* 25, no. 5 (1995): 537–57.

O'Neill, William R. *Reimaging Human Rights: Religion and the Common Good*. Washington, DC: Georgetown University Press, 2021.

Owen, John. *The Works of John Owen*. Vol. 3. Edited by William H. Goold. Edinburgh: Banner of Truth, 1977.

Padilla, René C. "The Fullness of Mission." In *Mission between the Times: Essays on the Kingdom*, 146–57. Rev. ed. Carlisle: Langham Monographs, 2013.

Palmer, G. S. "Appendix E." In Richardson, *Maria W. Stewart*, 118.

Palmer, Phoebe. "Entire Devotion to God [1845]." In *Phoebe Palmer: Selected Writings*, edited by Thomas C. Oden, 185–207. Sources of American Spirituality. New York: Paulist Press, 1988.

Parry, Robin. *Lamentations*. Two Horizons Old Testament Commentary. Grand Rapids: Eerdmans, 2010.

Pelletier, Kevin. *Apocalyptic Sentimentalism: Love and Fear in U.S. Antebellum Literature*. Athens: University of Georgia Press, 2015.

Pickard, Kate E. R. *The Kidnapped and the Ransomed: Being the Personal Recollections of Peter Still and His Wife "Vina" after Forty Years of Slavery*. New York: Negro Universities Press, 1968.

Polgar, Paul J. "'To Raise Them to an Equal Participation': Early National Abolitionism, Gradual Emancipation, and the Promise of African American Citizenship." *Journal of the Early Republic* 31, no. 2 (Summer 2011): 229–58.

Purvis, Robert. "Appeal of Forty Thousand Citizens Threatened with Disenfranchisement to the People of Pennsylvania." In Woodson, *Negro Orators and Their Orations*, 94–100.

Pybus, Cassandra. "Jefferson's Faulty Math: The Question of Slave Defections in the American Revolution." *William and Mary Quarterly* 62, no. 2 (2005): 243–64.

Quarles, Benjamin. *The Negro in the American Revolution*. Chapel Hill: University of North Carolina Press, 1996.

Raboteau, Albert J. *A Fire in the Bones: Reflections on African-American Religious History*. Boston: Beacon, 1995.

Radner, Ephraim. *Church*. Eugene, OR: Cascade Books, 2017.

Richardson, Marilyn, ed. *Maria W. Stewart, America's First Black Woman Political Writer: Essays and Speeches*. Bloomington: Indiana University Press, 1987.

———. "What If I Am a Woman? Maria Stewart's Defense of Black Women's Political Activism." In *Courage and Conscience: Black and White Abolitionists in Boston*, edited by Donald M. Jacobs, 191–206. Bloomington: Indiana University Press, 1993.

Roberts, Neil. *Freedom as Marronage*. Chicago: University of Chicago Press, 2015.

Roberts, Robert. "Texts for Meditation." *The Liberator* 1, no. 11 (March 12, 1831): 42.

Rosner, Brian S. *Paul and the Law: Keeping the Commandments of God*. New Studies in Biblical Theology. Downers Grove, IL: IVP Academic, 2013.

Rowe, C. Kavin. "Biblical Pressure and Trinitarian Hermeneutics." *Pro Ecclesia* 11, no. 3 (2002): 295–312.

Rugemer, Edward B. *Slave Law and the Politics of Resistance in the Early Atlantic World*. Cambridge, MA: Harvard University Press, 2018.

Ruggles, David. *The Abrogation of the Seventh Commandment by the American Churches, by a Puritan*. New York: David Ruggles, 1835.

———. *An Antidote for a Poisonous Combination*. New York: David Ruggles, 1838.

———. "Appeal to the Colored Citizens of New York and Elsewhere in Behalf of the Press (1835)." In *Early Negro Writings, 1760–1837*, edited by Dorothy Porter, 637–55. Baltimore: Beacon, 1995.

———. *A Brief Review of the First Annual Report of the American Anti-Slavery Society by David M. Reese, M.D. of New York Dissected by Martin Mar Quack, M.D. L.L.D. M.Q.L.H.S.O.S.M.F.M.P.S.&c.&c. of That Ilk*. Boston: Calvin Knox, 1834. Attributed to David Ruggles.

———. "David Ruggles' Letter in Reply to Wm. Whipper and Robert Purvis." *National Anti-Slavery Standard* (New York) 1, no. 17, October 1, 1840.

———. David Ruggles to Frederick Douglass and Martin R. Delany. Northampton, MA, January 1, 1848. The Fredrick Douglass Papers Project. https://frederick douglasspapersproject.com/s/digitaledition/item/5006.

———. *The "Extinguisher" Extinguished! or David M. Reese, M.D., "Used Up."* New York: David Ruggles, 1834.

———. "For the Colored American: A Boy Kidnapped." *Colored American*, September 16, 1837.

———. "New York Committee of Vigilance for the Year 1837, Together with Important Facts Relative to Their Proceedings." In Newman, Rael, and Lapsansky, *Pamphlets of Protest*, 145–55.

———. "A Plea for 'A Man and a Brother.'" *Colored American*, July 18, 1839.

Ryan, Judylyn S. "Spirituality and/as Ideology in Black Women's Literature: The Preaching of Maria W. Stewart and Baby Suggs, Holy." In *Women Preachers and Prophets through Two Millennia of Christianity*, edited by Beverly Mayne Kienzel and Pamela J. Walker, 267–87. Berkeley: University of California Press, 1998.

Ryan, Mary P. *Cradle of the Middle Class: The Family in Oneida County, New York, 1790–1835*. Cambridge: Cambridge University Press, 1981.

Sanders, Fred. *The Triune God*. New Studies in Dogmatics. Grand Rapids: Zondervan, 2016.

Schor, Joel. "The Rivalry between Frederick Douglass and Henry Highland Garnet." *Journal of Negro History* 64, no. 1 (1979): 30–38.

Schreiner, Thomas R. *Romans*. 2nd ed. Baker Exegetical Commentary on the New Testament. Grand Rapids: Baker Academic, 2018.

Schweninger, Loren. *Families in Crisis in the Old South: Divorce, Slavery, and the Law*. Chapel Hill: University of North Carolina Press, 2014.

Schwöbel, Christoph. "The Creature of the Word: Recovering the Ecclesiology of the Reformers." In *On Being the Church: Essays on the Christian Community*, edited by Colin E. Gunton and Daniel W. Hardy, 110–55. Edinburgh: T&T Clark, 1989.

Seijas, Tatiana. *Asian Slaves in Colonial Mexico: From Chinos to Indians*. Cambridge: Cambridge University Press, 2014.

Sexton, Jason. "Public Theology: The Spirit Sent to Bring Good News." In *Third Article Theology: A Pneumatological Dogmatics*, edited by Myk Habets, 421–41. Minneapolis: Fortress, 2016.

Shadd, Mary Ann. "A Plea for Emigration, or Notes of Canada West (1853)." In Newman, Rael, and Lapsansky, *Pamphlets of Protest*, 198–212.

Shorter-Bourhanou, Jameliah Inga. "Maria W. Stewart, Ethnologist and Proto-Black Feminist." *Hypatia* 37 (2022): 60–75.

Singer, Alan J. *New York's Grand Emancipation Jubilee: Essays on Slavery, Resistance, Abolition, Teaching, and Historical Memory*. Albany: State University of New York Press, 2018.

Smedley, Audrey, and Brian D. Smedley. *Race in North America: Origin and Evolution of a Worldview*. 4th ed. New York: Routledge, 2019.

Smith, James McCune. "The Abolition of Slavery in the French and British Colonies." *Colored American*, June 9, 1838.

Smith, Justin E. H. *Nature, Human Nature, and Human Difference: Race in Early Modern Philosophy*. Princeton: Princeton University Press, 2015.

Smith, Ted. *The End of Theological Education*. Theological Education between the Times. Grand Rapids: Eerdmans, 2023.

Sonderegger, Katherine. *The Doctrine of God*. Vol. 1 of *Systematic Theology*. Minneapolis: Fortress, 2015.

Spaemann, Robert. *Persons: The Difference between "Someone" and "Something."* Translated by Oliver O'Donovan. Oxford Studies in Theological Ethics. Oxford: Oxford University Press, 2006.

Spooner, Matthew. "'I Know This Scheme Is from God': Toward a Reconsideration of the Origins of the American Colonization Society." *Slavery and Abolition* 35, no. 4 (2014): 559–75.

Srole, Carole. *Transcribing Class and Gender: Masculinity and Femininity in Nineteenth-Century Courts and Offices*. Ann Arbor: University of Michigan Press, 2010.

Stewart, Maria W. "An Address Delivered at the African Masonic Hall." In Richardson, *Maria W. Stewart*, 56–64.

————. "An Address Delivered before the Afric-American Female Intelligence Society of America." In Richardson, *Maria W. Stewart*, 50–56.

————. "Appendix D." In Richardson, *Maria W. Stewart*, 118.

————. "Cause for Encouragement." In Richardson, *Maria W. Stewart*, 43–44.

————. Introduction to Stewart, Lee, Foote, and Broughton, *Spiritual Narratives*, 1–24.

————. "Lecture Delivered at the Franklin Hall." In Richardson, *Maria W. Stewart*, 45–49.

————. "Meditation I." In Stewart, Lee, Foote, and Broughton, *Spiritual Narratives*, 25–26.

————. "Meditation II." In Stewart, Lee, Foote, and Broughton, *Spiritual Narratives*, 26–27.

————. "Meditation VI." In Stewart, Lee, Foote, and Broughton, *Spiritual Narratives*, 31–33.

————. "Meditation X." In Stewart, Lee, Foote, and Broughton, *Spiritual Narratives*, 40–43.

————. "Meditation XIII." In Stewart, Lee, Foote, and Broughton, *Spiritual Narratives*, 47–49.

————. "Mrs. Stewart's Farewell Address to Her Friends in the City of Boston." In Richardson, *Maria W. Stewart*, 65–74.

————. "The Proper Training of Children." *Publications of the Modern Language Association* 123, no. 1 (2008): 156–65.

————. "Religion and the Pure Principles of Morality." In Richardson, *Maria W. Stewart*, 28–42.

Stewart, Maria W., Jarena Lee, Julia A. J. Foote, and Virginia W. Broughton. *Spiritual Narratives*. Schomburg Library of Nineteenth-Century Black Women Writers. Oxford: Oxford University Press, 1988.

Still, William. Preface to *Still's Underground Railroad Records: With a Life of the Author*. Rev. ed. Philadelphia: William Still, 1886.

————. "Self-Improvement." *Weekly Anglo-African*, March 17, 1860.

————. *Still's Underground Railroad Records: With a Life of the Author*. Rev. ed. Philadelphia: William Still, 1886.

————. *Still's Underground Rail Road Records with a Life of the Author: Narrating the Hardships, Hairbreadth Escapes and Death Struggles of the Slaves in Their Efforts for Freedom, Together with Sketches of Some of the Eminent Friends of Freedom, and Most Liberal Aiders and Advisors of the Road*. Philadelphia: William Still, 1883.

————. *The Underground Railroad: A Record of Facts, Authentic Narrative, Letters, &c., Narrating Hardships, Hairbreadth Escapes and Death Struggles of the Slaves in Their Efforts of Freedom, as Related by Themselves and Others, or Witnessed by the Author Together with Sketches of Some of the Largest Stockholders, and Most Liberal Aiders and Advisors of the Road*. Philadelphia: Porter & Coates, 1872.

———. William Still to Caroline Still Anderson, April 30, 1866. In the William Still Collection. Philadelphia: Temple University Libraries. https://exhibits.temple.edu /s/william-still/item/19178.

———. William Still to Caroline Still Anderson, February 1, 1876. In the William Still Collection. Philadelphia: Temple University Libraries. https://exhibits.temple .edu/s/william-still/item/19530.

———. William Still to Edward A. Wiley, October 13, 1873. In the William Still Collection. Philadelphia: Temple University Libraries. https://exhibits.temple.edu /s/william-still/item/19540.

———. William Still to Elijah F. Pennypacker, November 2, 1857. In *The Black Abolitionist Papers: The United States, 1847–1858*, edited by C. Peter Ripley, 331–34. Vol. 4. Chapel Hill: University of North Carolina Press, 1985.

Strong, Douglas M. *Perfectionist Politics: Abolitionism and the Religious Tensions of American Democracy*. Religion and Politics. Syracuse: Syracuse University Press, 1999.

Stump, Eleonore. *Atonement*. Oxford: Oxford University Press, 2018.

Suderman, W. Derek. "The Cost of Losing Lament for the Community of Faith: On Brueggemann, Ecclesiology, and the Social Audience of Prayer." *Journal of Theological Interpretation* 6, nos. 1–2 (2012): 201–18.

Sulzener, Britany. "Night of Death, Morning of Rebirth: Maria W. Stewart's Apocalyptic Futures." *Nineteenth-Century Contexts: An Interdisciplinary Journal* 4, no. 5 (2019): 623–30.

Switala, William J. *The Underground Railroad in Philadelphia*. 2nd ed. Mechanicsburg, PA: Stackpole Books, 2008.

Tanner, Kathryn. *Christianity and the New Spirit of Capitalism*. New Haven: Yale University Press, 2019.

Taylor, Charles. *Modern Social Imaginaries*. Durham, NC: Duke University Press, 2003.

Thiessen, Matthew. *Paul and the Gentile Problem*. Oxford: Oxford University Press, 2016.

Thiselton, Anthony C. *Discovering Romans: Content, Interpretation, Reception*. Discovering Biblical Texts. Grand Rapids: Eerdmans, 2016.

Tirole, Jean. *Economics for the Common Good*. Translated by Steven Rendall. Princeton: Princeton University Press, 2017.

Tolkien, J. R. R. "From a Letter to Amy Ronald, 15 December 1956." In *The Letters of J. R. R. Tolkien*, edited by Humphrey Carpenter, 273. Rev. ed. Boston: Houghton Mifflin Harcourt, 2000.

Tomek, Beverly C. *Slavery and Abolition in Pennsylvania*. Philadelphia: Temple University Press, 2021.

Torrance, T. F. *The Trinitarian Faith: The Evangelical Theology of the Ancient Catholic Church*. Cornerstones. London: Bloomsbury T&T Clark, 2016.

Tran, Jonathan. *Asian Americans and the Spirit of Racial Capitalism*. AAR Reflection and Theory in the Study of Religion. Oxford: Oxford University Press, 2022.

Treier, Daniel J. *Introducing Evangelical Theology*. Grand Rapids: Baker Academic, 2019.

Treier, Daniel J., and Euntaek D. Shin. "Evangelical Theology." In *St Andrews Encyclopaedia of Theology*, edited by Brendan N. Wolfe et al. August 10, 2022. https://www.saet.ac.uk/Christianity/EvangelicalTheology.

Vanhoozer, Kevin J., and Daniel J. Treier. *Theology and the Mirror of Scripture: A Mere Evangelical Account*. Studies in Christian Doctrine and Scripture. Downers Grove, IL: IVP Academic, 2015.

Vidu, Adonis. *The Divine Missions: An Introduction*. Eugene, OR: Cascade Books, 2021.

Volf, Miroslav. *A Public Faith: How Christ Followers Should Serve the Common Good*. Grand Rapids: Brazos, 2011.

Waters, Kristin. "Crying Out for Liberty: Maria W. Stewart and David Walker's Black Revolutionary Liberalism." *Philosophia Africana* 15, no. 1 (2013): 35–60.

———. *Maria W. Stewart and the Roots of Black Political Thought*. Jackson: University Press of Mississippi, 2022.

Watkins, Jordan T. *Slavery and Sacred Texts: The Bible, the Constitution, and Historical Consciousness in Antebellum America*. Cambridge: Cambridge University Press, 2021.

Watson, Francis. *Paul, Judaism, and the Gentiles: Beyond the New Perspective*. Rev. ed. Grand Rapids: Eerdmans, 2007.

Webster, John. "Christ, Church, and Reconciliation." In *Word and Church: Essays in Christian Dogmatics*, 211–32. Cornerstones. London: Bloomsbury T&T Clark, 2016.

———. "Evangelical Freedom." In *Confessing God: Essays in Christian Dogmatics II*, 215–26. Cornerstones. London: Bloomsbury T&T Clark, 2016.

———. *Holiness*. Grand Rapids: Eerdmans, 2003.

———. "Hope." In *Confessing God: Essays in Christian Dogmatics II*, 195–214. Cornerstones. London: Bloomsbury T&T Clark, 2016.

———. "The Self-Organizing Power of the Gospel of Christ: Episcopacy and Community Formation." In *Word and Church: Essays in Christian Dogmatics*, 191–210. Cornerstones. London: Bloomsbury T&T Clark, 2016.

Weil, Simone. *The Need for Roots: Prelude to a Declaration of Duties towards Mankind*. Translated by Arthur Wills. Routledge Classics. London: Routledge, 2002.

Wells, Jonathan Daniel. *Blind No More: African American Resistance, Free-Soil Politics, and the Coming of the Civil War*. Mercer University Lamar Memorial Lectures Series. Athens: University of Georgia Press, 2019.

Wells, Samuel. *Improvisation: The Drama of Christian Ethics*. Grand Rapids: Brazos, 2004.

Welter, Barbara. "The Cult of True Womanhood: 1820–1860." *American Quarterly* 18, no. 2 (1966): 151–74.

Williams, Rowan. *Why Study the Past? The Quest for the Historical Church*. Grand Rapids: Eerdmans, 2005.

Winch, Julie. "Philadelphia and the Other Underground Railroad." *Pennsylvania Magazine of History and Biography* 111, no. 1 (1987): 3–25.

Witherington, Ben, III. *Grace in Galatia: A Commentary on St. Paul's Letter to the Galatians*. Grand Rapids: Eerdmans, 1998.

Wolf, Eva Sheppard. "Early Free-Labor Thought and the Contest over Slavery in the Early Republic." In Hammond and Mason, *Contesting Slavery*, 32–48.

Wolter, Michael. *Paul: An Outline of His Theology*. Translated by Robert L. Brawley. Waco: Baylor University Press, 2015.

Wolterstorff, Nicholas. *Justice: Rights and Wrongs*. Princeton: Princeton University Press, 2008.

Woodson, Carter G., ed. *Negro Orators and Their Orations*. Washington, DC: Associated Publishers, 1925.

Wright, Nazera Sadiq. "Maria W. Stewart's 'The First Stage of Life': Black Girlhood in the Repository of Religion and Literature, and of Science and Art." *Society for the Study of Multi-Ethnic Literature of the United States* 40, no. 3 (2015): 150–75.

Wright, Theodore S. "Prejudice against the Colored Man." In Woodson, *Negro Orators and Their Orations*, 90–96.

———. "The Progress of the Antislavery Cause." In Woodson, *Negro Orators and Their Orations*, 85–89.

Wu, Siu Fung. *Suffering in Romans*. Eugene, OR: Pickwick, 2015.

Young, Robert Alexander. "Ethiopian Manifesto." In Newman, Rael, and Lapsansky, *Pamphlets of Protest*, 84–89.

Zahl, Simeon. "Non-Competitive Agency and Luther's Experiential Argument against Virtue." *Modern Theology* 35, no. 2 (2019): 199–222.

Author Index

Subject Index